PETER ALLISS

PETER ALLISS

REFLECTIONS ON A LIFE WELL LIVED

Lennard Publishing

Published in the UK in 2022 by
Lennard Publishing, an imprint of
Lennard Associates Ltd,
Mackerye End,
Harpenden,
Herts AL5 5DR

email: orders@lennardqap.co.uk

Hardback: ISBN: 978-1-78281-794-9
eBoook: ISBN: 978-1-78281-795-6

A CIP catalogue record for this book
is available from the British Library

Production Editor: George Harrison
Design: Paul Cooper

PICTURE ACKNOWLEDGEMENTS
Many thanks to Getty Images for providing many of the illustrations in this book and to
Rob Lear, Dave Cannon, Jo McCusker, Parkstone GC and Ferndown GC for their help
in sourcing or providing other photographs

Printed and bound in Italy by LEGO

CONTENTS

Prologue by Bill Elliott   07

'Oh Hell, What's He Doing Now?'   11

Born to Play Golf   18

Tea, Biscuits and Greatness   34

Television Beckons   51

The Masters is Glorious but ...   77

The Ryder Cup – Then and Now   97

Going Clubbing the Old Way   123

Swinging and Dancing witht the Stars   143

The Peter Alliss Hall of Fame   157

There's Something on My Chest, Doc!   177

A Return to Portrush   189

Eplogue: My Peter by Jackie Alliss   201

PROLOGUE: ON WRITING A BOOK WITH PETER ALLISS

Dear Reader,

YOU hold in your hands a book which has had the gestation period of a reluctant elephant. Covid, of course, is partly to blame, but so too is the happy fact that Peter and I spent so much of our time together engaged in enjoyable and deeply diversionary conversation. Entire evenings were given over to discussing the Goons and puzzling how it could be that malt whisky tastes so good from a decent glass and yet so average in your typical tumbler. Why is that? Either way, this is not quite the book we set out to create years ago, when Peter asked if I would join forces for this, his final project. Of course, none of us knew then that this book would be Peter's ultimate mark on the world. His death in December 2020 was as unexpected as it was blessedly swift and peaceful.

This was a book, Peter and I soon discovered, which would not conform to our expectations of it. It took on a life of its own, growing and changing beneath our pens as Peter reflected on his career, mulled over the great questions of the universe and raged at the eternally vexed problem of the A303 at Stonehenge. He requested from the start that I should throw in my own observations here and there. I was keen to oblige. Peter wanted this book to contain more than one voice, and I trust the inclusion of mine, at the beginning and end of each chapter, does not grate.

It was enormous fun to work on this book with Peter, but more than that, it was thoroughly interesting to sit back and listen to him do what he did best: ramble on about such and such in that famous voice of his, drawing sharp and funny observations from disparate quarters of life before inevitably tying everything neatly together and returning to the subject of golf. At times, getting information out of Peter was like trying to arm-wrestle a crotchety octopus, but it has been intriguing to record his vivid recollections of a life well lived. How wonderful it was to look back on that double-edged career in sport and media, one that is unlike any other and is surely never to be repeated.

Peter had, in fact, been planning to draw a line under that illustrious career. It was his intention to retire immediately after commentating on the 150th Open Championship at St Andrews, which would have neatly completed a circle that began so many years earlier.

'We'll walk towards the sunset together on that Sunday,' he had grinned. 'Probably take a couple of bottles with us.' The sun set sooner, of course, than any of us had hoped, but this book ought to serve as the proverbial glass raised in the great man's memory.

I first met Peter Alliss in 1978, when he was living in Yorkshire. In my capacity as a golf journalist, I was sent from my home in Manchester to interview him. Forty years and a firm friendship later, we both found ourselves living in Surrey and working on this very book, an exercise in patience and fact-checking (apologies in advance for any we might have got wrong) which stands now as a postscript to Peter's incredible life. I am grateful to have had the chance to properly get to know both Peter and his wine cellar. The result is a friendship I will always treasure.

I uncovered no unpleasant surprises while working with Peter on this book. While occasionally irascible (aren't we all?) he was instinctively a kind, generous and wise old soul. His memory for long-passed names and distant places remained extraordinarily sharp. He was also a man of his age, so naturally there were more than a few facets of modern life which he found confusing and exasperating. This, however, is surely true for any of us who have lived beyond the point where we wake up each day wondering what the hell we ought to do with our lives.

I agree with some of Peter's conclusions and disagree with others. And rightly so, since he was a self-confessed 'Tory Wet,' while I still cling to my status as a half-baked socialist. One of Peter's great strengths, however, was his inclination to listen to the opinions of others and always consider them thoroughly. When he was done mulling it over, he would usually lob the offending opinion into the kitchen bin, but still... it's the thought that counts.

Ideology aside, Peter was truly a monumental figure. He was a bit like the Queen, in that he had always been a constant in my life whether I wanted him there or not. Wherever I went in the world of golf, I would find him: observing this, explaining that, and throwing in a potpourri of off-the-cuff wit for good measure. His voice was the soundtrack to my career, as it has been for so many others who have paid even the scantest attention to the old game.

Peter always appreciated his good fortune at being able to make a living from his 'ramblings,' while at the same time possessing an acute awareness of his rare talent for finding the appropriate word or phrase while winging it over a television picture. His belief that sometimes silence is more eloquent than words – a view nurtured by the great Henry Longhurst, who mentored Peter as a commentator – flies in the noisy face of much modern broadcasting. Peter's listeners appreciated him all the more for sticking to this conviction and daring to hold firm in the face of changing convention.

Also unyielding was Peter's kindness, his steadfast concern for others. This trait is best summarised in an exchange from September 2018. Peter read the *Daily Mail* (a habit he balanced by subscribing to *Private Eye*) and commented one day that it had been several weeks since he last saw a column by the sports correspondent Charles Sale. When I told him that Charlie was seriously ill, he asked for a contact address, which I duly supplied.

Peter never got into computers and emails, let alone texts and WhatsApp. To him, TikTok was the noise a clock made, while smartphones were mysterious objects best left well alone. So Peter unsheathed his fountain pen and wrote a good old-fashioned letter expressing his concern and wishing Charlie a swift return to health. This was despite the fact that Charlie had, for many years, been one of Peter's most relentless media critics, never passing up an opportunity to accuse him of being too old and out of touch. More than once, he had called for Peter's dismissal from the BBC on those grounds. When I bumped into Charlie sometime later, after he had recovered, I nonetheless asked him if he had received anything from Peter.

'I got a very nice note,' he said. 'I didn't expect that at all after what I've written. It was very kind of him.'

Peter is gone now, but the spirit of kindness in which he lived his life reverberates still. The Alliss house, meanwhile, remains as rambling, as comfy and welcoming, as Peter was himself.

Here it is worth adding that there is nothing rambling about Peter's wife, Jackie. She was his rock, his advisor, his fiercest critic and most loyal defender. She is also probably the busiest woman I know, having spent years dashing here or there to promote his interests, her charities, or their joint projects. Now and then, when this book seemed like it might hit the buffers, Jackie was hugely encouraging (as well as occasionally chastising). I thank her for her support, as I thank my own wife, Valerie, for her unending and loving encouragement, coupled with those vital, consoling suppers. I thank Peter, too, for his time and effort and for involving me in the first place. He may be reading this somewhere, after all.

Most importantly, however, I thank you for reading this book. Peter really would be delighted. He always said that he loved how his career had transmogrified from that of a successful golfer to a lauded television performer and bestselling author.

I remember him saying, once: 'It's all been rather a pleasant surprise to me, and it never really felt like work. In fact, at the risk of sounding immodest, I've found it all rather easy. Don't tell anyone, will you?'

And we laughed.

Sincerely,
Bill Elliott

Bill Elliott first interviewed Peter in 1978. He has covered more than 100 Majors and is presently Editor at Large of Golf Monthly *magazine following a 40-year career on Fleet Street.*

'OH HELL, WHAT'S HE DOING NOW?'

IT is Sunday 18th July 1999, and the final round of the 128th Open Championship is about to take place. The setting is Carnoustie. At once forbidding and glorious, this linksland has been hosting Opens since 1931. That first year, victory was claimed by Edinburgh's Tommy Armour, one of a vast multitude of golfers whose fate will forever be one with this hallowed ground.

Golf has been played here, near the mouth of the Barry Burn, since the early sixteenth century. They know the game at Carnoustie Links, and they know also that their course is rightly regarded as the toughest on the Open rota. The 18th is particularly fiendish, probably the most challenging final hole of them all.

Peter Alliss knew all this – as did Alex Hay, his fellow commentator and friend. Having played in twenty-four Opens himself (finishing in the top ten on eight occasions) and having commentated on the Championship for nearly forty years, Peter thought he knew what to expect. He was, of course, very wrong.

That day, a little-known Frenchman, Jean van de Velde, was on the verge of embroidering his name on Open history, although not in a way anyone could have imagined. Peter's powers of observation and commentary, his ability to fill long periods of television time with wry comment, were going to be tested as never before. The old game was about to become enveloped in a bizarre mixture of tragedy and farce, a combination that would produce a moment of memorable television that echoes still with all of us who watch the great game of golf. I'll let Peter tell it...

DUE to an accident of birth, my whole life has revolved around sport. My father, Percy Alliss, was one of the world's top golf professionals in the 1920s and '30s. I just followed his example, like it was the most natural thing in the world.

Although I never seriously played another sport, I watched them all with a keen interest, taking in the highs, lows and cruel twists of fate which define competition at the top level. I was certain Devon Loch would win the Grand National, right until that fateful fall on the final straight. Don Fox had only to kick a goal from in front of the posts for Wakefield Trinity to win the Challenge Cup; Ed Sneed had only to par one of the last four holes at Augusta to be the champion. Like everyone else, I watched these sporting disasters through my fingers – watched in disbelief as these modern-day gladiators snatched defeat from the jaws of victory. But none, in my opinion, could ever compare with that Sunday in 1999 on the east coast of Scotland.

The day began in a nondescript way. The skies were dull, and a breeze swept in from the North Sea. It was forecast to turn a bit nasty as the day went on, but we'd all had that sort of experience at Open Championships before. During the week there had been many complaints about the thickness of the rough, which came in some cases right to the edge of the fairway. It was the same for everyone, though, and professional sportsmen have, on occasion, been known to go looking for things to whinge about.

As we made our way into the commentary booth by the 18th tee, Alex and I chatted about what the day might bring. Jean van de Velde was leading by five shots from the American Justin Leonard, who had won the Championship at Troon a couple of years before. Tied with Leonard was Craig Parry, the excellent Australian.

Five shots was a very good lead, but it was not insurmountable, and certainly not on a course as difficult as Carnoustie under the pressure of trying to win an Open Championship. It's that unpredictable edge that creates a sense of drama and lays the boards for theatrics. Therein lies the fun of the game.

I had homework to do ahead of a full day of broadcasting. We were on air hours before the leaders got going, and I had to make sure I was up to speed with who was doing what and where. There were the inevitable preview pieces to camera as well. As usual, I enjoyed it all.

Whether you're playing or watching, the sport of golf comes with a lot of time to think. For a commentator, this means there is also a lot of time to talk. It's not necessary to fill every second with chatter – indeed, it's important not to – but neither can one allow silence to reign for too long. This is particularly true if there are no interesting pictures for viewers to watch. The challenge is in striking the balance between talking the viewer's ear off and leaving them alone in a wasteland of dead air.

By the time the leaders got to the final few holes, the ending of this particular Open seemed to have been written, and I assumed the hardest part of my day was behind me. There had been a flurry of action over the first nine: van de Velde ran up a couple of bogeys and Parry made some birdies to take a one-shot lead. The Australian then hit his own problems while van de Velde got back on the straight and narrow. When they came to the 18th tee, van de Velde had a three-shot lead over Leonard and Paul Lawrie, the Scot, who had come from nowhere thanks to a splendid 67 that was nine strokes better than his previous day's score. Well done, I thought. It would be nice to see a Scottish player in the top five at the end of the day.

Then I looked away from my screen, down onto the 18th tee, and saw the first indication that we might be in for a bumpy ride to the finish. There was van de Velde, taking out his driver. What was he doing, I wondered? He could take an iron off the tee, another one up the fairway and pitch onto the green, where it would be two putts for victory. But maybe, being French, he wanted to finish with élan. Looking at things from a global perspective, I certainly thought a dashing, smiley Frenchman winning The Open in style would be a fantastic result for the game of golf.

In France the game was then, and indeed still is, an elitist pastime – a sport played by people more interested in how they look swinging the club than where their ball ends up. France boasted dozens of excellent courses, but many were hardly used. Victory for van de Velde had the potential to change this state of affairs. I intended to say all this when he won, as inevitably he would.

I was so certain of this because you could give a ten-handicapper a three-shot cushion up the last at Carnoustie, and nine times out of ten they would get the job done. So it was unthinkable that a professional would throw away such a lead. It seemed in the bag, so I had started already to wonder what I might have for supper that evening, with half a thought devoted, of course, to the appropriate wine pairing. But then out came that driver.

I glanced at Alex. I could tell by his face that he shared my bemusement. Out of bounds on the left and the blessed burn snaking its way down the right… hitting a driver – unless you had to – brought too much potential trouble into play.

Van de Velde hit his tee shot. He didn't have to worry about out of bounds left – but only because the ball went so far to the right. The burn came briefly into question, but only for a second, as – glory be! – it emerged that the ball had gone too far right even for that. He had messed up so comprehensively that he missed all the trouble. The golfing gods were with him, it seemed. Cue great sighs of relief.

'The lucky bugger's got away with it,' I thought, but I wisely chose not to say so on air. Now surely he would take an iron, lay up short of the water that guarded the green, pitch on and win The Open. Here his caddie should have advised him, but he didn't. He was far too young in golfing years to be of any use in this moment, and both he and van de Velde seemed to have stopped thinking. I said as much as the Frenchman took a 2-iron and went straight for the green. Out of bounds was only two or three yards off the green to the left, so this was a bold play. But there is a fine line between bravery and foolishness.

Once again, we watched van de Velde's ball fly to the right, this time heading for the grandstand, where thousands were sitting and watching the final moments. If it went into the stand he would get a free drop, and despite playing the hole carelessly, he would win. But golf, like life, is a perverse beast. The ball hit a stanchion, and instead of dropping to the ground it rebounded back across the burn into deep, deep rough. It was a stupid shot to take on in the first place, but no one deserved such freakishly bad luck.

'Now he is in trouble,' I said. But he was not yet buried, and I assumed he would at last pick the sensible course of action: pitch back onto the fairway, play on to the green, and take a couple of putts to win the Championship by two.

Instead, we all know what happened. He tried to be too greedy, too bold, too brave. Call it what you will, but ultimately he chopped the ball back into the burn as the tide was rising. The outlook went from bad to terminal as he contemplated his next move.

I was lost in that moment. I couldn't believe that a skilled professional was tearing up his thought process and throwing away his chance of winning The Open. Victory would have changed his life forever, although I suppose that's precisely why he wasn't thinking straight.

Time passed. Then, lo and behold, van de Velde took off his shoes and socks and stepped into Barry Burn. He needed help. Anyone, for God's sake? The tide was coming in, his ball was already half submerged and he was up against a five-foot wall. The shot was impossible and it seemed he had lost his mind. There was much to criticise, and I couldn't hold back. It was sad, and it was unnecessary, and I said so. 'Would somebody kindly go and stop him?' I asked. 'Give him a large brandy and mop him down.'

At last he worked it out and took a drop. Good sense prevailed. From there, he pitched into a greenside bunker. Then, to his great credit – no, dammit, to his enormous credit – he got down in two from the sand to put himself into a playoff with Lawrie and Leonard. That last hole must have taken three quarters of an hour or more, instead of the allotted fifteen minutes. By the time the flag was back in the hole, Jean was frazzled, and he wasn't alone. Play should have ended at about a quarter to seven. It was now past seven thirty and there was still a playoff to get through.

In the end, Lawrie won. In truth, he was the only one to play decently, but rather like Stewart Cink, who won The Open at Turnberry, he didn't receive the accolades usually afforded to winners of this great championship. Van de Velde and Leonard were fit for nothing after such a long wait; I'm sure they could have done with a lie down in a darkened room with gentle music playing.

Some seven million people watched our broadcast that day. Hopefully some of them found a few things I said amusing – and maybe even illuminating. I've always known it is impossible to please all of the people all of the time, but I do wonder if too many have lost their sense of humour in this confusing modern world. That evening, something had to be said while Jean was trying to gather his thoughts, and sometimes you have to say whatever comes into your head. It just so happened, in that moment, that I was thinking about dinner. I should have been sitting at home, enjoying a glass of malt in anticipation of a nice steak. That's what came into my head, so that's what I said.

I was thinking, also, about my father and the dramas he himself had been through at Carnoustie. In the 1930s he came to that feared 18th hole on the final day and hit his second shot out of bounds, ending in a tie for third with Gene Sarazen. He was just two shots behind the winner, Tommy Armour. That was the closest my father ever came to winning The Open. He never forgot that second shot to the final green – the ball just tiptoeing under those three strands of wire – but then, neither have I.

It was almost dark when the trophy was duly handed to Paul Lawrie. In my ear, the director's voice came at last: 'That's it, pass it back to Steve [Rider].' It hadn't been the hardest day of my television life, but it had been one of the longest. A group of us, including Alex, made our way out of the booth and headed back to the BBC compound, where we had a caravan that doubled as an office. We were all ready for one or two stiff drinks. It might have been three.

Not only were we thirsty, we were also very hungry. Someone suggested a fish and chip shop they'd seen on the High Street. As we dug in to a greasy feast I remember thinking how the public must imagine the glamorous lives we lead. In many ways, though, I have lived a glamorous life, and it's all thanks to the game of golf.

Did I set out to become a television commentator? No. I set out on the path of professional golf to try and make a living. It's as simple as that. Way back in the 1950s and '60s we didn't dream about being the world number one or winning dozens of championships. And how I got into the wonderful world of television remains a delightful surprise. A lot like my father getting into the world of golf in the first place, back in 1920, and setting me down a similar path before I had even been born.

PETER'S commentary of Jean van de Velde's Carnoustie meltdown lives on in infamy. Peter's observational gifts meant he was compelled to say what he saw – and what he saw that day was a man whose golfing brain had stopped working.

But not everyone reacted so well to Peter's scathing, if honest, criticism of the floundering Frenchman, and the press was vitriolic at the time. Scotland's Daily Record called him a 'prattling plonker,' while the eternally irritated Daily Mail called for him to be sacked. The Mail even polled its readers on the subject. Several years later I interviewed Peter for my newspaper, The Observer, and the hurt from that time was still evident.

'In those circumstances what the hell can you say?' he asked. 'The next day some people claimed I'd been cruel and said I'd taken the piss out of van der Velde. I didn't think I had. I've said many times that I thought it was one of the saddest moments I'd ever seen in the world of golf, but Jean did everything wrong, starting with his choice of driver off the tee. I've talked to him since and we're fine. But some of the press wanted my head. One of the writers on the Daily Mail led a crusade to get rid of me altogether, but I had a friend in their chief sports writer, Ian Wooldridge. He rang me to say, "Don't worry about the poll, old friend, it's 8-1 in your favour - you've stuffed 'em." I was comforted and very happy that I had so much support from the world of golf.'

The following remarks are taken from a tribute given by Jean van de Velde at the Service of Thanksgiving for Peter Alliss held at St Andrews in July 2022:

I WAS first introduced to Peter when I was thirteen years old. Not in person, but through the screen. My parents sent me to Britain for three years to learn English. The highlight of that time was not only playing golf every day, but also listening to Peter throughout the Open Championship. I could only understand half of what he was saying because his vocabulary was so amazing, but it really left a print. Especially the 1979 Open, when Seve happened to win his first Major.

Not only could Peter talk, he could surely play golf. And he was also very involved with the politics of the game. He believed in serving for the greater good – not for personal gain or for his own interests. I believe Peter would have a lot to say about what is going on today in the world of golf. He would have said it in his own particular way, of course; and political correctness is such a big thing today that I'm sure he would have got into a bit of trouble for it.

As a commentator, Peter described himself as an observer. His job was to work out the right thing to say - and to say it in the fairest way possible. He never minded telling us what he was thinking, nor was he ever scared of saying what he saw. We have an example of that in 1999, for which I want to thank Peter. I can only imagine that what happened to me actually triggered a few memories of his own past. He really identified with what happened to me that day, and he didn't mean to say it in a bad way. He just reacted the way he would have reacted if it had happened to him. Only players can appreciate this kind of thing, so I never held anything against Peter. On the contrary, you like

to hear what people have to say. You like to reflect on it. So, again, to me it was good.

I never met Peter as a player, but in 2002, in early July, one of my old knee injuries reappeared, and I was going to be off golf for quite a long time. A couple of days after finding out I had to have surgery, [BBC executive producer] John Shrewsbury called me. He said he heard I had a problem with my knee, and how would I feel about coming to work with them as a commentator at the Open in Muirfield? I said to John, 'How much do I have to pay you?'

Ten days later, there I was at Muirfield. I met all the team; I remember going to a kind of briefing as the new kid on the block. At the briefing, I was told it's quite simple; I will be brought in as an analyst, and when the lead commentator wants me in, he'll ask me a question. If I have nothing to say, or nothing to add, then I don't need to say anything; the images will speak for themselves.

My first forty-five minute rotation the next morning was with Peter Alliss. I was really nervous, but I didn't have to worry at all. I didn't say a word in the whole forty-five minutes; there was not a single question. So I came out of the truck and I was fuming. John saw me coming from a distance, and he said he would have a word with Peter. Two hours later, I came back, picked up my microphone and boom! Peter had his first question for me. I wasn't ready, but I had to answer, and thus began the best forty-five minutes as a broadcaster of my life. We just talked and chatted, the whole time. From then on, and in the years to follow, my impression as a thirteen-year-old was confirmed. I was in the presence of greatness, and I feel lucky to this day that I have been able to work with and know Peter. He brought joy to millions.

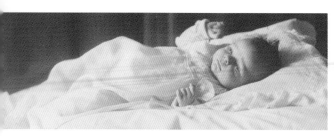

BORN TO PLAY GOLF

THE year 1897 marked Queen Victoria's Diamond Jubilee. Back then, Britain ruled not only the waves but a significant slice of the land – and a fifth of the world's population to boot. Naturally, the celebrations spread far and wide.

But that year was also significant for other reasons. It was a year for notable births, including Aneurin Bevan (father of the National Health Service), Anthony Eden (the prime minister who oversaw the Suez fiasco) and the children's author Enid Blyton. And there's one more we should consider. In Sheffield, Percy Alliss emerged into the world.

IT seems quite extraordinary now, in this confused twenty-first century, to say my father was born while Queen Victoria was on the throne. It seems extraordinary, too, that the Open Championship of that year was contested by twenty amateurs, alongside the usual contingent of professionals. The venue in 1897 was the Royal Liverpool Golf Club. Harold Hilton, a club member and amateur, won by a couple of shots from Scotland's James Braid. How different the Championship was then, in the year Percy Alliss was born.

I can tell you with certainty that my father was a delight – a kind man with a gentle sense of humour. I can tell you he survived four years as an infantryman in the First World War, and I can tell you he took up the job of assistant professional at the Royal Porthcawl Golf Club in South Wales upon his return. But quite how he became a professional golfer is a mystery to me. He surely couldn't have found much time to work on his swing between shellings on the Western Front. And where did he get his clubs? The truth is that I have no idea.

My father died in 1975, and it never occurred to me to ask these sorts of questions while I had the chance. It's only after one's parents are gone that one tends to realise just how many questions have been left unasked and unanswered.

What I do know is that my father was a very talented player, one of the top professionals of his day. In total, he won twenty-two titles and finished in the top six at the Open Championship in 1928, 1929, 1931, 1932 and 1936. He also played in four Ryder Cups, and when I, in my day, made the Great Britain and Ireland team, we became the first father and son pairing to have participated in the competition. I'm very proud of this family achievement, although it has now been matched by the father and son of Spain's Garrido dynasty.

As far as I know, there were no golfing influences in my father's family. When my father was a boy, his father (my grandfather) owned a small gardening business where the Hallam Tower Hotel stands today. A couple of my uncles worked for the firm, although Father never shared any of his brothers' aptitude for horticulture. Gardening may have been out the window, but Father needed to earn his pocket money somehow.

What to do, what to do? He settled, for whatever reason, on becoming a golf caddie, and from the ages of ten to twelve he worked at the Hallamshire Golf Club on the west side of Sheffield. This must have been the chance event which started him on the path to becoming a professional golfer. I can only assume that one of the members took a shine to him and gave him a couple of clubs. Then he must have found the time and a place to hit a few balls. Hardly the beginning of a glittering career, but still, there was an innate talent for golf in there somewhere.

Then came the Great War.

Father joined the war effort in 1914, aged seventeen-and-a-half. He and his brothers sought out a recruitment centre in Sheffield. The brothers were all over 6ft tall, while Father, at 5ft 9in, was the runt of the litter. He was reminded of this when the recruiting officer for a Guards Regiment uttered the immortal words: 'Sorry, we don't take short-arses like you. There's a Scottish Regiment recruiting round the corner – go and see them.'

Off my father went. He soon found himself signing up for the Argyll and Sutherland Highlanders, in whose company he saw a lot of action under fearsome conditions. When he was shot in the arm he was patched up and sent right back to the front to do it all over again.

Like many children of my generation, I never heard my father say much about those times. On one rare occasion, when he was meeting an old friend, I heard Father comment on the smell of death which had lingered in his nostrils. Human remains, rotting horses, mud and filth… four years of service and all this horror playing out no more than an 8-iron away.

Demobbed in 1918, Father went back to Sheffield to look for a job. Before the war he had been a keen cricketer: a promising slow, left-arm bowler and a number-seven batsman with a good eye and quick hands. He was the sort of player who could score thirty or forty runs in the wink of an eye. His cricket-mad brothers suggested he write to Yorkshire Cricket Club asking for a trial.

So there was always that option. But another option arose when Father spotted a job advert in a golf magazine. Where that article came from I have no idea; perhaps a friend in the Pro Shop passed it on, or perhaps Father dug it out from a wastepaper basket. Either way, he decided to write two letters: one to Yorkshire Cricket Club and one to Jock Hutchinson, the pro at Porthcawl, who was looking for an assistant. What a nerve! Where on earth did he derive the confidence to write two such letters? What could he possibly offer either of these fine clubs? I'm not sure many cricket matches were played at the front during the Great War, and I'm certain golf facilities were scarce amid the mud and gore of the trenches. So how did he think he could get away with it?

If you'll pardon the expression, my father's application to Jock Hutchinson was bullshit of the highest order. But – thank God! – Jock replied, offering my father the position of assistant professional. Did he ever get a letter from Yorkshire Cricket Club? I have no idea. But off he went to South Wales and the joys of Porthcawl. His future was settled, and in a way, so was mine.

I am baffled as to its origins, but Father evidently possessed an innate skill for golf. Within eighteen months of his appointment to Porthcawl he had not only won the Assistants' Championship but also the 1920 Welsh Professional Championship. As a result, he was offered the full professional job at Clyne Golf Club, a course beautifully positioned at the entrance to the glorious Gower Peninsula. He ventured into England to play in various events, and those in the world of golf were soon taking notice of him. He was then offered the job at Wanstead Golf Club, a thriving club in North East London. From there he won the Essex Professional Championship in 1923, 1924, and 1925.

Everything was going well, but Father had noticed something interesting: golf professionals on the continent were held in far more esteem than those in Great Britain. On the continent he would be a person of real stature, a 'professor' of golf who could charge two or three times more for passing on his knowledge. So when the professional position became available at Wannsee Golf Club, on the outskirts of Berlin, he applied. Father duly impressed the Germans and took the job. This was a rather brave (some might say foolish) thing to do when you think how, some ten years earlier, the locals had been the ones taking pot-shots at him on the Western Front. This was an endeavour they had pursued with vigour, and they were rather successful at it, too.

Thankfully, Father developed a neat and nasty trick for whenever he came across someone he really didn't like. He would send away these belligerent students with the biggest slice you've ever seen: one of those slices that hits you when least expected, a golfing horror to last the rest of your life. The chance to pay back any German unpleasantness in such a way would have appealed to my father's sense of humour.

But the life of a continental pro wasn't all lessons, and Father was soon back playing competitions – successfully, too. He won the German Open Championship in 1926, 1927, 1928 and 1929, triumphing against the might of the entire US Ryder Cup team: Walter Hagen, Gene Sarazen and all. He won again in 1933, a year he crowned off with victory in the Italian Open as well.

It was teaching that paid the bills, however, and it was to this that Father devoted most of his time. His Open successes were all the more impressive, I think, given how limited his practice opportunities must have been.

One of Father's most high-profile students was Joachim von Ribbentrop, who would later become Hitler's foreign minister. Ribbentrop held that post until 1945, when he was found guilty of war crimes and became the first high-ranking Nazi to be hanged. No doubt he died with an awful slice to his game.

More pleasingly, my father also gave lessons to the film star Marlene Dietrich and to Fritz Kreisler, the great violinist. Fritz loved golf, but Father worried he would damage his precious hands if he hit too many practice balls. So Fritz limited his game to putting, which he loved. I wish I could say the same.

I came along in 1931. From the knowledge I have gathered, I believe Father was earning as much as £8,000 a year at the time – a huge amount of money in the days when £600 was considered a good salary. The Alliss family lived then in a beautiful bungalow in the middle of the course at Wannsee. My arrival shattered the relative peace.

I was a sizeable baby, and my mother had to have two midwives looking after her, both of whom were very unsympathetic – or so I was told. The word Nazi hadn't been invented at that time, but they were certainly a 'nasty' pair. I don't suppose I helped, weighing in as I did at 14lbs 12oz. I was particularly huge considering my mother was only 5ft 3in and had never weighed more than nine stone herself. I know for a fact she didn't ride her bicycle for several months after I was born.

I was the second son. My older brother, Alexander Percy, had been born seven years earlier, in 1924. We never had a great relationship, Alec and I, and this is something which saddens me greatly. The war years and the age difference kept us apart, although we would eventually team up to run the delightful Parkstone Golf Club – overlooking Poole Harbour – after the death of Reggie Whitcombe in 1957. Reggie, the winner of the 1938 Open Championship, had been the club pro for many years, and Alec and I jointly shared the professional position after his death.

Those Parkstone days were certainly a very happy time. It was there that Alec met Joan Curry, whose father was the chairman of the company bearing her name. Joan and Alec fell in love and got married, and from then on I was left to put away the trolleys by myself each night.

But back to Father. The more I delve into his life, the more fascinating I find it. He hadn't been long on the continent before he began to move in sophisticated circles. He could read a French menu and knew how to hold a knife and fork. In golfing terms, he spoke German to a six handicap and French to fourteen. He was elegant, neat and tidy.

It's funny the things one recalls. I remember, for example, that he had beautiful hands and kept his fingernails immaculate. He always wore a shirt and tie, too – either the Argyll and Sutherland regimental tie or that of the Professional Golfers' Association. He knew about life, understood how things really were. And all that was coupled with a great sense of humour, which I hope I inherited.

But this is Germany we're talking about, and we all know what happened next. Hitler was on the rise and the persecution of the Jews had already begun. The storm clouds which had been gathering over the continent became black and leaden. Not long after I came along, my parents decided it was time for the Alliss family to come home.

Father made a final trip to the Deutsche Bank in Berlin, where he deposited around £8,000 – never to be seen again. At the end of the war he received some reparation, but it amounted to less than £100. Mother, meanwhile, made her great escape carrying me in her arms – and what a task that must have been. She crossed the German border with her bloomers string-tied just above the knee, allowing her to smuggle a good number of banknotes on her person.

Back in Blighty, Father took up residence at the Beaconsfield Golf Club on the west side of London. (Now there's a delightful course, and one where I'm proud to be an Honorary Member, along with Luke Donald.) But life in Britain took some adjusting for all of us. All that lingers from those times are my memories, at three or four years old, of going endlessly round Bekonscot Model Village – a magical attraction. It's still there today, so don't take my word for it.

The Alliss clan then moved to Temple Newsam Golf Club, a new thirty-six hole complex on the north-east side of Leeds. It was a very busy club, but again, for whatever reason, things didn't work out for my father. My one clear memory of those times is of going round the putting green with the steward's son. I have a feeling he beat me on most occasions.

In 1938 the professional's job became available at the Ferndown Golf Club in Dorset. Father applied and was called down for an interview with one other candidate: Johnny Fallon, an elegant Scottish pro. Poor Johnny's elegance came to nought, however, and dear old Dad secured the post.

Father remained at Ferndown for the rest of his life. It is a delightful course near Bournemouth with the sea to the south and the New Forest to the north. Sadly, this pocket of sheer beauty has been heavily commercialised over the past sixty years. But there are still few better places to live.

With Father installed at Ferndown, I started at the Queen Elizabeth Grammar School in Wimborne. This is one of the oldest schools in England and a place where children have been educated for over 500 years. But then war came along, and everything changed. Travel became difficult, so I was transferred to a small private school, Crosby House, on the north side of Bournemouth, about four miles from home. I was able to cycle to and from school, and in a strange way, this became for me a time of great learning.

Our Headmistress was a Mrs Violet Weymouth, an absolute Tartar. You certainly wouldn't have given her or any of her fellow teachers lip, as seems to be very prevalent in some schools today. I have dug out my final school report, which is resting on my desk as I write this. It reads:

'Peter has been an interesting pupil. He's lively and intelligent, with a good brain, which unfortunately doesn't get used as often as it should. His main interests appear to be golf and Iris Baker. I can't see any good coming from either of those activities. However, we wish him well.'

As it happens, it did indeed turn out rather well.

The war years were a strange and lean time. Bournemouth was far enough from Portsmouth and Southampton that we were not completely levelled by the Luftwaffe, but sporadic air raids still caused untold damage. I remember one particular Sunday when a fleeing bomber jettisoned his payload over the town. One bomb hit a church, which was absolutely packed. Another hit a restaurant, and the final bomb hit a cinema. Several hundred people were killed or wounded.

By this time my brother had joined the navy. He served as a wireless operator on a minesweeper in the North Atlantic. He learned his wireless skills at the Butlin's holiday camp at Lowestoft, which had been requisitioned by the powers that be and turned into a training centre. Alec came back physically unscathed, but something happened during those years which turned him into a different person, aloof and strangely independent. Thinking back on it now, I am really very sorry that we didn't have a closer relationship.

For all the turbulence in my personal life, things kept looking up on the golfing front. In 1946 my father entered me for the Boys' Championship, which was being played at the Bruntsfield Golf Club on the west side of Edinburgh. I arrived as Percy Alliss's son and was swiftly taken under the wing of Leonard Crawley, who was there as the Daily Telegraph's golf correspondent.

Crawley was a true sportsman. He was a fine cricketer and an excellent golfer, having reached Walker Cup standards. He thought I must be something too, especially as I had been picked to play for England Boys against the Scots in the international match that preceded the Championship. We won that match, which happened to be my only foray into the world of amateur golf.

Crawley took notice of me, and I was duly installed as the Telegraph's favourite to win the Boys' Championship. I made a good start, sailing through several rounds to the semi final, where I came up against a young fellow called Donald Dunstan. The pride of Manchester, Donald was a stocky boy with a rather poor complexion. He stood at 5ft 2in, and to my eyes he was mere cannon fodder. I would sweep him aside; I was sure of it.

He won three and two.

Still, I had done enough to convince Father that I ought to follow him into the family business. On the way home, he said, 'Whatever happens, I don't think you're going to be a doctor or lawyer. I think you have some golfing talent, so you can become my unpaid assistant.' Oh joy of joys – an unpaid assistant!

In those days there was no such thing as further education. Sure, if you were

LEFT: Percy Alliss in the Argyll and Sutherland Highlanders
ABOVE: Peter Alliss the 14lb 12oz baby
RIGHT: Growing fast in his mother's arms
BELOW: The young Alliss family: Percy, Alec, Peter and Dorothy

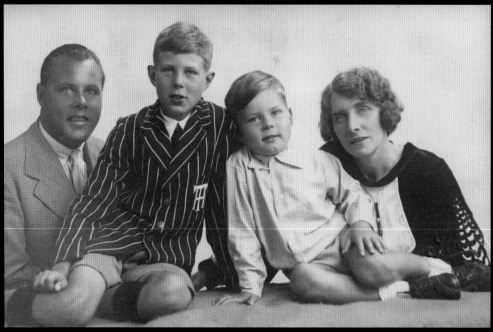

BELOW LEFT: Peter moves into his teens
BELOW: Academic success at age thirteen
RIGHT: Early days on the golf course with father Percy

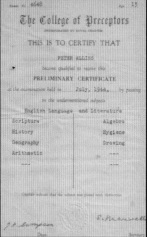

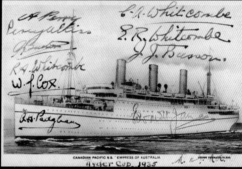

TOP AND ABOVE RIGHT: Good luck dinner for the 1935 Ryder Cup team on their way to the States on the Empress of Australia and autographed postcard

ABOVE: British Ryder Cup players support a charity day at Leatherhead in September 1935. Left to right: Charles Whitcombe, W J Cox, Ernest R Whitcombe, Reg A Whitcombe, E W Jarman, Percy Alliss, Commander Rowe and A Perry

RIGHT: Percy Alliss on the course at Wannsee and (below) in tournament action in England

CLYNE GOLF CLUB
BLACKPILL

SATURDAY, MAY 26th, 1945

Professional Exhibition of Golf
between famous British Open Championship & "Ryder Cup" players

18-Holes Singles at 2-15 p.m.

PERCY ALLISS
(Ferndown) v.

REG. WHITCOMBE
(Parkstone)

18-Holes 4-Ball Match at 5-15 p.m.

Percy Alliss & Mr. D. J. Bonnell
(FERNDOWN) (ASHBURNHAM)
v.
Reg. Whitcombe & Major M. R. Gardner
(PARKSTONE) (1935-1936 ARMY CHAMPION)

Entire proceeds in aid of the Lord Mayor of London's National Air Raid Distress Fund.

Course can be reached by Mumbles Electric Train to Blackpill (10 minutes from course) or by Swan Bus Services (three minutes from clubhouse). Marquee for refreshments.

Spectators Badges 2/6 (DONATION TO FUND) Souvenir Programmes 6d.

bright enough you might get into a university, but there weren't too many of those around. The alternative was to learn a trade. Plasterer, plumber, carpenter, painter, window cleaner... it didn't matter which; there were many ways to earn money if you had drive and energy. But with my father's words ringing in my ears, I knew I had already found my trade. I declared myself a professional golfer. Father sent away for the official papers, which were soon signed and sealed. And that was that.

By the autumn of 1946, I was earning around £10 a week, which was as much as my dear old Dad. There was little or nothing to sell in the shop, as no golf clubs were manufactured during the war. It wasn't until the John Letters Company produced an excellent copy of the McGregor line that things started to move very slowly back to normality.

Back then, I wasn't allowed in the clubhouse unless invited by a member. Neither was my father, even though he was a star. My status was nothing compared to his, but it wouldn't be too long before I started to move up in the world of golf.

In the meantime, I enjoyed my own version of a further education at Ferndown. I remember the days not long after the war, when I was playing off scratch before my fourteenth birthday. Those who knew a thing or two thought that I could possibly be the next Tom Morris Jr. If only!

You could say I was studying at the University of Life, thanks to a handful of members who did so much to broaden my horizons. One of my lecturers, as it were, was a retired dental surgeon by the name of Joe Close. Then came Thomas and Harold Wakefield, who were from an oil family, and Ralph Langton, whose family owned a brewery on the Isle of Wight. In the war, Ralph had been a tank commander, and he certainly looked the part. Standing at 6ft 4in, he was elegant and wonderfully louche – and what a character! He loved the ladies; he was a rascal, a rogue, a womaniser and an absolute delight.

And then there was Major Ruttle, a great supporter of mine. One of his companies was the Gresham Trust, which had been involved in Madame Tussauds and the building of the London Planetarium. He had a daughter named Maureen, who became Maureen Garrett. She captained a Curtis Cup team and received the Bobby Jones Award for services to golf. She was one of my dearest friends.

I used to go down to the practice ground at Ferndown when Maureen was having lessons from my father. The Major was always in attendance, and father urged him not to let Maureen have too many lessons, insisting she had to learn to use her own brain. I can still hear him saying, 'Find out for yourself, then come and talk to me. Tell me what you've seen; tell me what you've noticed. Learn to think for yourself.' Many of today's players lack the ability, or perhaps the willingness, to think for themselves. They seem only too happy to outsource decisions to their various gurus and coaches. It's not how my father would have liked it.

Come 1949, I was living a lovely life and playing lots of golf with these colourful characters. But National Service loomed. Thursday 16th June 1949 – the day my service began – is forever engraved in my memory. It was my first real solo journey away from home: from Bournemouth to London, up to Chester, then on to West Kirby on the Wirral. I remember standing in line as a chap in uniform looked me over before asking if I fancied being a gunner. I thought that sounded like a fine idea, serving in the Royal Air Force as a 'Tail End Charlie' – a tail gunner, stuck in the worst part of the plane if there was any real action. I gambled on a quiet period of service, supposing it would be a romantic time either way. I would enjoy the camaraderie and impress the girls. Whisper it, but I even nurtured visions of becoming a hero.

There was one vision that never came to pass. Instead, I found myself in the RAF Regiment, which turned out to be a cross between the Foreign Legion and the Pioneer Corps. They were wonderful days nonetheless, and I look back on National Service as a second education. There was a lot to learn: how to get on with people, how to look after your kit, keep time, clean shoes, be mindful of others. 'Think boy, think!' I went on to Catterick, a huge airfield to the side of the A1, just short of the eponymous village in North Yorkshire.

Catterick was the RAF Regiment's main depot. It is now under the control of the army, but I remember my winter there: months on end spiced with a mixture of nerves, joy, trepidation and affection. I made friendships which, at the time, were worth as much gold. From Catterick I visited a few other bases before ending up at Watchet on the North Devon coast. This was a small ack-ack gunnery school, and it was here where I completed my National Service.

There were only twenty-two regular staff at Watchet. It was a wonderful experience – one I shared with the distance runner Gordon Pirie, who was stationed alongside me at the time. He was then preparing for the 1952 Olympic Games and was awarded special privileges to help him maintain his training routine. I made sure I stuck closely to him and even managed to get a few crumbs from his table.

One of my greatest coups, however, came when I was allowed to exchange my boots for walking shoes, on account of my dropped metatarsals. This victory was eclipsed only by my successes with Molly, the girl whose parents owned the milk bar down by the harbour. She was a delight, and never more so than when she was teaching me how to French kiss. We never considered going further for fear of catching something itchy-scratchy or getting in the family way. Neither was a desirable option, so I made my peace with going to bed frustrated without ever really knowing why.

Alec was working then at Weston-super-Mare Golf Club. It was a lively place and home to some good players. Naturally, I was all too happy to get away from Watchet to visit my brother every now and then. The course was very pleasant, and I remember some of the members: Jim Payne; Donald Hood-Wright, the Secretary; E J Poole; Neville Jutsun; George Irlam… all fine golfers. They were all interesting and all had something to say about life, money and marriage. I'm not sure whether those sorts of conversations go on today, but I like to think they do.

Eventually, I came to the end of my service. I was offered the chance to sign on for another year and become a corporal, but I chose instead to go back to Ferndown, where my golf career would start in earnest. I picked up where I had left off, and soon golf expanded once again to fill my entire life.

My first Ryder Cup came in 1953. My selection was, in truth, a desperate move by the authorities. In 1947 and 1951, Great Britain and Ireland had taken a terrible thumping. In 1949 – when the matches were played at Ganton, a superb course in East Yorkshire – we should have won but fell at the last hurdle. The losses were mounting up. There were cries for change, and new blood was clearly needed. Only Bernard Hunt and yours truly were available at the time, and so we were given our chance.

Back then, The Ryder Cup was in deep financial trouble. The rights were owned by the Professional Golfers' Association, and they were virtually penniless. Without the financial help of the American fruit canning magnate Robert Hudson and Sir Stuart Goodwin of Neepsend Steel of Sheffield, the Ryder Cup might well have sunk into oblivion – like the Wightman Cup in tennis. How things have changed over the last forty years! I'm pleased to say the Ryder Cup is now one of the world's great sporting events, and I'm just as pleased to have played my own small part in its history.

That 1953 Ryder Cup was played at Wentworth, under the captaincy of the ever elegant Henry Cotton. We should have won but we fell short – due, in no small part, to my inexperience. We played thirty-six-hole matches in those days, foursomes and singles. A player could only win two points if he won both matches. And there I was, one up with three to play on the West Course at Wentworth.

My opponent was Jim Turnesa, the US PGA Champion that year and one of a big family of golfers. Somehow I managed to lose two of those last three holes, and we lost the match 6½ to 5½. The press, officials and spectators were all deeply disappointed and said so in no uncertain terms. Their disappointment weighed heavily on me for many years.

The PGA, in its wisdom, picked neither me nor Bernard Hunt for the 1955 matches, which took place in Palm Springs. It will give you a sense of how long ago that was when I say Palm Springs boasted only a few courses at the time. Today there are over 120. The United States won again, making it seven wins on the bounce.

Bernard and I returned to the team in 1957. The matches were played at Lindrick, a splendid course dissected by the A57. The road was temporarily closed, which caused much wailing and gnashing of teeth. But when Great

Britain and Ireland roared back, all was forgiven. Although I contributed nothing as far as points were concerned, I remember the joyous scenes as if they were yesterday.

Looking back, we were quite disadvantaged, and we won very much against the odds. Wives were not allowed to accompany us, and we were treated like novice monks. The Americans, on the other hand, arrived with all their ladies in all their glory: fur coats, high heels, jewellery, beautifully coiffured hair, full make-up… the lot. I'm not sure if our wives were left out because the PGA couldn't afford the extra cost, or perhaps they had to stay home because the authorities feared we might get up to a bit of hand holding (or worse) in the middle of the night. This, of course, might upset the rhythm of our putting or – God forbid – throw off our delicate pitch shots from a bare lie over a bunker to a downhill green. Who knows what they were thinking, but either way it didn't go down well. Some of us felt we were a couple down before we got to the first tee. The fact is we were poverty stricken compared to the USA team, but at the end of the day we won handsomely. Everyone was a hero – perhaps with one exception. Not that it stopped me enjoying the various beverages on offer. You couldn't fault my team spirit in that regard.

I did go on to have great success in the Ryder Cup, mainly with Christy O'Connor as my partner. I had some special moments in other events with Scot John Panton, a marvellous foursome partner. Bernard Hunt and I also enjoyed great success as partners over the years. Abiding friendships were formed – not just with teammates but also with men like Arnold Palmer, Jack Nicklaus, Billy Caspar and Doug Sanders. These were friendships which lasted forever.

Over the years, fraternising has sadly become less common. Afterwards it's okay to chat, but be careful not to give anything away during the match! It's almost as if we were guarding some great secret handed down by the golfing gods for our special use. How I wish that was the case.

Today, the media drives most developments in the world of golf, as it does with developments in the wider world. Newspapers may be struggling, but television is in rude health, and everyone seems to possess a telephone that will do everything except make you an omelette. Soon people won't even need to bother with school – a great pity for many young people who already struggle to write with a legible hand and for whom the use of grammar is a dying art. Am I beginning to sound like an old grump yet?

Anyway, I played in eight Ryder Cup teams and played ten times for England in the World Cup. I was lucky never to play in any of the World Cup matches closest to home. Don't think me rude, but not for me were Rome, Madrid, Dublin and London; instead I got to visit Japan, Australia, Mexico, South America and Hawaii. What bliss to have $500 in travellers' cheques and a seat at the back of the plane.

I remember how we would stop off in Hong Kong to play a couple of matches

ABOVE LEFT: Peter Alliss in 1949, a fast-emerging talent at eighteen
ABOVE: 1952 Exhibition match at Bridport and West Dorset with Max Faulkner
ABOVE RIGHT: Peter Alliss and Bernard Hunt representing England in the Canada Cup
LEFT: Percy and Peter at the Spalding golf at Worthing 1953
BELOW: Winning the PGA Closed Championship at Llandudno in 1957
BOTTOM: A spot of bother at The Open at St Andrews in 1957

ABOVE LEFT: More success at the PGA Closed Championship at Little Aston in 1962
ABOVE: Winning the Esso Matchplay at Moor Park in 1964
LEFT: Competing at the Wentworth Foursomes in 1965 and (below) at The Open at Carnoustie in 1968
BOTTOM LEFT: Telegram wishing Ryder Cup success from National Service friend and distance runner Gordon Pirie
BOTTOM RIGHT: Swinging well at the PGA Closed Championship at Royal Mid Surrey in 1961

at Fanling or Happy Valley. There I would have suits made for me overnight, although sometimes I wished the tailoring could have been done during daylight hours – particularly when nothing fit all that well. I'd buy beautiful, soft leather shoes for £10 a pair and ride up The Peak by tram for the view of Hong Kong harbour at night. All those blazing lights made for a magical scene – one which seemed impossibly exotic. In Hong Kong I lived like a millionaire.

I remember looking at new cars, stroking them and admiring them. I used to wonder if one day I'd be able to afford one. Daimlers, Jaguars, Rovers, Bentleys and Rolls Royces... this was long before the days of Lamborghinis and the like. But I'd have to work, and win, to ever make it that far. And that's what I endeavoured to do.

In the final accounting, I won twenty professional tournaments. Along the way I forged lasting friendships with the likes of David Thomas; Dai Rees; Max Faulkner; Bernard Hunt and his brother, Geoff; Italy's Ugo Grappasonni and Aldo Casera; and the Miguel brothers from Spain. The overseas players of the day had little success in the UK, but on home territory they were formidable opponents. Players looking back today have little concept of how good they were.

Earlier I mentioned Parkstone Golf Club, where I was the joint professional alongside Alec. It was during my Parkstone days in the late fifties and sixties when I had much of my playing success. I found club life to be enormous fun, so very different from my days at Ferndown. I won many major events during this period, and it was no coincidence that this success went hand in hand with my happiness at Parkstone.

My most enjoyable – and indeed, memorable – tournament win was the Esso Round Robin at the Moor Park Golf Club. It was a small field, and everyone played everyone for the £750 first prize. I found myself in a winning position with a round to go; I was already uncatchable, and what a joyous occasion that made for. Just fancy going out for the final round with the £750 prize already tucked away in your back pocket. To top it off, I was playing my great friend Christy O'Connor. Oh, the joy I felt when stepping onto that first tee for the last time! For once, it really was a walk in the park. Happy days.

PS While researching this book, I came across a contract my father signed in 1938, when he was the professional at Temple Newsam Golf Club. It's interesting to note that my father had expenses paid for playing in eight tournaments that year, from Newcastle in the north to Rickmansworth in the south. Total expenses were £57.17 (around £4,000 today), and his base salary was £5 a week – worth about £18,000 per annum in today's money. A club pro's salary in 2018 averaged £25,000 at your typical club and double that at more prestigious places. Of course, more money can always be earned by giving lessons and so on.

Another sheet of yellowing paper, this one from 1961, reveals that the PGA offered fifteen tournaments in which to compete, with entry fees costing a few hundred pounds. One of the biggest entry fees, £411, was for the Ballantine Tournament staged at Wentworth and won by Neil Coles. The total amount raised from the gate and car park charges was £1,917, which is around £50,000 now. That's still no fortune and far adrift of the monies raised when the PGA Championship is staged at Wentworth these days.

IT always amused Peter that quite a few people thought he had never played golf professionally and that his entire career had been on television. It is always worth reminding those who don't know the facts that Peter won those twenty significant titles, alongside eleven lesser events. Perhaps the greatest testament to his golfing prowess is the month of October 1958, when a sustained burst of brilliance saw him take the Italian, Spanish and Portuguese Opens in successive weeks. He won by ten strokes in both Italy and Spain and by six shots in Portugal.

Judged by anyone's standards, this is an extraordinary highlight reel, reflecting Peter's ability not only to play but to perform under pressure. The reward for that golden October was just £650, worth roughly £15,000 in today's money. Of course, this is rather better than the proverbial slap in the face with a wet kipper, but it does lag somewhat behind the approximate £1.5m such a hat-trick would earn today. Times change, of course, but nowhere is that change more evident than on the bank statements of today's most successful golfers.

TEA, BISCUITS AND GREATNESS

PETER became acquainted with golf's aristocracy at a very early age. How could it have been otherwise, when his father was a gilded member of that glittering brigade? Peter remembered coming home from school one day to find his mum and dad taking tea in the kitchen with no fewer than four Open champions: Alf Perry (1935), Alf Padgham (1936), Reggie Whitcombe (1938) and Dick Burton (1939). A fifth golfer at the table, Ernest Whitcombe, was runner-up in the 1924 Open. That's some tea party for an aspiring golf pro to quietly sit in on!

A young Peter listened in as these great golfers, all friends of the family, reminisced about this and that. He grew up surrounded by legends, and through a process of osmosis he became steeped in the rich traditions of our ancient sport. Is it any wonder, then, that he was destined to become an outstanding player himself, rubbing shoulders with so many of golf's true greats along the way?

I RECENTLY spent an afternoon leafing through an old *Golfer's Handbook*. I was amazed to discover that I have either played with or met all but eight of the winners of every Open Championship since 1900. Quite a remarkable little fact (even if I say so myself), and how curious that I'd never before realised just how many of these champions had crossed my path. The magical missing octet are Alex Herd, Jack White, Arnaud Massy, Ted Ray, Harry Vardon, Jim Barnes, Denny Shute and Jock Hutchinson – Father's former boss. All the others I've had the pleasure of meeting. Mind you, I did get off to an early start, playing in my first Open Championship at the ripe old age of sixteen.

Picture it. The year: 1947. The venue: Royal Liverpool, perhaps better known as Hoylake. It was the year of Fred Daly, the whistling Northern Irishman and, incidentally, the only Irishman to win a major until Padraig Harrington triumphed in the 2007 Open. Back in Fred's day, everyone, including the holder, had to qualify for the Championship. It was eighteen holes on Wednesday, eighteen on Thursday and thirty-six – yes, thirty-six – holes on Friday. We had to wrap it up so the professionals could get back to their clubs and look after their members over the weekend. Not a problem faced by today's professionals, of course. I didn't make it past the qualifying rounds that year, but I stayed on to watch the rest. How I remember those final moments, with the rugby-playing Australian Bill Shankland and the American amateur Frank Stranahan fighting to the very end.

This was, of course, the era of South Africa's Bobby Locke and Australia's Peter Thomson, who dominated the sport in the 1940s, '50s and '60s. And how beautifully they played. There was a certain aura about them, a quiet confidence rather than out-and-out ego. You knew they were good, they knew they were good, and because everyone else knew as well, there was never any need to shout about it.

In fact, there were very few – if indeed any – arrogant professionals in those days. It wasn't the case that golf players were uniquely saintly; sportsmen of all stripes just didn't have such big heads. Beside fame and the adulation of the public, there were no great rewards for most sportsmen back then. In the world of football, for example, £10 a week was the maximum wage for the top players. One or two bonuses crept in here and there, but the only distractions at that time came between racing pigeons, enjoying a pint of mild and bitter and going to the cinema. There were no glamourous women clamouring for your attention, and the greatest players in the world either cycled or took the bus to matches. Life then was very simple and understated. And although it wasn't quite that way for the professional golfers, it wasn't far off.

The great Fred Perry said he made up his mind to make tennis his profession when he walked past his local tennis club on the outskirts of Manchester. What did he see? A fleet of fine motor cars and a general air of affluence. He was already the world table tennis champion, but he couldn't resist the chance to go into a more upmarket sport. And it wasn't until Henry Cotton started to make a mark in the world of golf that our sport went down that same road. Professionals soon began to realise the importance of taking events seriously, dressing well, and maybe even winning The Open – a tournament which suddenly elevated its victors to the company of the high and mighty. Open glory also allowed you to charge more for your teaching services. In Henry Cotton's case, of course, it also helped when he married Isabel-Maria Estanguet de Moss, the daughter of an extremely wealthy Buenos Aries beef merchant.

Henry lived from then on in great style, in fine houses with servants, but he remained for his entire life a professional golfer. I am sure there are people who can remember going to buy some tees or balls at Penina Golf Club in the Algarve, a course Henry designed, and being astounded to be served by the maestro himself in the club shop. It's impossible to imagine Arnold Palmer, Jack Nicklaus or Tiger Woods in that situation.

You don't need me to tell you that the world of professional golf has changed hugely since I made my Open debut. In those days, a professional had not only to be attached to a club, but they had to be in full receipt of the shop's takings and any revenue from teaching. Books had to be kept, and bills had to be paid.

There were, of course, some great players who had it a little easier – for example, those fortunate enough to be attached to the Coombe Hill Golf Club. Here they pioneered a great scheme whereby talented young professionals could become attached to the club for a very low retainer, in some cases just £5 or £10 a year. In return, the professional could use the facilities of the club for practice and the name of the club when entering all golfing events. This was something of a win-win, and affiliation to Coombe Hill certainly made pros look far better than AN Other (Unattached).

These Coombe Hill professionals were the exceptions, though. In almost all other cases, golfers back then really lived a dual life – one moment a shopkeeper, the next a star. Then came a dramatic change in the early seventies. That's when the Professional Golfers' Association split in two, resulting in a divide between the golf professionals and the professional golfers. The former group stayed at home to look after the members and visitors, playing in local events and becoming very much an integral part of their club. The latter lot rode out like professional gamblers, their motto: 'Have clubs, will travel.'

This new wave of professional golfers carried no particular affiliation to a club. Instead, they took with them a mere endorsement as they travelled the world playing in various tournaments. They wagered everything on their ability to win a living; if they didn't win, they didn't eat. Little did those early pioneers imagine that the game would ever grow to such vast proportions as it has. The life of a professional golfer is certainly very different now. I'm not sure whether today's players are happier, but they're definitely richer.

That split in golf's professional ranks called for the establishment of a whole new organisation: the European Tour. Stars from across the continent appeared suddenly on the scene. The prize money grew with the Tour's reputation, and in time more players arrived from Australia, New Zealand, South Africa and the Far East. The prize pot kept growing, and like moths to a flame, out came the managers and agents, those men and women in their fine suits who sapped much of the individuality from the players. In fairness, this was sometimes a good thing, as many of the players had absolutely no business acumen – and why should they? These same players had been suddenly thrust into a new, very rarefied atmosphere. Something similar happened in football, and it didn't take long before the agents were virtually running the show.

Golf, however, is a slightly different beast. For one, it is much more simple than most team games. Simple, why? Well, for a start, if you don't play well, you don't earn any money. How's that for simple? In a team sport, meanwhile, you can be injured or out of form for months and still get paid.

On the other hand, I know the playing life of most sportsmen is really quite short, since time is the natural enemy of athleticism. It's a longer life in golf, especially with the growth of the Senior Tour, but you still have to earn your money; you still have to be more than competent to make a good living and, indeed, survive. Being self-employed is a good thing for many of us, but it comes with its own challenges, whether you are laying bricks, baking cakes or whacking golf balls.

When Arnold Palmer arrived from America in the sixties, I thought he had the aura of a man who was more than good enough to make it. He had a quiet air, but the look in his eye said he could beat anybody. I got to know Arnold very well and enjoyed his company tremendously. He liked a drink, a cigarette and a well-turned ankle. He was what you might call a discreet romantic. He was a true star, too, and a working-class hero to many. Then Jack Nicklaus joined him on the scene. The king was pushed slightly to one side and the public didn't like it.

Compared to Arnold, Jack wasn't such a looker. Arnold could have been a film star, and he had the added advantage of being an ex-marine. Jack, meanwhile, was rather tubby, sporting if not quite a shaven head then certainly a very severe crew cut. He had also a high-pitched, squeaky voice which seemed particularly unflattering next to Arnold's manly baritone. But Jack was wise enough to let his clubs do the talking, and there was nothing squeaky about those.

For a time, some of Arnold's fans treated Jack disgracefully, shouting as he swung and waving placards now and then urging him to 'hit it into the trees, fat boy!' Sooner rather than later, however, Jack won over the majority of his critics with the skill of his play and his instinctively sporting personality.

In truth, I've seen three Jack Nicklauses in my time. First came the original. Then, in the early seventies, he found a decent hairdresser, lost 30lbs, started dressing sharper and emerged with his own brand of film-star looks. All this complemented a strategically impressive game and a nerve that never seemed to crack – no matter how great the pressure. Finally, there came the mature old campaigner who suddenly spoke enormous sense and was well worth listening to. Today, Jack has honed his ability to explain complex things in a simple way. Younger players ought to listen closely when he speaks and take on board as much as they can. I'm sure some do, but I suspect many don't, which is a great pity.

The final member of the Big Three, as they were dubbed, was South Africa's Gary Player, who has a remarkable record and has won everywhere. I love Gary dearly, but he does have a tendency to exaggerate. I've always wondered why, when his great feats are plainly there to be read and admired. He really doesn't have to tell everybody how successful he's been, how many countries he's visited, how many miles he's travelled and how difficult it was travelling with an ever-growing family. He also liked to exaggerate in his tales of how much things used to cost. It's rather laughable to anyone who was actually there at the time, as I was.

One of Gary's best-known stories tells of his arrival at St Andrews for the Open Championship in 1955. He claimed he couldn't find any accommodation and slept on the beach. Later, he said he did find one room but it would have cost £50 per night. I'm not sure where he plucked that figure from, but in those days £50 would have got you a week at the London Savoy. Still, I admire and enjoy much of what he says and does, even if some of his thoughts on life, food, exercise and the widespread use of performance-enhancing drugs are, at times, bordering on fantasy. If anyone could produce a miracle drug to make you play better, many of us would be taking it tomorrow. Pinning individual successes on doping doesn't adequately take into account the way the human mind and body work, although there are some who would disagree.

Anyway, on paper, certainly, Gary's record is unparalleled, and he truly is the world's golfing ambassador. Yet, for whatever reason, I believe he's still yet to receive the full acclaim he deserves for everything he achieved – much of it against the odds.

For a few years, Tony Jacklin joined this pantheon of the very best players in the world. He lifted British golf in a way it hadn't been lifted since Henry Cotton's days, and much of that was due to the advent of television – especially the proliferation of colour broadcasts. His success also coincided with a general increase in media attention for our sport. Almost overnight, celebrity seemed as important as ability. More money came pouring in, and egos grew in line with bank balances.

Our Tony had one unfortunate trait, and that was that he tended to blame everybody and anybody except himself when things didn't go right. He also didn't appear to have any real grasp of how to deal with money, and he was very lucky to have shrewd women in his life to help him. His first wife, Vivien, sadly died of a brain haemorrhage while they were living in Spain. He then married Astrid, a Norwegian divorcee. Unlike Tony, these women understood money and what to do with it. Without them, Tony's feet may not have remained so firmly on the ground.

When his game ultimately went south, Tony pointed the finger at his agent, Mark McCormack – an American lawyer and the founder of the International Management Group. Tony claimed Mark had soured his game by sending him off to play all over the world in various tournaments and exhibition matches, instead of allowing him to settle down and practice. Tony also blamed IMG for allowing him to buy that great house in Gloucestershire in the early seventies, at a cost of well over £100,000. When the running costs of the house and other excesses started to overwhelm his life, Tony complained that Mark should have been more forceful in guiding him through his financial affairs. Tony ultimately had no choice but to sell up and move to Jersey.

He may not have a financial brain, but one thing Tony does understand is woodwork. His craft with a fretsaw is really quite superb, and if the BBC ever decides to do a series of programmes on the unusual hobbies and pastimes of famous people, Tony would be a natural choice for one of the slots. Sadly, he's now gone quite deaf, but he seems to be enjoying life in Florida, where he associates closely with Jack Nicklaus. The pair worked together on a magnificent course called The Concession, named after the famous putt Nicklaus conceded to Tony in the 1969 Ryder Cup. The matches that year were played at Royal Birkdale, and that famous putt resulted in a halved series – to the delight of many but to the great annoyance of some of Nicklaus's team mates. Although the halved match meant the Americans retained the trophy, they were robbed of a chance to actually win the match.

Looking back now and talking about the greats of yesteryear makes me think fondly about the life we players lived back then. Everything was much more friendly and collegial; we golfers travelled together and usually shared bedrooms while we were away. Remember: back in the fifties and sixties there were very few hotels with ensuite bathrooms. We all travelled with pyjamas, a dressing gown, a towel and a bar of soap. When we needed to, we set off down the corridor hoping to find an empty bathroom that had been left as one would wish to find it. Often they were not.

Compared to these gentler, simpler times, the modern player doesn't appear to socialise much. In fact, chit chat seems to have been a casualty of golf's success. Players nowadays either travel alone or as a family unit, and on the whole they're happy to keep their heads down and get on with their luxurious lives. Thirty-six holes in a day is now but a pipe dream.

The routine, these days, seems to consist of breakfast, settling the family, going to the course, hitting some balls, having a sandwich and then off you go. Eighteen holes later you come in, get back on the range and hit a few balls to cool down or try to find that elusive secret we've all been looking for since the dawn of the sport. Then it's back to the hotel, early supper, TV and then bed. And you're up again the next day for the same routine. It wouldn't have done for me or my playing friends.

In truth, today's golf stars can give the impression that they're rather a dull lot. They don't talk about much besides the game of golf, and I often wonder what hobbies they have – if indeed any. What are they good at away from the course? Do they read? Repair watches? Paint? It's all a bit of a mystery, although I can't imagine any of today's pros hunched over a workbench with a fretsaw quivering away in their hands.

It may be a good thing, however, that today's professionals live more cleanly than those in my day. Tom Watson has been one of the world's very best, of course, but there was a time when he really enjoyed a glass or two of whisky. Mind you, I also remember how Jack Nicklaus used to scrounge cigarettes off anybody who smoked. Then, when asked if he shared that habit, he would always say: 'Oh, good heavens, no. I would never dream of doing that.' It's like Gary Player, who insists he has very rarely, if ever, tasted alcohol. And God forbid he ever held a girl's hand besides that of his dear wife, Vivienne.

Tom Watson, incidentally, is one of very few players who, deep into his sixties, could still swing a club almost exactly as he did thirty years before. The only part of his game that has creaked a little with age has been his putting. No disrespect to Stuart Cink, but how I wish Watson had won The Open in 2009 at Turnberry – not just for sentimental reasons but because it would have shown the world that, when the conditions are right, it is still possible to compete at the highest level even if you're old enough to be classed as a pensioner. Oh, Tom Watson. There's a bright, cheerful breath of fresh air – a spring-in-the-step player of the sort that doesn't come around very often.

Nick Faldo, meanwhile, is one of those characters who inhabits a world of his own. When he first stepped into the golfing arena he was much lighter, with a willowy swing. He was very rhythmical and rather reminiscent of the late, great Tony Lema. After a pretty good start to his career, he decided that if he were to improve, changes had to be made. He discovered David Leadbetter, then a little-known coach, and off they went to do great things together, armed with a variety of rather bizarre aids. I'm talking about a beach ball between the knees or a golf ball under the left armpit… or was it the right? That sort of thing. As unorthodox as it might have been, the training regimen worked. Faldo changed and grew as a player, although it took him a year or two to get into the right mode. Mentally, he became very focused, which was a key component of his great skill. For the best part of a decade he was truly superb, and his aloof character added to the mix in a way that made him appear so dominant over his rivals.

Faldo certainly played three or four of the best shots I've ever seen. His iron shot to the 13th green during his victory at Augusta; his last four holes at Muirfield on his way to winning the Open Championship; that pitch up to the last green in the Ryder Cup at Oak Hill against Curtis Strange; the putt from four-and-a-half feet to win the point… they were all brilliant. And his final round at the Masters, when he beat Greg Norman so comprehensively, was undoubtedly, under the circumstances, one of the finest rounds of golf I've ever seen. At no stage during the eighteen holes did he display any triumphalism, which is to his great credit. That applied also to his great caddie and golfing partner for the day, Fanny Sunesson. All wonderful moments.

Faldo has always seemed to get on very well with young people, perhaps better than he gets on with adults. His association with his children, despite umpteen marriages, seems solid and loving. To me it's a pity that he so often comes across as such a cold fish with a weird sense of humour, which he mistakenly thinks is a cross between Bob Hope, Eric Morecambe and the Goons. His lack of charm is more than a little off-putting. I admire him in many ways, but I also think that if he and I were stranded on a desert island, we wouldn't be singing many songs around the campfire of a night.

Then there was Greg Norman, who I first encountered in the summer of 1977.

I was then filming a BBC instructional series called *Play Better Golf* at the Downfield Golf Course on the north side of Dundee. The series producer was one Gordon Menzies, a great figure in Scottish television and the man responsible for one of the most amusing delights in Scotch and Wry, a programme of sketches, music and dance which, in my opinion, has never been bettered.

Greg was on his first visit to the UK, under the watchful eye of my good friend Guy Wolstenholme, who found himself working at once as a mentor, bodyguard, tutor, taxi driver and all-round consultant on the ways of the world. This arrangement worked very well, and Greg immediately exhibited a great deal of talent and athleticism, topped off with a good putting touch. The only chink in his armour was his work round the green: his pitching, chipping and his performance in bunkers.

But Greg worked long and hard on those parts of the game and became, for a relatively short period, a giant. He played and won all over the world. But at the end of it all, perhaps he didn't quite fulfil his huge potential. On occasions he was robbed, on others he was desperately unlucky and on others still there was a touch of self-destruction stirred in with his innate talent. Regardless, he certainly left his mark on the game. Although he kept playing competitively into his fifties, he never made the senior circuit his be all and end all. Instead, he has become an extremely successful businessman, driven and determined, some might say ruthless in pursuit of greatness and the ever appealing dollar. Perhaps the grass really is greener on the other side, although I sometimes wonder at what true cost Not particularly good at the marriage stakes, granted, but he is someone who has left a considerable shadow wherever he's travelled and has had a significant impact on the game itself.

Over my many years in the world of golf I really have met so many of the world's greatest players. It's only when I stop and look back that I realise just how lucky I am to have been acquainted with all these stars in golf's firmament. It helped that I started young, of course. As a boy, I was surrounded by fame, and I didn't even realise it. Before 1950 – in the days when golfers were still shopkeepers – I don't think any of the sport's stars, apart from perhaps Henry Cotton, recognised just how famous they were. They'd all won the Open Championship, dammit, but in practice that meant rather little. They were club professionals who had taken a week off giving lessons to play and win The Open for a grand prize of 100 guineas. It's very hard to appreciate today, with all the money sloshing around our sport. Interestingly, all these people had a few traits in common. They all seemed (in public, anyway) gentle, kind and well mannered. In old fashioned parlance, they all knew their place and rarely, if ever, stepped out of line.

I was fortunate enough to meet Bobby Jones when I went to Washington DC to play in the Canada Cup, which later became the World Cup. Bobby was then in the early stages of his battle with arthritis, and those fingers which had once held a golf club so elegantly were already becoming swollen and twisted. One of my abiding memories is of the Ronson cigarette lighter which hung on a ribbon round his neck. I recall, also, the small ivory cigarette holder with which he was forever fiddling. I enjoyed his quiet charm and marvelled at the relatively small stature of this man (he stood at 5ft 8ins and weighed barely over eleven stone) who had been such a golfing colossus.

Back in Bobby's day, it was difficult for us mere mortals to grasp the success these players had achieved over the years. Fame was a very delicate subject; it had to be earned and then earned again (and perhaps again) before people became aware of who and what you were. Only the newspapers, radio broadcasts and newsreels carried reports of fame, and these reports travelled around the world slowly. The reality was that you had to become a giant in your particular field to be known globally. No wonder there were so few swollen-headed sportsmen and women in those far-off days. It also explains how some truly great players were allowed to fly under the radar.

That brings me neatly to Byron Nelson, perhaps the most underrated and certainly the most overlooked player in the history of the game. He was like the professional version of Bobby Jones, winning dozens of events before retiring early. He won eleven consecutive tournaments on the American Tour, such as it was in the early 1940s, and claimed victory in eighteen events in the year 1945. But they (whoever 'they' were) said his achievements were of no real consequence because so many other players were away fighting the war. Nonsense! You only have to look at the scores he put together over those eighteen tournaments to realise how brilliant he was. He averaged just above sixty-nine shots a round for every round he played that competitive year – a record which stood for many decades until Tiger Woods came along with far superior equipment on courses which were much better presented.

I played with Byron in the French Open in 1955 in Paris. He was on holiday with his wife and decided to enter, perhaps having been talked into it. He had hardly played for years, having retired when he was thirty-four ('I had just become sick and tired of competing,' he was later to admit). He won that week in France. Many people found it difficult to believe, but I was there and I saw it happen. He still had that familiar swing, that excellent balance, that sweetness of the strike... the years had not dulled them. Byron Nelson, a true great.

I remember also my first sighting of Peter Thomson. It was 15th June 1951, around four o'clock in the afternoon. How can I be so precise, all these years later? Well, it was the day I was discharged from the RAF Regiment, having completed my two years of National Service, so it's a date I'll never forget. The occasion was the Penfold Festival of Britain Tournament at the Queens Park Golf Club, one of two fine municipal courses in Bournemouth at the time. This was before the construction of the new road into Bournemouth, which took away a little of the course and the clubhouse.

I stood on the veranda looking down onto the 18th green and there he was, replete with white shoes, dark green trousers, white shirt and a white tennis visor. My father nudged me and said, 'There's a young fellow who could become good over the years. Peter Thomson is his name; he's an Aussie. You'll come across him sooner rather than later.'

How right my father was. Three years later, Peter and I played a practice round at Royal Birkdale, the scene of his first victory in the Open Championship. I finished a handful of shots behind him and never managed to get any closer to victory. But we struck up a friendship that lasted more than sixty years.

Peter was, in some ways, rather strange and distant. He spoke very little about his parents or his early life. There definitely was something about him that struck me as simply different. He liked to read the classics, and he was passionately interested in politics. Although these twin interests are not unique, they are rather rare on the golf circuit. Returning to Britain after a period in the United States, he had in his possession the complete recording of My Fair Lady, which was huge on Broadway then. He knew the words to every song, and although he was no Frank Sinatra, he would sing a tune, any tune, at the drop of a hat and with a smile on his face. He was also a great fan of Bernard Cribbins. Many times have I listened to "Right Said Fred," "Hole In The Ground" and other such delights.

Many Americans didn't think he had the game for their long, watered courses. When he was old enough he decided – perhaps, as usual, on a whim – to play on their senior circuit. 'I'll give it a go,' I can hear him saying. And give it a go he did, winning nine events in a year before waving goodbye and heading back to Australia with a cheery cry of, 'There, I told you I could play a bit!' He never returned.

Therein lies the strangeness of Peter Thomson. Done it, enjoyed it, won it… and so why bother to do it again? A weird concept, perhaps, but that was him. Sadly, he struggled with Alzheimer's for the last few years of his life. The strain on his family, particularly his wife, Mary, was considerable. But there was a man who maintained his uniqueness even as he fitted quite beautifully into his time. He was a dear friend.

Bobby Locke, meanwhile, was simply a golfing phenomenon. Standing at just under 6ft, he was gangly with a toothy smile. He had a swing all of his own, but his putting touch was surely handed down by the gods. He had been pursuing a first-class amateur career in South Africa prior to the Second World War, at which point golf had to be put on the back burner (as it was for so many). He served in the South African Air Force and, amongst other things, ferried bombers to and from war zones. There was little time for golf, but after the war he finally got his chance.

TOP LEFT: Friends and team mates of Percy Alliss, the 1929 Ryder Cup team at Moortown

TOP RIGHT: Fred Daly, Norman Von Nida, Henry Cotton and Bobby Locke at Moortown in 1949

ABOVE LEFT: Playing with Max Faulkner at Walton Heath In the News of the World Championships in 1958

ABOVE: Alf Padgham playing against Percy Alliss in an exhibition match at Sundridge Park in 1933 and (left) Peter Alliss playing with Bobby Locke at The Open at Royal Birkdale in 1971

FAR LEFT: The cost of an overnight stay in 1964

BELOW: Henry Cotton (left) congratulates Walter Hagen for defending his Open title at Muirfield in 1929

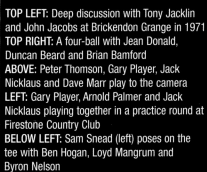

TOP LEFT: Deep discussion with Tony Jacklin and John Jacobs at Brickendon Grange in 1971
TOP RIGHT: A four-ball with Jean Donald, Duncan Beard and Brian Bamford
ABOVE: Peter Thomson, Gary Player, Jack Nicklaus and Dave Marr play to the camera
LEFT: Gary Player, Arnold Palmer and Jack Nicklaus playing together in a practice round at Firestone Country Club
BELOW LEFT: Sam Snead (left) poses on the tee with Ben Hogan, Loyd Mangrum and Byron Nelson
BELOW: Bettye Mims Danoff, Babe Zaharias, Louise Suggs and Patty Berg in 1950

Even as the ink was drying on the peace treaties, Bobby was on his way to the United States, where, from day one, he was very successful. He didn't play all year round, but he still won more than twenty tournaments between 1946 and 1949 – which was virtually unheard of at the time. He was competing then against Ben Hogan, Byron Nelson, Sam Sneed, Jimmy Demaret and a boatload of up-and-coming stars. The American professionals didn't like it, and they did all they could to get him banned. They brought in a number of weird and wonderful rules about overseas players coming to play on their shores and taking money out of their pockets. They made it so difficult that I'm not sure he ever went back after 1950, but he told me he had already made enough money during his American campaign to invest in a block of apartments in Johannesburg which, later on, became his pension. On the golf course he appeared very calm, but even though he had so much experience, he confessed that he was beset by nerves almost every time he went out to play. He had to take two Veganin tablets, a superior form of aspirin, before launching himself onto the course. I remember being with him on a day when his magic pills weren't available. I detected a slight but rising note of panic until a lady nearby produced something from her handbag, saving the day in the process.

A lot of nonsense was written about Bobby Locke. He played the majority of the time with a draw but could fade the ball when needed. They (yes, 'them' again) said he couldn't play when the ground was hard, but he won when many times under those conditions. They put the flags on the right-hand side of the green and a big tree in front so he couldn't get at the flag – but somehow he managed to do just that and won all the same. He wasn't very long, but he was long enough. He won on long courses, and he won on short courses. He was a golfing genius, no matter what they say.

The nearest thing to him today is probably the rather eccentric but very gifted Bubba Watson, although I do think a modern-day Locke would see off Bubba (and most of the others currently on parade) simply through his magical ability to keep the ball in play. He possessed an uncanny ability to judge distance, and he was a genius on the green in terms of his ability to read the line and judge the pace. I played dozens of exhibition matches with Locke, over the course of which he taught me a lot about golf and life. An interesting man and a wonderful player.

But to talk only about these great men would be to do a great disservice to the many great women who excel at our funny old game. Times were different when I was growing up, of course, but I still remember seeing many women in the Pro Shop during my early days at Ferndown Golf Club. I would press my ear to the door as they chatted with my father. Of course, I used to spend time at the club with my good friend Maureen, but Ferndown was frequented by many other women besides. They tended to show up on weekdays, particularly in the 1940s and '50s, when few women went out to work. For a long time, members of the fairer sex were conspicuously absent at weekends, which was a time for their menfolk (who often played thirty-six holes over two days).

Things began to change later in the '50s, when Bill Branch, the professional at Ganton in West Yorkshire, decided, along with his wife, to allocate a small area in the shop to cater for female golfers. Mrs Branch had a good eye for fashion, and twinsets suitable for golf were stocked alongside various other colourful and joyous offerings. Mrs Vivienne Jacobs, mother of John, did much the same at Sandy Lodge.

This proved to be a very smart and lucrative innovation. A change swept through the golfing world, with the humble Pro Shop gradually transmogrifying into an oasis for female fashion after so many years of bulletproof Harris Tweed. There were no women professionals in the UK or Europe back then, although the American Women's PGA Tour had been going since 1950. The Americans were blessed in this regard, since they had the four best female players in the world already signed up and raring to get the show on the road. Patty Berg, Babe Zaharias, Mickey Wright and Louise Suggs formed this magnificent quartet. What a foundation of excellence for their Tour.

Women golfers in this country, however, still had nowhere to go (beside the Pro Shop). There was no concerted effort to professionalise the women's game, even though I well remember the ladies of Dorset and Hampshire, alongside many others from the West Country whose names were already fabled in our sport. From Dorset there was Pat Crow, Esme Stuart-Smith and Connie Bannister – all of whom would, in my opinion, have played in the Curtis Cup had they lived in a more fashionable golfing county. Muriel Roskrow, Hilary Trant, Beryl Lowe (later Mrs Green) and the Honourable Joan Gee were all formidable competitors and glorious golfers.

I was fortunate enough to meet and play golf with our first female professionals: Jean Donald, Jesse Valentine and Wanda Morgan - two Scots and a Southerner. The two commercial sporting giants of the day, Dunlop and Slazenger, had the idea of offering these pros the job of going round various golf clubs demonstrating their companies' wares. The money would have been handy, as opportunities for these pioneering female professionals were very limited at first.

I remember also Angela Ward, who was a tall, elegant and strikingly powerful player. She married Michael Bonallack – five-time British Amateur champion and the man destined to become Secretary of the R&A. Then there was Lancashire's Frances Stevens, who was deceptively powerful with her slow, deliberate and well-balanced swing, and Philomena Garvey, a true Republican from Ireland. Like so many Irish players – both men and women – she had a swing all of her own, but boy, could she play. And then there was Jeanne Bisgood, a qualified barrister and three-time winner of the English Women's Amateur Championship. She was a great supporter and friend to me and my brother when we were the joint professionals at Parkstone.

And what of the continent at that time? Well, they had some delightful players who seemed to look at life and golf rather differently from our home-grown talent. There was the Vicomtesse de Saint Sauveur, better known as Lally, who, by all accounts, exuded beauty and confidence beside her rather dull husband. She had her own slant on life and became a friend to many – and how I envied them. Ilsa Bevione, along with her brother, was a formidable figure in Italian golf. They were oh-so elegant, but I was never quite sure whether they knew the correct way to mark the ball on the green. Henri de Lamaze, of the family who owned the Michelin tyre company, played by the same rules. There was a lot of talk in the amateur ranks, but they all possessed rhinoceros-thick skins and sailed through their golfing lives unscathed.

Many years later, the Ladies European Tour was formed. Although I was its first president, I'm ashamed to say I know very little of how the Tour came to be or who exactly was involved. I do know that when I was raised to this high position, I let it be known that any of the women (we used to call them 'girls' in our politically incorrect time) who signed up for the Tour and wanted help only had to contact me and I would do my best to be of service. Perhaps arrogantly, I was disappointed that not one of them got in touch. I really felt I could have been of some assistance with their game or with any business contracts they were about to sign. I remained president for a few years and then moved on after contributing very little to the future of the women's game. I was disappointed with how that role worked out. At present, the Ladies Tour is struggling, but I felt it could have become a giant.

After all, when you consider all the companies making products for women, I was sure many would have become sponsors if we provided a large enough stage. We had a promising couple of years or so, but we weren't able to generate enough good players to keep the show successfully on the road. We attracted some excellent players from the continent, particularly Scandinavia, but we weren't able to offer them enough continuity to keep them on our shores.

Obviously, the weather in Northern Europe factors into how our sport is played. Realistically, we Europeans have only an eight-month season at most – even if you take into account southern Portugal, Spain, Italy and Greece. But as the game was slow to take off in the Old World, women's golf in the sunny United States was going from strength to strength, and I could only watch. It was getting much easier to become a member of their Association and thereby play on their Tour. Mind you, it wasn't all milk and honey, and when Asian golf caught up it was the Asian players who came and swept everything before them. Their impact was staggering and not totally welcome.

At one time there was a very negative feeling towards the women competing from Asia. Many didn't speak much English and appeared not particularly grateful for the opportunities on offer. For a few years, the Women's Tour lost its magic. It had overtaken the Men's Senior Tour in the TV ratings, but now, with very little home-grown talent on show, the ratings dropped dramatically. Things only began to change when new players from Europe, Australia, South America and Mexico appeared and began to do well. That's not to say Korea, Thailand and Japan stopped producing wonderful players. Indeed, they still do.

Inbee Park and her compatriots were still competing at the highest level, but suddenly we were looking also at Lorena Ochoa, the golfing genius from Mexico; Karrie Webb, a wonderful player from Australia; and the cool, accomplished Annika Sorrenstam from Sweden. Catriona Matthew and Laura Davies flew the flag for Britain, while Michelle Wie and Lydia Ko, whose ascent of the ladder of golfing fame was nothing short of magical, added some youthful sparkle to the scene.

But what of the American players who had consolidated those early foundations – the likes of Pat Bradley, Jo Anne Carner, Hollis Stacey, Amy Allcott, Judy Rankin, Nancy Lopez, Julie Inkster and Carol Mann? Well, few people can be said to have contributed more to the growth of the women's game. Their legacy endures today, and you can see a testament to the success of women's golf in almost every Pro Shop in the country.

I've still got a few years to go, but I'm hoping I might just get a telegram from King Charles on my 100th birthday. To celebrate I would like to visit a Pro Shop or three and marvel at the amount of attractive, soft and high-quality merchandise on view. Today's offering really is so different from the days of Mrs Jacobs and Mrs Branch and all the other professionals who continued their crusade to make sure the lady golfers of the world were well catered for.

Irritatingly, however, there are still some clubs where women are considered a nuisance – particularly women who work Monday to Friday and so whose only chance to play is at the weekend. Still, women – supported by more enlightened men – are slowly and surely winning the battle for equality in golf.

The R&A has decreed that if a club wishes to remain on the Open rota it must have women as members alongside men. And quite rightly so. The golf scene is changing, and at many clubs it has changed already. Critics still attack the game for being sexist, hidebound and generally out of touch, but this criticism is increasingly unfair. Although some pockets of resistance remain, the game is generally a much more family-friendly and indeed female-friendly scene that it was even ten years ago.

Still, I wonder sometimes why it seems so difficult for people to work together towards a common goal. We all saw how difficult negotiating was during the Brexit days, but thank God, golf isn't quite as difficult as that. Or is it? Sometimes, despairingly, it seems like it, but we continue to live in hope.

IT is astonishing to read Peter's recollections of all the golfing masters he has known. He spent much of his life in the pursuit and observation of golf, so perhaps the depth and breadth of his knowledge shouldn't come as a surprise. Still, it is delightful to read his grand history of the game, anecdote by anecdote, one legend at a time.

Peter's telling of golf's modern ascension starts with Henry Cotton. I myself visited Penina in Portugal many times and played golf with the maestro on several of these occasions. Henry had inevitably lost length off the tee, but he turned deadly whenever he got anywhere near a green. I never did manage to beat him.

I asked him once, as we ambled towards our drives, how much harder it had got as he grew older. Henry stopped, put his hand on mine and adopted a very sad face. He said, 'The problem, dear boy, is that the bloody thing has got softer.' He was a great, pioneering golfer and a delight to know – even if very difficult to beat.

TELEVISION BECKONS

PETER was in good spirits as he flew over the Irish Sea with a group of friends and fellow professionals. He had just competed with great success in the 1959 Irish Hospitals Tournament, emerging from Woodbrook's tricky acres tied for second with his great friend Dave Thomas. Playing in Ireland was always a joy, the huge crowds as much of a certainty as the stiff drinks and fulfilling conversations afterwards.

Peter spent the flight regaling his pals with stories from the past week, offering his usual, sharp observations of this and that and provoking gales of laughter from the posse of pros eagerly listening in. Typical Peter. It wouldn't become apparent until later on, but that conversation set in motion a chain of events that would change his life. If he had been sitting in a different part of the plane, if he had fallen asleep or quietly buried himself in a book, then everything would have turned out differently.

But that's life, isn't it? Turn left and you hit disaster, turn right and you embrace triumph. We all need some luck now and then, and on that flight home from Dublin, Peter was handed the biggest slice of good fortune he ever enjoyed. More than a year passed, however, before he first began to realize this happy fact.

FOR most people, television is something which is just there. But it wasn't always so. Although a few hundred people in the London area had access to television in the late 1930s, it took a long time for this new technology to filter through to the masses. Radio remained king for many years after strange, flickering boxes began to appear in the corners of London living rooms.

The Queen's Coronation in 1953 changed all that. When it was announced that the event would be broadcast live, there was a sudden rush to buy a television set. That's certainly how the Alliss family came to acquire our first TV. Looking back, the programmes (all in black and white, of course) were a great mixture of wonder and corniness, but the mere fact that we had moving pictures in our front room was magic enough.

The BBC ruled the airwaves, then, although commercial television was preparing to launch itself on an unsuspecting public. The day's television would end at around eleven o'clock each night, beginning again the following morning. It's hard to imagine all that dead air now, in our age of twenty-four-hour viewing across hundreds of channels. We didn't even get a full daytime television service on the BBC until 1986.

Sport and television are a natural pairing, so it didn't take long after the proliferation of television for the proliferation of televised sport to catch up. We were, of course, well behind America in the breadth of their television productions, but demand was growing apace for football and, to a lesser degree, rugby and cricket. Tennis and golf were rather on the slow side, but the public interest was still there.

Various cinema newsreels – Movietone, Pathé and the like – carried all the sports news for the masses. How well I remember a plummy English voice announcing the arrival of a great ocean liner bearing the American Ryder Cup team, followed by the usual pictures of our American cousins all lined up and looking very elegant, most with a posh trilby hat at a slightly rakish angle. They had come to do battle. I watched all this with great interest but, of course, never dreamed that televised sport would become such an enormous feature in all our lives – and especially mine.

The television world caught up with me in the August of 1960 as I sat opening my post in the pokey pro's office at Parkstone Golf Club. There was one letter in particular that caught my eye – not least because of the little BBC logo printed in the top left. It was from a gentleman called Ray Lakeland, a senior producer based in Manchester. As I later found out, Ray was man of great import at the BBC, responsible for producing the Grand National, Test Match cricket, great football occasions and, of course, the Open Championships played between Hoylake on the Wirral and Royal Lytham and St Annes to the north. The letter was brief, but it was more than enough to pique my interest.

'Dear Peter,' it read. 'I was sitting behind you on a plane returning from some tournament or other. You were with Peter Thomson, Bernard Hunt, David Thomas, Dai Rees and Ken Bousfield. You were regaling them with stories of your four days' play. It was bright, cheerful and amusing, and I was wondering if you would care to join the TV team for the Open Championship which will be played next year at Royal Birkdale. Please contact me as to whether this is of any interest.'

I wasn't quite sure what to do, although I was rather flattered that someone of Ray's stature thought I might be bright enough to join the team. After much thought, I dialled his number.

'Mr Lakeland,' said I. 'Thank you for your letter, but next year I will be thirty years of age; I'm hoping to be very much in contention for winning the Championship. I'm not sure how I would be able to fit in.'

'No matter,' he replied. 'If you're drawn to play in the afternoon you can join us for half an hour or so and tell us what you're looking forward to. Talk about dangerous holes, the speed of the greens, who you're playing with, the quality of the field, the number of spectators and so on. Tell the public something about the day ahead. If, on the other hand, you play in the morning, then come up in the afternoon and tell us how it went.'

My mother was a great public performer. She loved music and dance, and she was an accomplished pianist. At one time, she even had her own dancing school. I have, therefore, always possessed a splash of theatrical blood in my veins. For that reason, television appealed to me. I have never been one to wear out a practice ground, so I wasn't too wary of jumping into television for the first time. I thought it would be interesting and amusing.

As I mentioned earlier, these were the days when golf events finished with thirty-six holes on a Friday, owing to the obligations of a busy weekend back at the club. I had some friends who lived only a couple of hundred yards from the clubhouse and with whom I always stayed when I was playing in the Southport area. I told Mr Lakeland that I planned to arrive on the Sunday prior to the Championship.

'That's perfect,' he said. 'Come and find us on Monday morning. You'll find our studio not far from the 18th green.'

On the aforementioned Sunday I arrived and parked myself with the Wormalds – dear friends going back to the Boys' Championship in 1946. I strolled over to the 18th tee and didn't see much except a green shed on stilts some 150 yards down the fairway. I stuck my head in the Secretary's office and asked if he could direct me to the BBC studio. He pointed to the shed and said, as far as he knew, I was looking at it.

Off to the shed I went. Little did I know where those few steps would take me, what lay beyond that door which I opened with some small measure of trepidation. There, standing in front of a large hand-painted board, was the BBC presenter and broadcasting doyen Cliff Michelmore. To my right was the great golf guru John Jacobs, and to my left was Ben Wright of the *Manchester Guardian*. In the corner I saw Bill Cox, the professional from Fulwell Golf Club in Middlesex, while sitting quietly to the side was Henry Longhurst, the man who'd kept the *Sunday Times* going (or so he said) for the last ten years. This illustrious crowd was getting ready for a rehearsal, but when Cliff saw me he called me in and told me to take a seat.

All around me was a Gordian tangle of cables; everywhere the shed was rammed with battered bits of furniture and electrical doodads. To my untutored eye it seemed a chaotic scene. I suspect that even to the tutored eye it would have seemed chaotic, but that was just how television was back then. I joined in the chatter, talking about this and that, and I told Cliff that as soon as I knew my starting time I'd pay them a visit.

If memory serves me right, I opened up with a seventy and qualified easily. Remember: this was long before the leaders went out last. As I'd qualified to play the final thirty-six holes all day Friday, I was obviously not able to do any television work on that final day, but I found plenty of time for the BBC on the other days and very much enjoyed my ad hoc introduction to broadcasting. Of

ABOVE LEFT: Ray Lakeland, who first asked Peter to say a few words on air
ABOVE: On the receiving end, Peter handles the press in Melbourne
LEFT: With the Duke of Edinburgh and Henry Longhurst at Blackpool North Shore in 1963
BELOW: In the box with Mark McCormack at the 1974 Open at Royal Lytham and St Annes
BELOW LEFT: The Mustang that Henry Longhurst bequeathed to Peter

THE RYDER CUP 1977
Royal Lytham & St. Anne's G.C.
PRESS

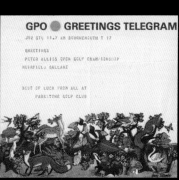

LEFT: A message from Parkstone Golf Club ahead of the 1971 Open at Muirfield and (far left) Peter's own summary of his performance that year
BELOW: Interviewing Seve Ballesteros before the 1987 Ryder Cup at Muirfield Village, Ohio
BOTTOM LEFT: A splash of colour in the box at the 1985 Open at Royal St George's
BOTTOM RIGHT: Entertaining Cliff Michelmore and others at son Simon's christening at Moor Allerton in 1975

course, I didn't have a clue what was going on or how anything worked. However, I swiftly realised that it was all about the precision of the timings, and I went away thinking how wonderful it was that those sporting pictures had been beamed directly into so many homes – and how delightful to have played my small part in that.

So the Championship ended, and all in all, I had a pretty good week, finishing as I did in the top ten. As I was climbing into my car, Ray Lakeland suddenly appeared, waving his arms and shouting, 'Peter, a word! A word!' I cranked the window down (you did in those days, of course – no electrics) and up he came. 'Did you enjoy that?'

'I did,' I replied. 'I hope you felt I added something.'

'Yes indeed, you did.' I felt a wash of relief. He added, 'We have another event we're televising in a couple of weeks time; would you like to join us? Oh and, by the way, I think we should pay you.'

This Alliss, renowned for his business acumen, responded by saying, 'No, no, no, I've enjoyed it enormously. It's been wonderful. I've never spent hours on the practice ground and I dislike practice putting enormously, so you're doing me a great favour by giving me an opportunity to fill my day.'

'That's fine,' said Ray, 'but you must be paid. I can offer fifteen pounds for each rehearsal day, twenty-five pounds for the first two days and forty pounds if, God forbid, you don't qualify and are free for the final thirty-six.'

I swiftly did some mental arithmetic. That made at least £80, plus a little for expenses. And that, believe it or not, was almost equivalent to the prize money for finishing in fifth place. Oh joy of joys! What a lovely back-up if the clubs or the golfing brain were taking a week off. And that is the story of how it all began for me at the British Broadcasting Corporation.

At that time ITV, the great rival, was separated into a number of companies – an amazing conglomeration of various styles and interests. I was never interested in leaving the BBC at any point in my broadcasting career, but in all truth, ITV never asked me anyway. Nor did Sky, when they eventually came along. Perhaps they all thought I was too rooted in the BBC – which I was – or maybe they just fancied new blood. Whatever the reason, I never had to consider another offer from a rival broadcaster in the UK, and that was absolutely fine with me.

Fifty-eight years I have spent with the BBC. It has been a wonderful journey. Looking back, I was extremely fortunate to have worked with some of the great BBC presenters: hugely talented communicators in the form of Cliff Michelmore, David Coleman, Des Lynam, Harry Carpenter, Steve Rider, Hazel Irvine, Frank Bough and the terrific team of men and women behind the cameras who make it all happen. Their names remain unfamiliar to the public, but I marveled at the skills of men like Slim Wilkinson (a wonderful producer) and the would-be Fred Astaire, Bryan Cowgill – a softly spoken Lancastrian from Clitheroe. At least, he thought he was softly spoken! There was also David Kenning; the New Zealander Harold Anderson; John Shrewsbury; Alan Mouncer; Ricky Tilling; Alastair Scott; and John Phillips – a posse of directors and producers who conjured up all the technical magic. All these individuals played, in their own way, a significant part in the story of sport on television. How much I enjoyed working with them all. I felt then, and still feel, that I am but an amateur in comparison. Perhaps I can be a rather glorious amateur on my better days, but nevertheless I simply couldn't compete on the level of the television professionals.

I learned one of my greatest lessons when we were filming at Royal St George's on the Kent coast in advance of the 1981 Open Championship. It was the year of Bill Rogers, the little-known American. I can't remember what the sequence was about, but it was a beautiful day, we were in the middle of course and everything in the world was lovely. The sun was out and the skylarks were in the heavens. Oh, those skylarks – those bloody, noisy skylarks.

If you inhabit the world of television, you're lucky if you find yourself working with those who want to produce a work of art. My sound engineer on that day was like that. Those skylarks were in his earphones like the London Philharmonic, and we had to do take after take after take in the hope that they would shut up for a few minutes. I found myself wondering if we would ever get the job done.

Now, I'd been with the BBC for several years by this time, and already I thought I knew a thing or two. I got a little bit huffy, and I remember saying, 'Come on, come on, that'll do. This place is renowned for skylarks; what does it matter?'

This maestro of a sound engineer turned, slowly took off his headset, and fixed me straight in the eye. 'Peter,' he said. 'All I'm trying to do is make you sound good.'

That shut me up. I've never forgotten those words, and now in difficult situations I just sit back and keep my mouth closed (unless I'm supposed to be talking). In the end, this philosophy has worked out rather well.

It was during my first few years at the BBC that I was approached by Mark McCormack, the American lawyer behind the IMG sports agency. He was one of the pivotal men who did much to change the face of golf and its various business channels. So it was a big deal when he told me he had been approached by ABC, the American TV network, who were asking if I would like to join them. They wanted me for up to twelve events a year, and I'd be working in harmony with the BBC when the broadcasters were at the same event – meaning I wouldn't have to abandon the Beeb. It was a no-brainer.

Mark and I worked out a very successful business relationship, and he went back to America to give ABC the thumbs up from me. To an outsider, his commission may have looked excessive, but he only earned money on work he found for me and which I wanted to do. Without Mark's input, many offers would never have come my way.

It helped that I enjoyed Mark's company very much, even if he did have one or two interesting traits. For example, he was a very poor drinker. Having said that, I never saw him even the tiniest bit tiddly, although he would often have two Mai Tais (a rum based cocktail, if you were wondering), a beer and a gin and tonic or a glass of red all in one sitting. He had also a number of facial twitches, which could be unnerving until you got used to them. And he had a soft spot for pretty ladies, but I think all he ever did was look.

His first wife, Nancy, was like so many incredible women who are married to very successful men. Throughout their marriage, she stayed in the background, bringing up the children and maintaining a solid base. The story goes that when Mark and Nancy eventually divorced, Nancy's lawyers drew up a financial settlement which would have suited her. Mark refused to sign and basically ripped it to shreds because she had been such a wonderful wife for so long and he thought she deserved so much more. It came to pass that she walked away from the marriage with enough to be more than comfortable, but I feel, sadly, that she was truly heartbroken.

My own association with Mark took me not only to America but also to Australia and Canada. Every journey was memorable: first class all the way, with a ramble about golf, one or two good titbits of insider knowledge from Mark and some serious money in the back pocket for my troubles. Sheer bliss and good work, if you can get it.

At the age of eighty-eight, as I write this, I'm still hugely enjoying my involvement with the world of television. Although my physical movements have slowed down, I like to think I'm still able to observe and give my opinions as adroitly as ever. I may no longer be able to sprint, but I can think quickly enough. I only wish I could do it all over again.

Certainly it has been a privilege to work for the BBC for so long. There are always critics of our great national broadcaster, but I hadn't been with the Corporation for very long before I realised just how much soft power this organization grants us worldwide and how well it represents our country abroad.

Everyone who worked for the BBC seemed to possess a certain presence. You felt they should be walking around with a badge, proudly worn on the chest, stating: 'I'm with the BBC.' To many, broadcasting was looked upon as a vocation, so for them it was never about the money. Of course, bills had to be paid, but in some ways those broadcast pioneers were a bit like those who went into the nursing and education professions. It wasn't quite the same, but that analogy really isn't far off. For many BBC bods I met, their work really was a calling – and since there was no competition, back then, it was BBC or bust.

All this was to change, of course, with the coming of commercial television and, later, subscription services such as Sky. Offers from these new boys flew around like confetti at a wedding, and they were tempting offers, too. Salaries were twice as good elsewhere, and there was a period when the BBC, for all its reputational might, was rather thin on the ground when it came to the real workers – those whose combined efforts put the show on the road.

I've never been in the inner sanctum, but I've mixed with plenty of BBC types ranging from the ground floor to the sixth floor, where all the big decisions were made. And I have no doubt that many of the changes undergone by the BBC have been politically motivated. When Margaret Thatcher was the prime minister, a revolution started. John Birt was brought in as Director General, his main objective being to slim down the organization. The most dramatic change was the new rule that at least a quarter of all programmes had to be made by independent production companies.

Over time, many departments were sold off or disbanded. Make-up, costume, and other core departments were privatised. The move to Manchester, in many people's eyes, was catastrophic, but that too comes under the heading of a political move. It cost the BBC many millions, and this at a time when the power (and therefore the cost) of various entertainment and sporting agents was rising. And suddenly there was a load of new expenses the BBC had to pay. The World Service, until then funded by the government, now had to come out of the BBC's budget. Free TV licences were given to the over seventy-fives, and the cost of moving up north – coupled with these new developments – soon became astronomical.

Fair to say, then, that there have been many changes since 1992 – and not all for the better. But the BBC still carries a certain aura – even if, due to the internet revolution, that aura is starting to look a bit pale compared to the old days. It saddens me, in my world, to meet people who don't seem to know that the BBC is still very much involved with golf on TV. One does one's best to explain that the highlights of several major golfing events are shown during the year, but the BBC doesn't seem to advertise that fact in the same way as Sky, which floods the airwaves year-round with ads highlighting its latest golf offerings.

I think back now to the flight in 1959 which started it all. As I was heading back from Dublin all those years ago, these developments were still very much in the future. But while I certainly enjoyed some good fortune on account of my yakking away, I wasn't always so charmed in my other endeavours.

I remember standing in the clubhouse after the prize-giving for that Irish Hospitals Tournament. A small, very inebriated Irishman wandered over and, slurring every word, congratulated me on my good play. Even better days would come, this stranger insisted. Then he pushed a small piece of paper into the top pocket of my jacket.

A few days passed before I rediscovered the piece of paper, on which was written: TARA EXPLORATION. I put the paper to one side until, by chance, I met one of my members who worked as a stockbroker. I passed on the name of this company and asked him to do a little paperwork. A couple of days later he came back to tell me he had found a Canadian firm with that name. Tara Exploration, he said, was engaged in boring for minerals in Southern Ireland.

Shares were available at 1s 10½d each. Rather flamboyantly, I asked him to buy £250 worth. I told several people of my acquisition but time went by with no success. Then I had another tip, this time from a friend in Nottingham who told me a certain shoe manufacturer was about to undergo a major expansion. I rang my stockbroker friend, and while we were talking he let me know my Tara shares had dipped to 1s 6d. In grand tones I heard myself saying, 'Sell! Sell! Buy! Buy!' like a proper City slicker. My broker wound down my position, and I chalked it all up to experience.

I soon forgot all about my share dealings. A few years later, however, I was approached by Brian Davison, who ran the Professional Golfers Co-operative Association and from whom club pros used to buy their goods at discounted prices. He gave me a big hug and told me the embrace was from his mother, who'd bought some Tara shares years ago for a few shillings and had just sold them for £62 each. I think I lay in a darkened room for several days after that, and I never again entered into the arcane world of stocks and shares. However, I shall forever live with the headline of the financial section of the one of the papers at the time, which read: BONANZA IN IRISH FARMER'S FIELD. Sadly there was no bonanza in the Alliss field, just a few more weeds.

If I was unlucky with the shares, I was more than slightly fortunate in having so many terrific colleagues alongside me in the broadcast booth. Certainly, I enjoyed my relationship with Alex Hay very much. Alex was an ever elegant man, with a ready wit and the neatest, cleanest size-seven shoes you would wish to see. He was overjoyed when the BBC offered him a role in their team – especially as it got him to Augusta, his dream venue. He was also an excellent after-dinner entertainer, and it was he who passed on the following piece of good advice: 'Never speak to anyone or anything other than a golfing audience.'

Alex had evidently had a nightmare at a rugby dinner or something of the like. His advice has stood me in good stead over the years.

Harry Carpenter was the BBC's main golf presenter throughout most of my early career in television. Small in stature and furnished with a whole suite of nervous habits, Harry was a man of twitches here and twitches there, and yet as soon as the red light went on, he sprang into action in the most competent and confident way. He was relentlessly professional, and he possessed good knowledge of a number of sports besides golf. His boxing commentaries, to this day, remain masterclasses in the art. It was a privilege to work with him, and I remember how I would spend hours transfixed, with something cooling in front of me, as he reminisced about the world in general and discoursed on its many problems – all of which we would surely solve in a matter of days, given half the chance.

Then there was Dave Marr, an American golfer good enough to have won the 1965 USPGA Championship. Dave rather reluctantly joined the BBC, but having been passed over from ABC, the Beeb gave him an opportunity to be seen and heard in a role which he ended up enjoying very much. It took Dave a couple of years to get into his stride – not least because in the States he had only been allowed to speak in brief soundbites. The BBC offered him the time and space to express himself at leisure, and once he got into the rhythm of things he became a true force, with that delightful Texan drawl and a hefty catalogue of homespun tales. Dave was as unique as he was fun to work with.

Bruce Critchley was another fine colleague. He was from interesting stock, and his family had been larger-than-life figures in the world of golf and beyond. Brigadier General Critchley, for instance, was the man who introduced greyhound racing into this country from America, while Bruce's mother, Diana, was a formidable golfer and the winner of many championships. Bruce himself was a beautiful striker of the ball, yet he only played once in the Walker Cup. Obviously there were one or two frailties in his game that held him back. Even though Bruce had gone to Eton, while my own education was much more modest, he and I struck it off in great style, and how many wonderful hours we spent just talking about life. He and his wife Hazel now live on the border of Somerset and Dorset. He tries to get down to single figures at bridge, and she just oozes goodwill and charm. By golly, can she whip up a good meal!

Howard Clark, meanwhile, was one of the best strikers of a ball I've ever seen, but he seemed to be held back from true greatness as a player by his own thoughts. He was so cripplingly critical of his own efforts both on and off the course, although I have no doubt that, with a little tweak here and a little tweak there, he could have been one of the world's great stars. Instead he brought real insight to his broadcasting career. In my opinion, he walked away from this calling much too early for whatever reason. And, to be fair, he had already enjoyed a very successful playing career, regardless of his shortcomings.

The inimitable Ken Brown, meanwhile, didn't make the best of starts in the world of professional golf. Under the captaincy of John Jacobs during the Ryder Cup at The Greenbrier in 1979, he and Mark James were on the verge of being sent home after their childish antics in West Virginia. But they were both young and hot-headed, and more than enough time has passed for redemption.

I've worked with Ken for many years with the BBC, and I have always thought of him as an imaginative and progressive individual. When everything comes together, a night out with Ken is a total joy. I'm only sorry he has lost his nerve. He tells me he doesn't feel able to play a proper round of golf if anyone is watching him, and yet when he's doing his *Ken on the Course* pieces they are

RIGHT: Peter Alliss, Tony Jacklin, Lee Trevino, John Fenton, Renton Laidlaw and Alex Hay at Woburn in 1987

BELOW RIGHT: Ken Brown, Renton Laidlaw, Alex Hay, Peter Alliss and Seve at Wentworth with army volunteers from the REME

ABOVE: Bruce Critchley at the microphone in 1989
BELOW: BBC team at Loch Lomond in 2003: Ken Brown, Wayne Grady, Alex Hay, Peter Alliss, Steve Rider

TOP LEFT: Harry Carpenter interviews Jack Nicklaus at the 1978 Open
TOP RIGHT: Hazel Irvine interviews Luke Donald at the 2011 Scottish Open
ABOVE: Howard Clark commentating on the PGA Championship at Wentworth in 1999
RIGHT: BBC's Alastair Scott and John Shrewsbury at the 2013 Open
BELOW: Des Lynam at Sunningdale for a charity day in 2003
BELOW RIGHT: At the Masters in 2007: Wayne Grady, Ken Brown, Gary Lineker, Sam Torrance and Peter Alliss

quite brilliant. His touch on the green remains outstanding, an art given to few.

It was difficult, meanwhile, for an outsider like myself to understand how the BBC lost the services of Steve Rider. In my opinion, he was one of the great presenters, alongside Harry Carpenter, Cliff Michelmore, Hazel Irvine, Des Lynam, David Coleman and Frank Bough – to name some of the crème de la crème. Steve had a wonderfully dry sense of humour, and I have never seen him flustered.

Hazel Irvine is another of those presenters with an innate air of calmness. No wonder, I suppose, when everyone she ever worked with was amazed at her extensive preparation. I once asked her why she spent so many hours putting together information that might never be used, and she said she liked to have a safety net. She carried it all off with a gentle charm that was very infectious.

America's Judy Rankin was a slight figure, but what a glorious player she was. She started on the LPGA Tour at just seventeen and went on to win twenty-six titles. I first saw her playing at Sunningdale in the Colgate Tournament, which she won. She fell in love with the area and, for a time, talked about nothing other than the possibility of buying a small house there where she could spend her retirement. It never came to pass, but I know her love for the club never diminished. She has become an outstanding, no-nonsense broadcaster who is never shy of criticising or making suggestions – even if her comments go against the run of play. She is a dear friend.

Then there was Wayne Grady – a wild, extremely likable, colonial boy and the winner of the US PGA Championship many moons ago. Rather like Dave Marr, Wayne made much of that single major victory, and good luck to them both for being able to do so! His knowledge of the game makes him well worth listening to, while his turn of phrase is engaging and his love of life is enormous. A wonderful working companion, and a kind and generous soul.

But those are just the people you see on one side of the camera. Throughout my career, I have known so many other BBC staff behind the scenes who were tremendously helpful and kind. I think we all got on so well because I had no pretensions about becoming a know-all about how everything else worked. I did my bit and they did theirs, although I knew I couldn't have done my bit without so much professionalism and enthusiasm on their end.

For a long time, Jonathan Martin was the BBC's Head of Sport. Jonathan may have been a small man, but he was huge as a promoter of the BBC and its sports department – although it was always sad to think he wasn't always appreciated by his colleagues. Just before his retirement he gave me a long-term contract, for which I will be eternally grateful. He now lives quietly with his wife, Joy, and their horses on the south-west coast of Wales. There have been moments over the past few years when many wished he'd been back at the helm.

Barbara Slater, having climbed all the way up the ladder from her initial role as an assistant producer, came in to take charge of the BBC's sports offering at a very difficult time. This was back when the BBC was being roundly beaten in many departments by the aggression and sheer wealth of Sky, and it happened to coincide with more and more agents becoming tangled in the mix, driving up fees considerably. But Barbara was a top sportswoman herself and, being an Olympic gymnast, managed to navigate these difficult times with agility and poise.

And what about Paul Fox? Now Sir Paul, of course, he was a big influence in the world of television. He was controller of BBC 1 from 1967 to 1973 and edited Panorama, Grandstand and a myriad of other first-class programmes. The BBC was shaken to its roots when he upped stakes and left to run Yorkshire Television. He was a great television figure and loved by his staff.

The great Henry Longhurst will be remembered, also, for many things – not least the brilliant *Sunday Times* column he wrote so charmingly for twenty-five years, filling inches with his insights on golf and life. But his influence extends beyond even that. If you ever get a chance to look at a television manual setting out the rules and regulations for outside broadcasts, you'll find a section headed, 'Longhurst Ladders.'

Many years ago, near the 8th tee at Wentworth, there was a television tower maybe eighty feet high. Every ten feet or so there was a platform, and tied to the tower was a builder's ladder. Watching Longhurst standing at the bottom, looping a rope under his arms, and setting off on that dizzying vertical journey was a truly terrifying sight. Health and Safety would be apoplectic today. In America, however, they were already very conscious of these things, so when accommodating their commentators they arranged for five-foot-wide stairways with handrails on either side to be built against their television towers. They were christened 'Longhurst Ladders' and remain so to this day. Henry rather liked that.

Henry was an inspirational figure and a man who never lost his sense of fun. For many years, the Piccadilly Match Play at Wentworth marked the end of the professional golf season in October. It became a tradition for Henry to arrive with his friend John Blackwell (of pickle and jam fame) and park up close to where the first tee of the Edinburgh course is today. Henry would open up the boot, and lurking inside would be a hamper. Blackwell always supplied some wonderful game pie, along with bottles of sherry and other delightful appetizers, and when the weather was decent we'd sit down and enjoy all these goodies, living life to the full as we chatted and gorged ourselves on a wonderful picnic. What a joy amid the autumnal splendour of the West Course.

So much was different, of course, in my playing days. During my professional career, and continuing into my early months in the world of television, there was very little social contact between players and the top journalists of the day. After all, these scribes seemed rather mystical figures, and they thought themselves much too grand to associate with us professionals, who were really only two or three steps up from our caddies.

However, not long after the death of Henry's son and son-in-law – both in tragic accidents, one in east Africa and one in the middle deserts of Australia – the great columnist appeared at my shoulder and started talking to me. Once I got over my surprise, I found he was very pleasant to talk to. Perhaps he felt that I, in some obscure way, helped to fill the void left by the deaths of those two young men. We never discussed it but it did appear that way. Certainly, I was greeted with a look of real delight when I later asked him if he would be godfather to my eldest son, Simon.

After that first conversation we began to spend more time together. And although Henry was much more famous than me, it was I who appeared to be the leader of our friendly duo. I fondly remember how we would walk past the various hospitality pavilions at golf tournaments up and down the land and wait for him to be recognised. It usually happened at about half past ten in the morning. I can hear them now, shouting, 'Henry! Henry Longhurst! Over here!' Those words would always be accompanied by some very senior member of some great corporation, beckoning from the veranda.

'Would you like a cup of coffee?' was always the question. This, cunningly, is where I would take charge.

'That would be nice,' I would reply, 'but a glass of champagne would be better.' The thinking was that a nice glass would get us just a little lubricated ahead of our lunchtime broadcast. I'm sure Henry wondered at my cheek, although he always enjoyed the bubbles, and our friendship grew in spite of whatever reservations he might have had. My first visit to his home, situated on the hills overlooking the village of Hassocks, remains a vivid memory.

Here Henry had built a modern structure between two windmills he called Jack and Jill. His was an upside-down house, with bedrooms on the ground floor, a sitting room upstairs and a veranda which gave the most splendid views all the way round. I went there first with Dai Rees and Bernard Hunt when we were on our way to play an exhibition match in Brighton. Henry, naturally, insisted we have a glass of bubbly. As he fiddled away at opening the bottle, Dai asked how long he'd lived in the house. Henry mumbled that it had been eighteen years or so.

'It really is a delight,' I said, 'but I bet it doesn't half blow up here.'

At that precise moment the champagne cork popped. Henry muttered under his breath, 'That's why they put the bloody windmills here.' How often he must have said that.

One of our most memorable journeys was to Washington DC on Concorde. We were flying out to do some work with ABC, and Henry had worked out that our first class return tickets (courtesy of the broadcaster) could be traded in for a trip outwards on Concorde and back in economy. As it worked out we were upgraded on the return journey, so it was Concorde out and first class on the way home. Brilliant. It was another lesson from the master to his pupil.

Concorde was then a new phenomenon, and there was considerable excitement when it touched down in Washington. We were picked up and whisked out to the course, where our ABC friends were all waiting to hear about our journey: 'How long did the trip take? Do you notice how fast you're going? Can you see out of the windows? How's the food? Is it really that good?'

Now, I have had the privilege of flying on Concorde a dozen or so times. I was always amazed by how comfortable it was, even though I am 6ft tall and blessed with what you might call a rather sturdy build. I've never sat in a more comfortable seat on any aeroplane, but nobody wanted to know what I thought. They all wanted to hear from the great Henry Longhurst.

These questions rained down on Henry. I can hear his voice now as he replied, 'We got here in two hours and fifteen minutes. The 747 is very comfortable but takes five-and-a-half hours, but then you could travel on the Queen Mary, which is ultra comfortable but takes five days. Take your pick.' He turned and moved to another group, leaving bemused looks on the faces of a number of young Americans. I heard him mumble as he moved away, 'Two and a quarter hours... hardly enough time to get pissed.'

Henry was one of the most pompous looking men I have ever seen, but the amazing thing about him was that he was, in actuality, the least pompous person in the world. In fact, he loved to prick pomposity, and he did so in such a way that those being pricked often never even felt it. He is someone I think of almost every week. I recall the situations we found ourselves in, and our many discussions about family life, motor cars, TV, income tax… you name it, we had an opinion on it. Henry really was a great man.

When he died in 1978 he willed to me his Ford Mustang (left hand drive, convertible). I worked hard to restore it, and when I eventually had to let it go I felt another deep sense of bereavement. It was like losing the last physical tie to a beloved colleague and friend.

I learned a great deal from Henry about broadcasting, but probably the most important thing he ever taught me was the value of silence when commentating. It might sound a bit silly to trumpet the virtues of saying nothing when the job is all about talking, but it's true that viewers tire swiftly of anyone who feels the need to babble endlessly over pictures which could tell the story well enough on their own – if only they were allowed to. The trick is to shut up at the appropriate moment and then start talking again at exactly the right second. It helps if you have something interesting, or at least apposite, to say at these times. I always tried to get this right, and I think I did on a few occasions.

Henry was only sixty-eight when he died. I still miss him, for he was always an interesting companion who saw the world in a very fair way. He'd done a lot with the years he was given: put on a deep sea diver's suit and explored the ocean bed; zipped down the Cresta Run; skied a bit; played golf for Cambridge;

won the German Amateur; wrote a number of delightful books; and, of course, his weekly essay on the back page of the *Sunday Times* was unmissable for many. I still have a prized picture of him standing on a mound at the Moor Park Golf Club, near Watford, doing one of the first golf broadcasts for television in 1938. TV has certainly come a long way since then.

It was another dear friend, Terry Wogan, who said to me one lunchtime at our house in Surrey, 'Don't let anyone know how easy you find it.' I wasn't quite sure what he meant at the time, but I think I do now, having read of people being sick before going on the stage or making public appearances. The great Bobby Jones was said to become physically ill on many occasions before going out to play. Perhaps that's why he was so good, although I'm glad to say I was never troubled in the same way.

Of course there were a few nerves on occasion – that's only natural. But I always enjoyed my TV work so much that I never suffered any real anguish before a broadcast, no matter how big the audience.

Really, I was just doing what came naturally... but please don't tell anyone I said that.

IT is worth recalling, at the end of Peter's telling of his career on the small screen, how much more difficult it was to televise golf all those years ago. Cameras were large and heavy, requiring the strength of an elephant to move them from one fixed position to another, with a maximum cable length of around 400 yards. For a long time there would only be fourteen fixed cameras on site, so coverage of tournaments (played, obviously, over large fields) was necessarily limited. On the production side, it was imperative to run around turning on the cameras some four hours before the broadcast was due to begin; that's how long they took to warm up. And it did not help that there was no instant recording of the action, so a well-executed shot or an important holed putt could not be shown and re-shown seconds or even minutes after it had been played. Everything was live, and if you missed a vital moment of action once, you missed it forever. The great innovation of recording play as it went along can be credited to Alastair Scott, the BBC cameraman-turned-director who Peter describes as a crucial behind-the-scenes influence. Alastair is among a raft of broadcasting giants to pay tribute to Peter's skill with a microphone and look back fondly on the time they shared.

Peter Alliss: Broadcaster and Friend

Peter's broadcasting career touched the lives of millions of viewers. He also had a profound effect on the colleagues with whom he shared a studio. Here, some of those who worked closely with Peter remember his sharp wit, generosity of spirit and incredible talent.

Paul Azinger, golfer and broadcaster, writes:
I WAS lucky enough to broadcast the Open Championship and the Masters alongside Peter for many years. It was the thrill of my broadcasting career. He had such a command of the English language; I hung on every word that came out of his mouth. He was such a great entertainer, and I will always remember him conducting himself the same regardless of whether he was on or off-air. He's a national treasure, and I miss him.

Sports presenter Steve Rider recalls the huge impact Peter had on the BBC:
IT was the mid-nineties at BBC Television Centre in London, and we were fighting to hang on to long-term broadcasting control of the Open Championship. It was one of many rear-guard actions we were fighting at the time, but this one was serious. The whole department had been mobilised to produce marketing videos and dig up any kind of evidence that might persuade the R&A to resist the greater commercial opportunities presented by the giant independent producers. The presentation in Studio Three had gone well, but we were running out of ammunition. Then came a question from a gentleman representing the Welsh Golf Union.

'Mr Alliss, we know your loyalty to our great Championship. Can we assume that you will continue to provide your wonderful commentary no matter who is delivering the pictures?'

To paraphrase Peter's reply: 'No, sir. Yours is a great Championship, not least through the efforts of my colleagues at the BBC. As long as it is their coverage you will have my commentary. I have no desire to work for any other UK broadcaster.'

It was a wonderful moment, although with hindsight, it was just delaying the inevitable. But within a close-knit team at BBC Sport, that episode just cemented the reputation of Peter Alliss – the finest of colleagues and most loyal of friends. This, of course, went alongside his public reputation as one of the greatest sports broadcasters of his time.

Peter was a genius, and he had already brought golf to new audiences before anyone else even thought to do so. In the seventies the favourite programmes of my aged parents were *Pro-Celebrity Golf* and *Around with Alliss*, especially if they were scheduled on BBC 2 alongside *One Man and His Dog*. For myself, as an aspiring journalist and club golfer, Peter's broadcast work showed how a sport could expand and engage beyond its normal competitive range. That is only possible in the hands of an outstanding communicator and listener, and Peter was certainly that.

Fast forward to 1986. By this time, by luck more than qualification, I had been a sports presenter on ITV and Channel Four and had already presented three years of the Masters before the contract switched to the BBC. Ever the opportunist, I moved across as well, excited to work alongside the likes of Peter Alliss.

On the Tuesday morning of Masters week, Peter suggested that we take a stroll down to Amen Corner. Peter had not been to Augusta for a few years, and as we walked down the slope toward the famous 12th, he put his hand on my arm, looked across wistfully at the 11th green and said, 'Lets stop here for just a moment. This is where it all went wrong in 1966...'

Peter proceeded to tell the story of how his Masters challenge had imploded when he had taken five putts from six feet. He recounted it with such humour, although the memory was clearly still raw.

'I think we marked it down as a nine but it could well have been fourteen or fifteen. I remember Gene Littler saying, "What the f*** are you doing?" and I said, "I don't know!" There might have been a whiff in there and a double hit, maybe a complete air shot. I don't know. All I know is I walked off that green a different person, and my confidence as a golfer was gone.'

Peter also came off that green with the experience he needed to turn him into an outstanding commentator. He certainly bore scars from golf – and a few from life as well – that fed into his approach to commentary. His philosophy appeared to be that golf is a strange little game, a sport where humour and respect both play a role. You shouldn't take it too seriously, but sometimes you have to.

Take Carnoustie and Jean van de Velde. Off came the shoes and socks, and it seemed the whole world was laughing – but not Peter Alliss. He was the one who recognised that Van de Velde's misfortunes were turning into the kind of experience that could haunt a player for the rest of his life.

The papers next day rejoiced in ridiculing van de Velde, with some accusing the 'miserable' Peter of 'failing to see the funny side.' But to my mind, no one read that situation with more depth and sympathy than Peter, and it was probably his finest commentary – mainly because when Jean van de Velde climbed out of the Barrie Burn in 1999, there was Peter Alliss walking off the eleventh green at Augusta in 1966.

But, my goodness, Peter could also make us laugh. He took great pleasure in smuggling the odd non-pc nugget past the BBC's internal harbingers of good taste. Once, Dave Marr called for Peter's assistance in trying to explain the complexity behind Chris Di Marco's putting grip. 'The last time I saw a grip like that,' Peter said, 'was round the back of Kings Cross station.' This golden line was away and gone before the editor, or any of us, could work out exactly what he meant.

I would often look into the back of the commentary box and see the likes of Bruce Forsyth or Jimmy Tarbuck hanging around. They weren't there to get out of the rain, or because they wanted a better view of the golf; they were so transfixed by Peter because he was a master broadcaster and they wanted to see his impeccable comedic timing at work.

Despite the jokes, Peter was a professional. He never lost sight of the fact that he was there to describe the golf and embellish the coverage. To my mind, he was a kind of jazz pianist – the sort who could go off on minutes of complex improvisation but would always return to the main theme with respectful timing, just as the tee shot was being addressed or the putt lined up.

From the presenters' point of view, however, Peter often got the adrenaline pumping. He would lie back in his chair and close his eyes as you were in the process of handing to him, and you were never certain that he wasn't asleep. On one occasion, he was.

American audiences loved him too, although he said to me once, 'No one really understands what I'm talking about.' I remember listening to him on the commentary team at the Heritage the week after Mike Weir had won the Masters. Peter was asked to assess the scale of the achievement of a left-hander winning at Augusta for the first time. Peter gave the question the answer it deserved.

'People don't fully appreciate how difficult it is to play left-handed,' he said. 'I've tried, and it's almost impossible.' There followed a po-faced analysis of why exactly it was so difficult to play left-handed, with Peter chuckling away in the corner of the studio all the while.

Peter's work for charity was unassuming but legendary – in particular his work to provide powered wheelchairs for children. He helped raise over £7million, changing hundreds of lives in the process. He also helped set up the DEBRA Golf Society and worked for many other golf-related causes, never as a mere figurehead but always energetically involved.

Away from the broadcast environment, I treasure the nights we had at Augusta and other places around the world – particularly when the red wine came out and the stories started to flow. I treasure also the memory of joining Peter on an Augusta supermarket expedition to make sure the team had all the right provisions. We ended up spending $700 and still had nothing for breakfast!

But more than anything else, I think of those Sunday evenings when the sun was starting to dip below the treetops and the final pairing was climbing the hill at the 18th, ready to take whatever fate had in store. These were the moments that were the most special, and how lucky we were to share it all with not only the greatest commentator in the sport but also the finest friend and companion anyone could wish for.

IMG's Sarah Wooldridge recalls warm Christmases with the Alliss family:
I GOT to know Peter Alliss while working for IMG from the early seventies, and how I miss his amusing telephone calls catching up with the latest golf gossip. Mark McCormack was very fond of Peter, and they had a great rapport together.

Only Peter and Jackie could be so thoughtful and kind as to invite me and my son, Jorge, to their amazing Boxing Day luncheons after my husband, Ian Wooldridge, died in March 2007. At Ian's memorial in June that year, Peter read "Seaside Golf" by Sir John Betjeman. His wonderful voice boomed around the Guards' Chapel. It was very much appreciated by the congregation and so special for me and the family.

On Boxing Day they always invited the same group of close friends. Peter would be wearing his latest cashmere cardigan and would recount amusing stories with us all gathered around the table. The buffet was delicious, and we used to look forward to the fillet of beef, the gammon, dauphinoise potatoes, celeriac salad, the chocolate roulade, pavlova and all the other goodies every year – all beautifully cooked by Jackie, of course. There were log fires burning in every room and Christmas trees everywhere. All the children and grandchildren were there, and it made for such a wonderful family scene.

Peter was just the greatest friend. Whenever he telephoned, he launched right into it, and of course I always knew who it was on the other end of the line! I miss him so much, but it was wonderful that he nearly reached ninety and was still broadcasting.

Producer and director Alastair Scott recalls his BBC golf journey with Peter:
I GOT to know Peter when we worked together on *Pro-Celebrity Golf* back in the 1970s. I was then a junior member of the production team, and Peter invited me one night to join him for dinner at his hotel. We soon struck up a bond, and our dinners became regular events, often lasting late into the night.

I remember Christmas Day 1977, when I was on my own in Pinner and feeling sorry for myself. I was about to go out for lunch when the phone rang. One thing you must remember with Peter is that you never got a 'Hello, Peter here!' This time, he started with: 'I was just wondering… how does a man on his own pull a Christmas cracker? Do you jam one end into the door frame? Do you tie it somehow to the bed and give it a tug?' We both roared with laughter, and I immediately cheered up. This was typical of the care that Peter demonstrated for other people. He always made time.

In the 1980s the BBC televised the Piccadilly World Match Play Championship, held over the West Course at Wentworth. Every year, there was the same lady checking our entrance passes. Everyone got to know her. We got talking one year and she said, 'Do you know that Peter Alliss? I had my purse stolen yesterday and he's just given me a £20 note!' We're talking about quite a lot of money in those days, but that was the Peter Alliss I knew.

I moved on up the BBC Sport production ladder and directed *Around With Alliss* as well as many European Tour events and all the golf majors. In 1990, I asked Jo to marry me and I asked Peter to be my best man. I must admit, I was slightly apprehensive as to his speech, but he was very gentle with me. Jo's grandfather was a vicar and there were a few other dog collars there, too. Peter told me afterwards that he had to completely change his speech.

As a commentator, there was nobody like Peter Alliss. His great skill, apart from his knowledge of the game, was his power of observation. He seemed able to see things others didn't. Of course, it's one thing to see them, another to then make the appropriate comment.

I am now an official European Tour starter, which meant I was often able to enjoy Peter's company at the end of a day's work. There are so many moments of commentary magic I can recall, but one of my favourites is the time a man streaked naked across the last green during The Open at St Andrews. There was a lot of kerfuffle before Peter quietly said, 'Such a lot of fuss over such a small thing.' It was just perfect.

Peter's final visit to a golf course was on Swinley Forest. He was in a buggy watching me and son George play with my good friend John Shrewsbury and his son, Jonathan. Peter saw that George 'could play,' in his words, and he took a keen interest in his game, clubbing for him the whole way round. It was a fantastic experience, with quality advice and entertainment from the maestro of golf. That was one of those days which will never be forgotten.

Barbara Slater, Director of BBC Sport, writes:

PETER was a true one-off, and the witticisms that entertained the audience on-air were just as funny, generous and warm hearted off-screen. He offered so much more than just calling the golf play. You could always rely on Peter to complement the TV pictures with his uncanny knack for spotting the quirky and the unusual. He had a huge passion for the game of golf and wanted to share that with everyone. With his great wit and quick mind, he brought the coverage to life, ensuring that whether you were a fan or just a casual viewer you could enjoy the broadcast just the same.

Golfer and broadcaster Ken Brown recalls Peter's unique commentary style:

WHEN you first start commentating with Peter Alliss, you know you're going in with the Jack Nicklaus of commentators. The Beeb does it a slightly different way to Sky, for whom I'd been working previously, and I went in with a slight nervousness. It's worked out quite well, but then, if you're partnering Jack Nicklaus in a competition, you'd expect to do well enough, wouldn't you? Peter had a raft of great strengths, including his voice, his timing, his observational skills and his wit. He spotted things the rest of us simply don't.

Because he tended not to bother with stats and figures, Peter never cluttered up what we saw on the screen. I suppose the highlights format didn't play to his greatest strengths of observation, but he was still supreme. His timing was breathtaking. I think in those twenty years of broadcasting together, we maybe talked over each other five times.

When the BBC was showing a lot more live golf, both professional and amateur, we developed a real conversational style, during which I was very happy to play Ernie Wise to his Eric Morecambe. Those were great days. Peter is a genius at this game; his knowledge, experience, and his natural ability as a raconteur marked him apart, and that's why he was quite rightly treated with reverence wherever he went. It was a joy to work with him. A real joy.

ABC Producer Terry Jastrow recalls working with the very best;

I CAN'T begin to express my love and thanks for Peter, who was such an important figure in both my professional and personal life. I also can't stop thinking about all the great times we had in the UK, USA and many more places around the world. Simply put, Peter was a terrific fellow for multiple reasons: he was the best of friends, an unrivalled diner companion and golf partner and clearly among the greatest golf commentators of all time. I cherish his friendship and fellowship, and I will forever hold him close to my heart.

Presenter Hazel Irvine pays tribute to a dearly missed colleague and friend:

'IF you can't be a ray of sunshine, don't be a dark cloud.'

Even in the advice he dispensed, Peter Alliss painted pictures with words. He effortlessly and gloriously elevated any broadcast. He was a joy to listen to, and it was always a thrill to share a commentary booth with him. Not only was he a fascinating person to learn from, but he was fun to be around. He was greatly loved and respected by his colleagues. He was, without question, one of the people who has most influenced my career – and my life.

Peter's approach to broadcasting was so unlike anyone else's. He made no bones about not knowing the answers and not having every statistic up his sleeve. Rather, he likened the discipline of commentary to sitting up on a hill with a friend, looking down on the unfolding story, and having a chat. That's why he'd pepper his observations with statements like, 'In technical terms, he's making a real pig's ear of this hole!' Or, famously, 'You'd need Carol Vorderman to work out his score today. Ah, Carol Vorderman. I like Carol. I was watching Countdown the other day and I got aroused. That's seven letters, very good.'

In his playful moments, Peter's whimsical talent shone through. But he was equally cogent in times of maximum pressure during a broadcast. The world seems to turn particularly quickly during the back nine of any major championship, and Peter's ability to succinctly encapsulate the unfolding drama was brilliant. I remember the moment when Rory McIlroy walked off the 12th green at Augusta in 2011. He'd just 4-putted there and his chance of a Green Jacket looked to have gone. 'His head,' Peter said, 'is like guacamole.' Before that, in 1996, there was Greg Norman's final round 'stall' at Augusta. As Nick Faldo roared past the White Shark to win the Green Jacket, Peter said, 'Faldo looks a young man again. And poor old Greg? Well, he looks ready for his bus pass.'

Peter may have given us the impression that he was just sitting and musing on that imaginary hill, but don't be fooled by his deliberately anecdotal style. He watched everything. He knew the stats, but to my mind at least, he chose to use them sparingly or only when they best suited his point. It told me that Peter knew he was broadcasting not simply to golfing aficionados but also to people who had perhaps tuned in by chance, or those who are only captivated by golf now and then. He understood how to create drama and interest for them, too.

In the last few years of his broadcasting career, the live golf broadcasts were replaced more frequently by edited highlights. Those programmes are not easy to do. Frankly, they're a lot less fun, involving less time and freedom to express yourself. They're also highly pressurised, with tight timings and complex sequences. Yet even amid these constraints, Peter remained an incredibly disciplined, sharp and focused broadcaster. He was a very, very good operator – pithy, crisp, concise, and thoughtful, in spite of the time restrictions.

But in the good old days when everything was live, Peter really knew how to pick his moments. He always enjoyed having enough space to ramble, and he would playfully elevate the most ordinary camera shots of spectators, landscapes, planes, trains and automobiles to produce moments of commentary magic. He weaved them throughout the long days of coverage – often over twelve hours a day – with so much light and shade, enduring humour and a miscellany of observations. Who can forget his fly-on-the-wall descriptions of ice-cream eaters at the Open, or Miguel Angel Jimenez' cigar-in-mouth warm-up routines?

In 2011, in a tiny commentary booth we shared at the Walker Cup at Royal Aberdeen, I remember sitting opposite Peter's commentary station when Paul, our director, cut up some shots of very hardy kite-surfers off the coast in the North Sea. It was a wild, wet and windy day. 'Oh, look at that,' he said, looking over at me with a wink. 'You know, I really miss *my* kitesurfing days.'

Speaking of the Walker Cup, that competition also produced one of his best commentary lines, one often recalled by my colleagues on the golf team. It was two days of edge-of-the-seat, heart-on-sleeve, honest endeavour between two sides: the USA versus Great Britain and Ireland. What a match it is, and on one famous occasion, Peter signed off with the words: 'And not a penny changed hands.' There it was. The essence of the Walker Cup in six words. It was a quite superb summation.

Peter was such a keen observer of the world and of the people in it. He was fascinated by other people, and he liked their company. He asked genuine questions of them and was always interested in the answers. Both he and his wonderful wife, Jackie, treated everyone in our production team the same way, with kindness and with interest. Everyone.

Of course, Peter could be uproarious, waspish, irreverent and downright hilarious. But he quietly offered insight and wisdom, too. I remember one of the first times I was anchoring the BBC's broadcast from the Masters in Augusta. Peter was our guest in the studio. With just a few moments until we went on-air, there was a great kerfuffle taking place all around me; changes were happening, with last-minute tweaks to the nominal running order. It was the usual, seat-of-the-pants broadcasting stuff. I was feverishly making script changes, head down, trying to process it all as various voices came rushing through my earpiece. I must have looked a little stressed.

I looked up and Peter calmly asked me, 'Do you like your job, Hazel?'

To which I mumbled, 'Sometimes, Peter.'

Then it hit me. He was trying to tell me to slow down, take it all in, breathe deeply and enjoy what was, and is, a wonderfully privileged ring-side seat. He was right, and it was an important piece of advice, cleverly delivered in Peter's own style.

It was not the only piece of guidance he gave me. I remember how he took me aside in my fledgling golf ventures to offer advice and encouragement. I really valued that. In fact, I was thrilled that he seemed to see some promise in me. I often looked across at him in commentary booths or studios over the twenty-five years thereafter and told myself to remember those times, and his morning greeting: 'Hey kiddo. How's it going today?'

Peter's voice will never leave my head. He was a ray of sunshine, not a dark cloud. A superb golfer in his own right, a brilliant wordsmith and story teller, a clever, funny and technically superb broadcaster. Often opinionated, he was always true to himself. And when we look back on some of the key moments in the history of golf, what Peter said about them is as much a part of our memory as that which we actually saw. Not many broadcasters are as closely woven into the fabric of their sport as was Peter Alliss.

It was a honour to learn from him and the greatest privilege to know him. I miss him greatly.

THE MASTERS IS GLORIOUS, BUT ...

WHATEVER else the Masters may be, it is a glittering testament to the power of marketing – an event conjured up by some of the sharpest minds in American business. Its success is also testament, as it happens, to the careful imagination and ambition of Arnold Palmer and his close pal, the journalist Bob Drum.

Bob was a larger-than-life character in every sense. For many years he was both Arnold Palmer's travelling companion and diarist. He was once asked how many Palmer stories he had written since his early days on the Pittsburgh Press, when he first spotted Arnie's genius as a high-school golfer. 'I reckon about 5,000,' Bob replied. 'I quoted him in every one, and half the time I couldn't find him. Palmer still thinks he said all those things.'

But why am I writing about Bob Drum, Arnold Palmer and the Masters? It's a story that starts in 1960, when Palmer won both the Masters and the US Open. Later that same year, during the trip to St Andrews to compete in his first Open Championship, the two men began talking about what might comprise a modern Grand Slam to equal Bobby Jones' 1930 triumph in all four of the US and British Amateurs and Opens. The Masters had been gaining in popularity throughout the 1950s but was still significantly short of Major status. Meanwhile, the USPGA had moved its date to August so it no longer overlapped with our Open. Several beers into the flight, Palmer and Drum settled on the Masters, the two Opens and the PGA as their answer to the question of what constituted the new professional Grand Slam.

Drum immediately began working the Grand Slam angle in his copy, billing Palmer as an all-American hero on the cusp of golfing history. The story was irresistible, and this line was swiftly picked up by other sportswriters. Palmer ultimately finished second, a shot adrift of Kel Nagle, but his great triumph of that Open was to establish the reputation of the professional Grand Slam. The Masters never looked back, and neither did our own great Championship, which had largely been ignored throughout the 1950s by many top American players – until that PGA date switch and Palmer's intervention.

By 1967 the new Grand Slam was firmly established among both players and the public as the old game's Holy Grail. It may be an improbable dream – although Tiger Woods proved with his 'Tiger Slam' in 2000/2001 that it is doable – but it is one worth tilting at and certainly one that captures the imagination. As it happens, 1967 was also the year that Peter played in his second (and final) Masters, suffering through one of the worst moments of his career. Perhaps even more significantly, 1967 was the first year that the BBC broadcast live from Augusta.

THE Masters began in the early 1930s with a less-catchy name: the Augusta National Invitation Tournament. This venture evolved out of a meeting of several minds, led by Bobby Jones, who was then arguably the most famous golfer in the world and still basking in the glow of his 1930 Grand Slam. He was joined by Clifford Roberts, a typically sharp New York financier, and Dr Alister MacKenzie, a former British Army doctor who had segued brilliantly into course architecture. Their partnership, of course, didn't happen all at once, but these were the Three Musketeers who basically put the whole scheme together. I'm sure they had no idea that their Augusta National golf course, created on an old nursery of some 350 acres, would become one of the world's most celebrated sporting arenas. Today, the invite for this great April jamboree is perhaps the most sought after in all of sport, never mind golf. But as with most things, it was not always milk and honey.

Between the early days and the mid-1950s, Augusta National Golf Club had some mighty struggles. It might seem very strange to think now, but there were periods of great financial embarrassment for the club before it became the titan it is today. Success came neither swiftly nor easily, and for a period, Dr Alister MacKenzie, the course designer, was so broke that he couldn't even afford a train ticket from the west coast of America, where he was based at that time. Money was flowing like glue, but they all weathered the storm, and look how things are today.

Essentially, the idea behind the Augusta National Golf Club was to create a sort of winter haven, a place where sports writers, golfers, baseball players, footballers and the like could escape the chilling rigours of a northern winter. Augusta, Georgia, is practically next door to northern Florida, which is where one could find almost all the winter training camps of the main American sports teams. The setup was rather like those modern-day English football clubs which ship their players out to Dubai, Spain or Portugal for winter training, away from the fog and the frosts of northern Europe.

Although the grand vision might have been a touch extravagant, there were enough initial investors, attracted by the name and fame of Bobby Jones, who were ready to back the ambitious project. As a former nursery, the clay soil was not ideal, and the land was very undulating, but there were plenty of well-established trees and plants to give it some early mature character.

Gradually the course took shape. Of course, they didn't use the sort of modern earth-moving machinery you see today, and much of the work was done by hand. It was very hard labour, no doubt. But it is one thing to construct a great course, and quite another to spread the word and attract members. As a means of promoting their new course, Bobby Jones and his pals came up with the idea of an annual event featuring America's most lauded golfers. They wanted it to be a celebration of the game, a sort of grand garden party with a spot of golf and a half-decent prize fund attached. This event was to be an invitational, so there would be no qualifying, as there is today. Crucially, they also didn't want a large field, preferring instead to invite just seventy or eighty of the day's top professionals and leading amateurs. By attracting newspaper coverage to this exclusive 'club tournament,' Bobby Jones and the gang believed they could create a word-of-mouth phenomenon. They had no idea.

As it happens, Bobby Jones knew my father well. I have already mentioned that I was privileged to meet him on that occasion in Washington, when he was in the very early stages of the debilitating spinal disease that would eventually take his life. What I did not mention earlier was that this was not the first time our paths had crossed.

Bobby Jones was not playing much golf when I encountered him in 1954, but he still remembered playing with my father at Parkstone not long after the war. This game was the occasion of our first meeting. I was fourteen years old, then, and I had no real idea of Jones's immense fame. Neither had I any idea that Alec and I would one day become the joint professionals at that very same golf club. It's funny how the same names and places can recur with regularity in a person's life story.

As for Bobby Jones, he ultimately fell out rather grotesquely with Clifford Roberts, the financier, because they had different ideas about the direction the Masters was going. Not many are privy to the actual details, but Roberts is said to have made Bobby feel unwelcome at the club, particularly when his body started to fail him. Somehow, Roberts felt that the image of Bobby in a wheelchair did not fit with the aura he was trying to cultivate at Augusta. That's outrageous if true, and how sad that their friendship should end the way it did. By the time Bobby died in 1971, their relationship was so broken that Roberts did not attend the great man's funeral in Atlanta.

Clifford Roberts, meanwhile, became a close friend of President Dwight D Eisenhower. The former US Army General was a keen golfer and played regularly at Augusta as Roberts's guest. It is reported that, through various investments, Roberts made Eisenhower a wealthy man. He was certainly a shrewd businessman, and he drove a hard bargain. His personality is best illustrated through the story that goes along the following lines...

The year was 1964, and the now-famous Butler Cabin had just been completed. Roberts was the man behind the construction of the rather grand 'Cabin,' which was to serve as a lodging house and interview venue. A certain member of some stature and wealth told Roberts that he thought it was a very good idea; he said the building was excellently done and gushed about how it enhanced the property. Then the season ended, the club wound down, Christmas came and went and the club reopened and primed itself for the next Masters. The member who had admired the Butler Cabin found himself back at the club and was informed that Mr Roberts wanted to see him when he had a moment. He duly presented himself at the office, and after a friendly handshake, Roberts handed him an envelope. In it was a bill. I'm not sure how much the bill was for, but let's say it was around $20,000, a huge amount in those far-off days.

'What's this for?' asked the member.

'You admired our cabin,' said Roberts, 'so we have built another one just for you. You can afford it, so thank you very much.'

I'm sure these words were said in such a way that the member felt that if were he to decline this 'offer,' his membership would not be renewed. Such was the arrogant, autocratic power of Clifford Roberts. Love him or hate him, the truth is that Roberts was largely responsible for the glorious rise of the Augusta National Golf Club – a glory which resonates still today.

Right from the start, the Masters has been embroidered with great elegance. Although today's event is not totally invitational, the organisers still have the right to invite certain players if they so desire. Over the years, this policy has been the source of a certain amount of annoyance. The invitation itself is no more than postcard size, with deep black writing on brilliant white paper announcing the event and inviting you to participate. It looks like the sort of thing you might receive if you were asked to a fancy dinner, and it's still done that way today.

For current professionals, it would be out of the question to even think of turning down an invitation to play at the Masters. Such a move borders now on sacrilege and would surely constitute a form of commercial suicide. Over the years, however, a number of players have resisted the temptation to play for a variety of reasons.

Neil Coles, for instance, did not enjoy flying. That is why, in January 1965, he travelled to New York by boat, before going by train to San Francisco, where he hired a car and spent the next three months playing in various tournaments across America until he arrived in Georgia to play in his first Masters. In the second round he reached the turn in 41, before whizzing back in 31 to make the cut. Frustratingly, he went down with flu overnight and had to withdraw – after all that effort to get there. It may not come as a surprise that Neil never returned.

I'm not sure why Christy O'Connor Snr declined his invites. Perhaps he thought that, between the expense and time of getting to Augusta, he might have been able to earn more at home.

And as for yours truly, it was typically a question of cost, time, family commitments and other bits and pieces that swayed my thinking. (In those early days, in the late 1940s and through the '50s, Ryder Cup players were automatically invited.)

My time to shine came eventually, but not until 1966. I thought it rather ridiculous that I had reached that fast and loose decade without having seen what the Masters had to offer. Arnold Palmer had appeared on the scene by then, and various journalists were going out of their way to praise the event – perhaps far beyond its value. But that's the way it was then, and that's the way it's still considered to be. If you criticise anything at Augusta, you automatically find yourself on very thin ice.

It sounds rather ridiculous now, but I can't really remember how I made that long journey to Augusta. I certainly didn't go by sea, so I must have flown. But to where? I can recall that no ships or trains were involved, but it's extraordinary how the mind has the ability to close out certain aspects of life. I don't remember heading down Magnolia Lane, nor checking in, and I've no idea where I stayed. One of the few things I do remember is that I was allocated a very sullen (and very large) caddie. He was at least 6ft 3 and must have weighed north of eighteen stone. He had no idea who I was, of course, and he made it clear enough that he wasn't happy to be stuck carrying my bag.

I suspect this unfortunate caddie thought I wouldn't be generous enough and that I was unlikely to play all seventy-two holes. Sadly, this latter prediction came to pass. I should have learned my lesson, but I went back the following year, 1967, to try it all again – with the same result. The truth is that I have never been anywhere in the world of golf where I was made to feel less welcome. I'm not sure how much of that was my fault and how much was just the general aura of Augusta. Everyone seemed sullen, unsmiling, unwelcoming. The clubhouse staff were almost rude. It was as if they had to really make an effort to be of service.

But perhaps all that was just down to me. I recognise that in some respects I have great confidence, while in others I'm self-effacing, bordering almost on subservient. This has changed as I've grown older (and inevitably grumpier), but up to the age of forty I would never have told someone to go forth and multiply. In my quieter moments, I often wonder what a psychiatrist or a psychologist would make of my ramblings. It may seem ridiculous, but my impression was of an Augusta constructed almost entirely of smoke and mirrors, like a great illusionist's masterpiece that millions come to marvel at without ever really seeing the truth.

An example: when the area suffers late frosts, and all the wonderful azaleas and dogwoods are blitzed, they dig the lifeless trees up, bring in new ones and plant them around the greens as though the frosts never happened. Another example is the year a great storm swept through the course; there was widespread flooding, and Rae's Creek was virtually obliterated – as was the area in front of the 12th green and alongside the 13th fairway. Hundreds of venomous snakes were washed onto the course, but all was repaired and tidied up over the next few weeks so that by the time the Masters came around, nobody knew anything had happened. One of the trees at the back of the clubhouse overlooking the course was severely damaged, and I'm talking about a great big 30ft whopper of a tree. What did they do? They dug it up, removed the roots, and brought in a huge crane to swing a new tree over the top of the clubhouse. When they were finished, all was as before.

This operation, you understand, was top secret. Nobody talks about these things at Augusta; they just happen. Greens are made bigger, bunkers appear here and there. If something doesn't fit, it's removed in such a way that you can't even see the seams.

Some fifty years ago, they changed the grass on the greens. The way it was done, so I was told, was that the greens were covered with plastic sheeting, and a poisonous gas was injected to kill the grass. Then the greens were dug up and re-seeded, and within a year they were playable – if not perfect. Can you imagine anything like that happening in Britain, Northern Europe or indeed anywhere else in the world? Augusta is a law unto itself, and in many ways, I think that's wonderful.

View it how you will, but Augusta National and the Masters is a very complex mix. The nearest comparison must be the All England Club – or Wimbledon, as most of us know it. Two great events held at the same place every year, backed by not so much a magic money tree as a whole magic money orchard. All this obviously creates problems of its own, but it does put the organisers in an overwhelmingly powerful position.

In spite of this, much of Augusta has changed, blown with the winds of professional golf. When I went, you had to use the club's caddies, and those caddies had to be black. Players now bring their own personal Sancho Panzas – of any race, of course – and they are treated right royally compared to way back when.

For a long time, Augusta was also renowned for its wine cellar. Fine vintages were collected, but not many were quaffed, so the collection grew ever bigger. Certainly, by the mid-1960s, they were selling wine at the club for far less than its true value, so there was either great ignorance or great generosity in that department. I'm not sure whether they still have some of those wines from half a century ago. I was privileged to go in that cellar once. It was no larger than a child's bedroom, with racks on either side. Not half as romantic as the cellar you might find beneath your average French chateau, but it sufficed.

The clubhouse is similarly modest when compared with many of today's monsters. After all, it was but a plantation house – built in 1854, back when Augusta National's acres were covered in indigo plants. Much has been added over the years, of course, but today's clubhouse remains in keeping with that earlier style. How wonderful that the building's understated elegance has survived the onslaught of modernity.

The Grill Room, meanwhile, has its own special magic: fine comfortable chairs of the tub variety, dark heavy wood, nice panelling and a handsome carpet. It's a wonderful place to while away an hour two with a glass of something refreshing.

Some years ago, there were protests outside the club regarding the right of women to participate in these aforementioned delights. It wasn't that big a demo – perhaps a few hundred protesters – but the media (and the major sponsors) noticed. After a suitable pause, the club did invite several women to join – most of whom were very famous and lived very far away. The club certainly didn't turn Tuesday into Ladies' Day, with the Lady Captain being the wife of a local taxi driver. That really would be progress, but we shouldn't hold our breath.

Today, the membership includes Condoleezza Rice, one of the most influential women in the world during her days as Secretary of State to President George W Bush. Miss Rice is a charming woman who loves the game of golf. She has written that her great-great grandmother bore five children to five different slave owners. So much for the 'white golfers and black caddies' shtick at Augusta, and good riddance, too. On reflection, she'd make a hell of a good Lady Captain. She's got my vote.

There is much to like about modern Augusta. For one, the honest price of admission is ridiculously fair. So too the price of refreshments on the course, with a couple of dollars seemingly enough for a beer or sandwich of your choosing. Compare that to the prices charged at our Open Championship, or indeed at any Premier League football match, and Augusta National looks like a charity. Somehow or other, tickets tend to crop up second-hand on the open market, where they can cost astronomical amounts. I don't know whether the club allows this, but some agencies also sell rip-off trips to the Masters in return for many thousands of pounds.

This was unheard of years ago. Back then, if anyone was caught selling their ticket for profit, they were banned from the course. Like Wimbledon, the club has built a system through which it allocates tickets to various individuals, many of them Augusta families who have been attending for generations. To the regular patrons who have been going to Augusta and Wimbledon for many years, their tickets are like gold and much too valuable to ever be sold.

As for the players, for that one special week they truly are lauded, and all that matters is their happiness and comfort. That's true for the handful of amateurs as well as the professionals. The field is still small today, and I don't think it has ever gone past the 100 mark, although it's not far off. This means the starting time is sensible, which is another feature that makes this tournament more civilised than most. No 6:30 a.m. starts here!

However, the organisers at Augusta do still like to bring an element of fear into the proceedings. By that, I mean the players all know that if they really go over the top, they won't be invited to play next year, regardless of their qualification.

Over the years, Augusta has had its share of run-ins with the Professional Golfers Association of the United States. There was a time when the prize money at Augusta was not considered official. The Augusta committee was told that if they weren't more open and welcoming, the PGA may well withdraw its labour. A golfing strike, you might call it.

What did Augusta do? They simply said, 'Fine. You do what you feel you have to. We'll run our tournament, and we'll invite who we wish. Those who want to play will be more than welcome.' I'm sure there were more negotiations but that was the end of that! Classic Augusta.

The club itself is open for only half the year. Almost as soon as the Masters ends, work starts to get things ready for the following year. This involves re-seeding the course, as well as various painting, repairing, gardening and tidying up. The work never stops, and the results are magnificent.

You could argue, however, that the location is not very salubrious. Have you ever wondered why you so rarely see aerial shots of the course? It's because this wonderful oasis is not surrounded by the likes of Hyde Park or Sherwood Forest. Instead, Washington Road, on which the club sits, is a hurly-burly strip of fast-food restaurants and bars. Perhaps that makes it all the more commendable that this golfing Mecca has been created from next to nothing. Can you imagine a club in the UK buying upwards of thirty or forty neighbouring houses and knocking them down just to create a car park for its patrons? That's what they did at Augusta, and I'm sure they would do it again if they had to.

Every year, come the Masters, the whole city begins to buzz. This hype is elevated to fever pitch by various golf equipment companies and by the locals, who know they have a golden week each year in which to make their fortunes – an annual bonanza. It should come as no surprise, then, that the price of everything in the city is hiked when the golfers, their entourages and the spectators come to town.

As for those spectators, it's hard to land on an exact figure of just how many turn out for the big event. On tournament days, the galleries swell with somewhere between 30,000 and 40,000 patrons, while on practice days it's come one, come all. Sales of merchandise are mind-boggling, and while the committee allows guests to be fed and watered out on the course for very little, they certainly make up for that with the prices they charge for their various golfing accessories. But having said all that, I think it's wonderful that there are people within our sport who still have the power to wag a finger at the multi-millionaire prima donnas and tell them, 'If you don't change your ways, you won't be welcome here.' Bravo!

Over the years, I've made several documentaries about the Masters for both the club and the BBC. This hasn't earned me any extra privileges, and however reluctantly, I must admit I rather like that. In truth, Augusta is not a place where I've ever felt particularly privileged. Although I've thought about it a lot, I still can't explain quite why I always felt so uncomfortable, edgy and out of place there as a player. After all, by the time I arrived on those famous lawns, I had already been playing at the top level for a dozen years. Yet here I was often overwhelmed – and that showed in the quality of my golf. I struggled to break 80 and never looked like threatening to finish in the top ten.

In 1967, my final playing visit, my first round was 76. However, I was level par when I stood on the 11th tee with a chance of qualifying for the final thirty-six. I was playing with Gene Littler, a gentle, charming man and a beautiful talent. I was on the edge of the green in two, some ten yards from the hole. I putted up six feet short, but then God knows what happened.

 My next putt went fifteen feet past; the next ended up four feet to the right; the next missed the hole by a good six inches… this dreadful exhibition seemed to go on for ever before eventually, my brain all scrambled, the ball dropped at last. There was an awkward silence before Littler remarked, 'What the fuck are you doing?' He must have been shocked, because he was a man who rarely swore.

I replied that I had no idea what had just occurred, nor indeed how many putts I had taken. My mind was a storm of panicked nothingness, a total blank. It came to pass that I had got the yips. It was strange and miserable moment, and something I would not wish on my worst enemy (although, maybe, I might be able to make one exception).

'How many was that for the hole?' Littler asked. I think we eventually settled on six putts, and so a quadruple-bogey eight for the hole. I assumed that would be the worst score ever recorded on the 11th, but to add insult to injury, I wasn't even that good at being bad. Dow Finsterwald had set the bar even lower (or should that be higher?) with nine in 1952. Since then he has been joined by several luckless others, most recently by dear Sandy Lyle in 2017. Maybe that means I'm a bit better than I think. Or should that be worse?

Far greater tragedies, however, have taken place at Augusta National Golf Club over the years – including some which have eclipsed our sport entirely. Perhaps the greatest involved Clifford Roberts, out of whose mind and business skills the whole thing came to be. Roberts killed himself down by the short course. He got out of bed one day in September 1977 and, in his dressing gown and pyjamas and with a 38-calibre pistol in his hand, wandered down the hill to the edge of Ike's Pond. He was a very sick man by then and didn't have long to live. He had resolved that a swift ending would be preferable to a drawn-out affair. Both his parents had also committed suicide. One shot and it was over.

That particular pistol then took on a life of its own. The story went round that a couple of club employees (according to the *Washington Post*, it was official photographer Frank Christian and head of security Charles Young) somehow obtained the firearm and offered it for sale. It went through various hands until it was sold in Japan. Christian and Young were fired, then rehired. Make of that what you will. Somehow or other, I believe the gun found its way back to the

TOP LEFT: A view of Fruitlands Nurseries in 1890, land that was later to become the site of Augusta National
ABOVE LEFT: The architect's drawing of the Augusta National Club House.
ABOVE: Bobby Jones, Fred Corcoran, and Jimmy Demaret share a laugh during a Masters in the 1930s
LEFT: Byron Nelson, President Dwight Eisenhower, Ben Hogan and Clifford Roberts enjoy a round ahead of the 1953 Masters Tournament
BELOW: The Butler cabin at Augusta National in the 1990s

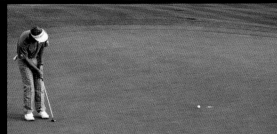

TOP LEFT: Nick Faldo and Greg Norman in relaxed mood before the start of their third round in 1996

TOP RIGHT: Peter McEvoy blasts out of the bunker during the 1978 Masters

ABOVE LEFT: Two Masters-winning putts for Tiger Woods (top) in 1997 and for Sandy Lyle in 1988 (below)

ABOVE RIGHT: Maurice Bembridge at Augusta in 1975

RIGHT: Johnny Miller, Jack Nicklaus, Tom Watson and Seve Ballesteros at the presentation ceremony in 1981

club. Where it is today I have no idea, but it's not the sort of thing you'd put in the trophy cabinet. Augusta, typically, has never made any comment.

When I found myself back at Augusta with BBC Television in the 1970s, the greatest changes were yet to come. The players were still white, the caddies black. I was less in awe and no longer had the feeling of impending failure I'd endured when I was playing there. I did still, however, feel a bit second class. All the BBC team did.

The TV compound was based close to the wonderful Par 3 Course and well away from the madding crowds (sorry, your honour, I mean patrons!). Here was the usual madcap array of trucks and cables, jostling for space alongside not a few egos. Look around and you would see men and women rushing hither and thither – setting up this, fixing that – as we prepared to broadcast to the world. It's always an exciting (if occasionally chaotic) scene and one I have come to love.

I say that we felt second class, and by that I mean we were looked down upon by our American colleagues at CBS. At Augusta, it was they who ruled the roost. They even had their own canteen, which was said to be rather grand. At least, I understand it was a nice eating place; I wouldn't be able to say for sure because no one on the BBC team was allowed in there. And if we couldn't make it into the clubhouse then it was cheese and pimento sandwiches all round. Not exactly a hardship, I agree, but it was still rather irritating and something which contributed to our ill feeling.

CBS had umpteen buggies, and we had none, because the BBC wouldn't pay for them. We have a couple now, and I promise you, that represents huge progress. Our original studio was a simple office, built out of breeze-blocks. CBS had a large structure cloaked in Augusta green. They still have commentary towers behind some greens, while we have never had that luxury. The nearest we get to the actual course and the action is some 250 yards away. Of course, CBS was paying big bucks compared to the BBC, but it rankled nonetheless.

That said, I always enjoyed my time beside the course with Ken Brown, Andrew Cotter and, recently, guest commentator and former Ryder Cup skipper Paul Azinger. We have a couple of screens showing us what we have to talk over, but otherwise the studio is a bit like a war room, in that you know the action is taking place and that you're very involved, but it all seems to be happening one remove away. It takes a while to get used to, but get used to it we all do.

When in Augusta, we always used the 'tradesman's entrance,' but the proper entrance to the club and the long drive down Magnolia Lane is as magnificent as you would hope. That sparkling white clubhouse sits at the end like a leftover prop from *Gone With The Wind*. Along with the R&A's clubhouse in St Andrews, it is surely one of the most recognisable clubhouses in the world. But what transpires within those white walls? Well, in reality, the power at Augusta is held by perhaps no more than thirty people – and what power they have!

A few years ago, they moved the media from an impressive HQ by the side of the first fairway to an even more impressive place a bit further away. Our new base looked out over the splendid practice ground, which itself had only recently been plonked down in place of a car park. There this grand edifice now sits, looking like some luxury Southern hotel. All that effort for a building which is home to a few hundred writers and photographers for just one week a year.

One year the media centre wasn't there, the next it was – all suited and booted and framed with mature landscaping to give the impression it had always been there and you had just never noticed it before. It is said to have cost some $65m, and it looks like it cost a lot more. As you walk around you can't miss an inscribed Bobby Jones quote that reads: 'To gain any fame it isn't enough to do the job. There must be someone to spread the news.' News, surely, has never been spread from a finer venue.

Here the television teams are given a little pep talk by the club each year. Everyone is told the rules: there must be no talk of prize money, no running, no phones and no mention of crowds, only 'patrons.' The emphasis, we are told, is on *courtesy*. And I can add that it's best not to forget one's pass. I once left mine back at our digs, some ten miles away, and as I was grovelling for a new pass I was made to feel very small, like I was at the assistant headmaster's study for a dressing down. As for the commentary, I wouldn't say I am apprehensive about what I say at Augusta, but I am more conscious of what is coming out of my mouth there than anywhere else. And in that regard, I am not alone.

In 1966, Jack Whitaker was the CBS anchor for the Masters. He fell rather hard from grace one Monday during an eighteen-hole play-off between Jack Nicklaus, Gay Brewer and Tommy Jacobs. It wasn't the usual Masters crowd that day; many of the patrons had left for home on Sunday and handed their tickets to fans who had never been on the course before. As the three players approached the 18th green, the fans began racing up the hill. 'Here comes the mob,' Whitaker drily remarked. Back in his office, Clifford Roberts became incandescent with rage. He phoned CBS and told them Whitaker was banned. It was five years before he was allowed back in, but by then he had lost his anchor role. He eventually moved to another network.

In 1994, television suffered another casualty when Gary McCord was tripped up by his own penchant for laconic, irreverent commentary. He was up the CBS tower behind the devilishly tricky 17th green. He was watching a group putting when he observed that the green was so slick it looked like it had been 'bikini waxed.' Then, as the camera panned across the back of the green, which had been newly landscaped, he said the bumps and hollows looked like so many 'body bags.' Apparently, Tom Watson's then-wife took offence, and Tom complained to the club. Remember, America at that time was still reeling from the human cost of the Vietnam War. McCord, too, soon found himself frozen out. Unlike Whitaker, he never came back.

I've visited Augusta more than forty times, and I'm pleased to say I have, thus far, survived these trips with my reputation intact. It is indeed a wondrous place, one that so often throws up golfing drama over a back nine filled with risk and reward. So many great memories, but if I had to pick my top Masters moments they would be Jack Nicklaus winning in 1986 (aged 46), Sandy Lyle winning in 1988, Tiger Woods's extraordinary success in 1997 and Nick Faldo's unlikely victory over Greg Norman in 1996.

Nicklaus's win was amazing. It was a Masters that seemed to be Seve Ballesteros's, right until he caught his approach to the 15th green heavy and found the water. Seve so desperately wanted to win this Masters to dedicate it to his father, who had recently died. Jack, meanwhile, was considered to be long past it as a great player. Nobody in the golfing world gave him a chance. Yet somehow he found the inspiration that Sunday. With his son Jackie as a caddie – surely a sign that even he didn't think he could contend that year – and with his mother there for the first time, he sealed his great career with an eighteenth Grand Slam victory.

Sandy Lyle's success – forever marked, of course, by his 7-iron recovery shot out of the bunker at the last hole – made him the first British player to win the Masters. I've always found Sandy to be a charming bloke as well as a most natural golfer, and I was delighted for him. Growing up as the son of Alex Lyle, the professional at Hawkstone Park in Shropshire for many years, Sandy is one of the last stars to understand the many benefits of club life. I loved the silly little jig which marked Sandy's moment of victory. That dance was so him – so innocent and charming. It is disgraceful that he was never made Ryder Cup captain, a role he surely deserved after such a glittering career.

Tiger Woods' victory was simply astonishing. After all, he had turned professional less than a year earlier. I'd seen him play in various amateur events and marvelled at his precocious talent, but like many others, I thought he would look less impressive when he measured himself up against the big boys. When he limped to the turn in 40 on the first day I felt rather smug. Well, let me say, that was the first and last time I've ever felt smug about Tiger. He roared back in 30, six under par, and proceeded to decimate the field. His final score of 270 – eighteen under par – is remarkable and set the bar for much of what was to follow. Such a pity we eventually discovered quite how flawed he is as a human being.

But Faldo's victory over Norman – that ambush! – marked the most compelling Masters of my time. Quite astonishing. I know Norman has since said that he was fighting a swing fault that week, but to my eye, he did very little wrong in a final round that he had entered with a seemingly invincible six-shot lead. Okay, he hit maybe four poor shots, but that was about it. On balance, he was desperately unlucky on several occasions. Faldo, however, was magnificent. Totally focussed, he and his terrific caddie, Fanny Sunesson, simply stalked Norman from the off, chipping away at his lead.

It was the greatest round of golf I've ever seen – absolutely sensational, under the circumstances. I also found the whole day very emotional. On the one hand, I was lost in admiration for Faldo's golf, and on the other I was greatly saddened for Norman, who, with just a wee bit of good fortune, could have won so much more than his two Open Championships. I was also hugely impressed with Faldo and Sunesson's handling of the whole situation. This was not only the Englishman's greatest ever round, it was his most thoughtful and gracious hour. Grinding Norman down that afternoon in Georgia must have taken so much out of him, but to his eternal credit, there was no triumphalism or nastiness. The embrace of his beaten foe on the final green was its own eloquent testimony to one of the greatest sporting occasions of the last century. Oh, it was simply terrific.

There are other great memories, of course. Some are of winners, but many are of personal achievement in this most demanding of arenas. Take Maurice Bembridge's course record of 64 – still the joint best score, equalled only by Jack Nicklaus and Lloyd Mangrum. It was Bembridge's second tilt at the Masters, the invite coming via the Ryder Cup route, and the Worksop-born golfer set off on the final Sunday aiming to finish in the top twenty-four to guarantee inclusion the following year.

Looking at it logically, Bembridge's game did not seem suited to Augusta, fine player though he was. He didn't hit the ball a huge distance, and his natural ball flight was low. Common sense told you the Masters wasn't for him, but that Sunday he defied logic with one of the truly great rounds – one that included a very dangerous episode indeed.

Following birdies on the 10th, 11th and 12th holes, he found the fairway on the long 13th. It was then that his caddie stopped some fifty paces before the ball. 'He's waiting to kill you,' he said, pointing to the water moccasin which lay curled nearby on the fairway.

Intrepid Maurice walked to his ball and took one look at the snake. He came back to his reluctant caddie, picked out a Slazenger 2-iron and gave the snake a 'bop' on the head. 'He wriggled about a bit and I caught him on the end of my club and tossed him into Rae's Creek,' he later said. 'I didn't know at the time that they are very dangerous. I had a plane to catch, so I couldn't hang around.'

Bembridge then considered his next shot. He decided it looked like a 2-iron anyway, so he whacked his 'snake iron' on to the green and, two putts later, walked away with a fourth successive birdie. He was now six under for the day and inside the top ten. A wedge to a couple of feet at the 15th brought another birdie, and so it stayed until the final hole where his 6-iron approach hit the top of the front bunker and dashed to the top tier. The hole was now some thirty-five feet beneath him, but fate rode with him that memorable day and he holed it for his 64. In doing so, he became the first player to traverse the back nine in 30 blows. He finished tied for ninth place and secured his place for the following year, when he would tie for twenty-sixth. Tremendous stuff.

An honourable mention, too, for the great English amateur Peter McEvoy, who in 1978 became the first British amateur to make the cut at Augusta. McEvoy has since done much in golf, including skippering the Walker Cup team, designing golf courses and writing eloquently about the game. But nothing befits him more than his performance that year at the Masters. Other players who I admired were Peter Butler, Ramon Sota and Peter Oosterhuis.

So, there you have it. To use an old phrase: Augusta, I love almost everything you have and almost everything you've done, but somewhere along the line it's also true to say bullshit baffles brains! Mind you, I still love going and these days I feel much more comfortable there. Even now, I approach it with a mixture of amusement and amazement. It really is like nowhere else.

My Last Masters

MY journey to the Masters in 2019 was, in some ways, rather strange. I'd attended the event many times, and yet I felt this might be my last. The BBC was beset by problems with their Augusta contract, and the great spectre of Sky Sports was looming. Sky was demanding far more for their money – and why not? Over the years they had contributed millions to the sport, and they were after exclusive rights.

Perhaps the days of live golf on the BBC have passed, but should that be the end of the BBC's golf offering entirely? I don't think so. The BBC is able to offer highlights of play with no commercial breaks and, if put on at a sensible hour, these will always draw a good audience – even if the actual results are already known.

The 2019 Masters was electrifying at times, and we got very gratifying ratings for our live broadcasts over the weekend. No wonder, when you had all the best players ready and willing to fight, with dear old Tiger Woods among them somewhere, written off by many but still looking good. And at the end of the day, it was Tiger who proved victorious. A number of very good players stumbled and lost ground at critical moments, allowing (if that's not too loaded a term) Tiger to come through and win.

He showed remarkable composure in the heat of battle, and then he showed such raw emotion after the final putt, when he greeted his family behind the 18th green. But never a tear. I would have bet money that if Tiger had asked someone for a tissue, blown his nose, smiled and excused his emotional moment, everyone would have been even more with him – but regardless, with him they were.

He did, however, show more humility than I'd ever seen from him, and that's having watched him since his late teens. To me, he just never looked as if he was enjoying his eighteen years of total domination. Is it too late for him to win again? It's certainly possible, but the years tick by. He's got to win another four Majors to pass Jack Nicklaus, and that's a big deal with so many very good players now in contention. It could be argued there have been greater victories, more hard won than this Masters. Three pars to win the Open Championship, for example – how often has that not been done when the opportunity was there? But for those few days in April 2019 at least, Tiger was back. Who knows what a revitalised Tiger Woods will now go on to achieve. A lot? A little?

While we all wait to find out, there can be no doubt that he gave the game of golf an enormous boost. I, for one, hope he continues. The problem he has now is deciding when to retire. Does he keep going, in an effort to beat Nicklaus's record, or if nothing happens in the next three or four years should he call it a day? Only he can decide. I hope he makes the right decision at the right time.

They're forever making changes at Augusta these days, many of them quite dramatic. During my time there in 2019, I was sure I felt the winds of change blowing stronger than ever before. I'm told, for example, that they have a new three-year plan which may involve moving the television area – trucks, commentary boxes, and all – off the property entirely. The club has already bought several acres of land to make room for this big move. Work is also scheduled to start on a tunnel underneath Washington Road. It will have to be at least 100 yards long. And I'm not sure of the height, but those wagons containing all the necessary TV equipment can be truly huge.

It's often been said that those within the Masters hierarchy do things their way, and that continues to be true. For example, for such a high-powered event, watched in awe around the world, it's always surprised me how simply and how amateurishly the tournament starter goes about his business. I have an idea that the starter alternates between members. In a voice that doesn't carry too far, you hear the cry: 'Quiet please, Rory McIlroy now driving.' That's it; there's no great build up, and only those within twenty feet can hear. It's the same in the now luxurious media centre. There's an excellent interview area, and it's all handled by one of the members, who sits alongside the interviewee. The member will do the introductions and butt in occasionally to ask a question, but there's no great ring of authority. Michael Parkinson they ain't. But does it matter? It's the Masters; they do it their way.

Every year there's talk about the places occupied by the old champions. Many come and don't participate, but several do and play well for their age. Indeed, some play very well, although there are others who make it look like very hard work. I've often wondered and suggested to some: why not have a nine-hole contest every day, starting at the tenth, while the young bucks start off the first? The older players could use a golf cart. I would make it a thirty-six hole competition for some lovely pieces of Waterford. The patrons would have a chance to salute the past champions and their favourite players, and even if some of them didn't play, they could still go round and accept the applause and warmth of the crowd. This would be a means of ensuring the old champs are still very much part of the occasion, but without them taking up a valuable spot in the draw when they know there's no hope of winning.

So many things went through my mind during that last week at Augusta. I wondered not only if it would be my final visit but also whether it would be the last time the BBC had any sort of presence on site. Incidentally, I recently found out a little bit about how the BBC's finances work. Let's take the Masters: the network pays its fee to the club, then after the event you get the viewing figures – how many people tuned in to your broadcast and when. Somehow, you link that up, per person, to the amount paid for the rights, and if it doesn't make economic sense then the powers that be (in this case, the accountants) say the rights are too expensive. Cut down, cut down! No matter that the BBC must be getting fees for showing their pictures around the world, making it all balance out. Europe, Africa, the Middle East, the Far East, Australia, New Zealand, the Caribbean, South America... so many countries showing golf, and at one time or another, this must have contributed to the BBC's coffers. Things do change, and it all gets so complicated, but I have faith in the BBC and in the future. Let's hope I'm right and that viewers can continue to watch golf ad-free on the BBC.

One of the good points this last year was the refusal of the Tournament Committee to allow competitors to carry maps showing all undulations, mounds, lines et cetera on the greens. The club likes to mention the legacy of Bobby Jones, his great integrity, and I can only applaud that. I've thought for some years that the USGA and the R&A have let certain things in the world of golf go too far.

For example, I was listening recently to an interview given by Bryson DeChambeau, who was saying what fun it was to learn to read a green. When I heard those words, I perked up. DeChambeau then told the listening world that he'd only ever used a green map and that he had no idea how to go about looking for tell-tale signs on the greens for speed and direction. Imagine that! Years ago it was considered a great skill to read the greens. It was all part of the game, like judging distance for your second shot. The first helpful signs I remember were painted posts about 4ft high, driven into the edge of the fairway to show the players how far out they were – whether they were 200 yards or 150 yards or whatnot.

On some courses they put taller poles in the rough, so players would have some idea where to look for their wayward tee shots. From there, things have progressed. Well, some people would call it progress, but I believe these innovations have taken away much of a player's skill. My father used to tell me that Alfred Padgham, the 1936 Open Champion, was the best judge of distance he had ever met. Bobby Locke, meanwhile, could not only judge distance but also read greens better than any machine. Sir Bob Charles was another who had a God-given gift when he found himself on the green. There have been many others at various times, all of whom stood out like beacons. Nowadays it's hard to find a poor putter, or even a shaky one.

One last thought: my wife Jackie and I arrived on the Sunday, just in time to see the end of the women's three-day event, culminating with the final eighteen holes on the tournament course at Augusta. Surprisingly, it was shown on the NBC Network. Why is that a surprise, you might wonder? Well, for many decades, the televising of the Masters has been looked after quite brilliantly by CBS. Yet now, just three days before the 2019 Masters, a rival network was putting out pictures of this unique golfing day: top female amateurs competing over the Masters course. That in itself is remarkable, but it also throws up another point of interest (at least, it does if you have a touch of the Hercule Poirot about you). I have no idea as to the Masters' contractual television arrangements, but it does seem rather odd that a company that has been working with them for so many years should not get this plum opportunity. It could, whisper it, be just another way for the club to let the general world of golf know that they are in absolute charge of their own destiny. Either way, it all adds to the mystique of the Masters.

SECOND only to The Old Course in terms of global fame, the Augusta National is obviously a gem. It's also a very private gem and a club that fiercely, almost cultishly, protects its exclusivity. This is one of the reasons why, quite rightly, it lags a long way behind St Andrews, which is effectively public property.

Peter's estimated quadruple-bogey at the 11th was just one of many unfortunate episodes to befall great players over the National's many acres. It is also further evidence of the old game's tendency to drive us all bonkers at some point. The worst score to par was Tom Weiskopf's ten-over 13 at the devilish 12th in the heart of Amen Corner. On this occasion in 1980, the tall, irritable American memorably lived up to his nickname of 'Towering Inferno' by angrily dunking five balls into Rae's Creek. In fact, if you add up the worst score for each hole at the Masters you end up with the staggering total of 167 – ninety-five over par. It could have been worse, had Billy Casper not torn up his card after recording 14 on the short 16th.

By the way, Peter's story of Gary McCord's banishment for his 'bikini wax' remark had a happy ending. No, he never returned to the Masters, but the incident greatly increased Gary's fame and popularity across the United States, and he has been in demand ever since. Talk about having the last laugh.

And as for BBC Television at the Masters, one of my favourite quotes came from a chat I had with a senior Beeb man who had just emerged from a meeting with then-Augusta National chairman Hord Hardin. They had been talking about renewing the broadcast contract for the following year. As is the way at Augusta, these contracts are renewed annually, and our man from London had just pleaded for a longer contract, making the case for budget preplanning and so on.

Hardin just smiled and said, 'Sir, you should know that here at Augusta National we're very much in favour of long-term relationships, but we're even more in favour of short-term contracts.' That's superficially polite, hard-nosed Augusta right there in a few words.

THE RYDER CUP ... THEN AND NOW

WHILE the true aficionado may well prefer stroke play and the grinding challenge of seventy-two holes over four days, the wider public understands and reacts more enthusiastically to match play. The non-golfer cannot be expected to appreciate the subtlety of a well struck 2-iron off a hanging lie, but show them man versus man and, as long as they can count, golf suddenly becomes not only more accessible but also more exciting. While the time taken to play the game remains a point of debate, the sublime irony is that this very painstaking pace is what allows even a casual observer to absorb the character and instinctive nature of a competitor. After all, walking, thinking, standing still, perhaps eating a banana... these are the activities which take up ninety-eight per cent of the time during any eighteen holes. Simply watching this non-action, more often than not, offers a telling insight into the character and personality of any given player and how they react to those two imposters, Triumph and Disaster. Even today's stars, too often hiding behind a cap and dark glasses, cannot help but allow the occasional glimpse of the gladiator beneath the armour.

And what event could better encapsulate this strategic tug-of-war than the Ryder Cup? When Peter was playing in the old rumble (eight times, remember), the Ryder Cup was important, but it was not the money-spinning, attention-seeking, overwhelming titan it has evolved into over the last forty years. Peter's participation, first as a player and then as a commentator, means he has bridged the gap between the Ryder Cup that was and the Ryder Cup that is. Today, the Ryder Cup brings golf to a huge section of the world's population who would not otherwise give the game much, if any, attention. And Peter has seen it all.

FROM the beginnings of the tournament almost a century ago, the Ryder Cup has evoked an air of excitement and anticipation. There are always going to be debates about the where, how and who of it, but one thing is for sure: the Ryder Cup has become one of the world's great sporting events.

My father should have played in the very first matches in the late 1920s, but this was back in his Wannsee days, when he was living and working abroad. The rules then stated that for a player to represent their country, they had to live there. Father was therefore ineligible, so Great Britain, as it was then, played the might of America without one of their best players for the Ryder Cup's first half-a-dozen years. That rule looks rather ridiculous today, when one considers how the game has grown.

The first matches after the war were played at Portland, Oregon, in 1947. They were bankrolled by Robert Hudson, a fine man of business whose family ran a fruit canning empire. Fortunately, he loved the game of golf. Without him, the Ryder Cup may well have passed into golfing history (into the can, if you will) – that's how close the tournament came to bankruptcy. Of course, those days are now long forgotten, rather like the days of financial difficulty at Augusta.

Great Britain received a dreadful beating in those 1947 matches. Leonard Crawley, the *Telegraph* man who had taken a shine to me at the Boys' Championship a year earlier, led a subsequent crusade against the team – the main thrust of it being that we desperately needed new blood. Where, however, would we find it? The war years had prematurely brought to an end many a burgeoning sporting career, and thus talent was thin on the ground wherever you looked. I was offered up as a possible combatant, alongside Bernard Hunt and Tony Harman. A few articles were penned as to the why and wherefore of the situation, and the consensus was that we were almost certainly due another beating when the Americans arrived in 1949. But beating or no beating, we younger players would have no part in it. There were several things that conspired to keep us from competing in that team, but the most important one was that we were all concerned with completing our National Service.

The matches that year were played at Ganton, a delightful course in East Yorkshire. I still remember my games there with great affection. Huge banks of gorse in full bloom, tremendous bunkering, wonderful turf... it was all rather grand in the nicest possible way, and the membership swelled with a contingent of wealthy Yorkshire farmers who wanted for nothing. In fact, the club was run on (dare I say it?) almost feudal lines. Ganton owned several properties within the confines of its grounds, and from these houses came many members of staff responsible for running the club. They all did it quite brilliantly, for Ganton was their home – even more so than for the members who paid for the privilege of playing. I remember still the Ganton cake, a fruity affair like a really good, moist Christmas cake without the icing. It was sheer bliss – wonderful after a win and just as good at purging the taste of defeat from one's palate.

Anyway, Ganton was the venue that year, and contrary to all expectation, the GB team put on a rather good showing. After a very good victory in the foursomes, things looked set fair for a home victory... but it wasn't to be. The victorious visitors, by the way, were captained that year by Ben Hogan, who wasn't playing on account of his recent road accident.

In 1951, the matches returned to the United States, and although there were one or two good British performances, the home side won handsomely. In those days, every newspaper in the UK had a golf correspondent, and this coverage was complemented by a good number of golf magazines in circulation at the time. These various publications made it easy for us back home to read about the goings-on across the pond, and the sheer volume of coverage created, in the UK at least, an air of prestige around the tournament.

Come 1953, both Bernard Hunt and I had completed our National Service. Tony Harman, meanwhile, was settling into the life of a club professional. All this meant it was surely time to introduce the new blood Britain had been craving for so long. Bernard and I were duly selected, and the excitement was almost immediately overwhelming. All these goodies soon started coming our way: shoes, trousers, Ryder Cup-branded blazers, shirts, sweaters, a raincoat, a golf bag, an umbrella and a set of head covers. We thought we were millionaires. (Incidentally, my gifted Ryder Cup bag currently resides in the Hall of Fame museum in Florida. I confess it looks rather sad, slouching as it does beside many magnificent and more modern golf bags.)

Henry Cotton was our captain. We stayed in accommodation right opposite Sunningdale clubhouse, which was then used as an overnight stopover for BOAC workers flying out of Heathrow early the following day. Although the guns had long fallen silent, there were still many restrictions on food, drink, clothing and transport. But thanks to all his weird and wonderful connections, Henry managed to get the team some steaks and some very drinkable red wine. He insisted we drink a glass every night along with dinner, washed down with copious bottles of Perrier. I think that was the first time I ever saw bottled water; I should have bought some shares.

Looking back on the matches, played that year at Wentworth, I concede it was all a rather sedate affair. At the time, however, it was sheer magic. For the practice rounds before the event, Captain Cotton made us put 10 shillings (50p) in the pot, with the best scorer winning the day. As for our putting competitions, let me say it was amazing how one's concentration improved when there were a few pounds on the line! Evening meals saw us all sitting at a big table together, with Henry telling wonderful stories about the people he had met and the places he had visited. We were captivated by tales of his life and work in the UK and the South of France. He was a master storyteller, well ahead of his time.

I remember one particular story of Henry's about mentoring one of his various assistants in the Pro Shop. He said he always encouraged his assistants to pick up a smattering of French, learn the foxtrot and make a decent acceptance speech if they happened to win one of the local competitions. Many of these ideas were laughed at. But looking back, it was very good grounding, particularly when you consider the pathetic efforts made by many when called upon to make any sort of acceptance speech – and I don't care whether that's for winning an Oscar or growing the prize turnip at the village fair.

However, I digress. I partnered Harry Weetman in the foursomes that year. We played thirty-six hole matches in those days, both foursomes and singles. I was surprised at how nervous Weetman was, considering he was a seasoned campaigner. We had a competitive match but lost two and one against Ed 'Porky' Oliver and Dale Douglas.

The singles were delayed for over an hour because of early morning mist. My opponent was Joe Turnesa, that year's US PGA Champion and one of a great family of golfers. I was one up and three to play on the West Course, and all seemed rosy until I made the most monumental mess of those last three holes – a series of errors which have lingered bleakly in my memory ever since.

It started with a misjudged second shot to the 16th, which landed in the front bunker, twenty-five yards short of the flag. I couldn't do better than a 5, while Turnesa won the hole with a 4. Then his drive at the 17th went way to the right, while I drove out of bounds left. He ultimately won the hole with a 6, meaning he was one up after thirty-five holes. I then hit a cracking drive up the last hole, while Turnesa (again) went miles into the trees on the right. Colonel Tony Duncan, a man very well known in the amateur ranks of golf, was our referee. 'You've got him now,' he said.

From at least thirty yards in the woods on the right, Turnsea had found a lie in a clearing. He pitched back just short of the little ditch that crosses the fairway. I hit a good 2-iron but missed the green by a good ten yards on the left, almost pin high. He rather messed up his third shot and ended up well short of the green. Now all I had to do was to play a nice little pitch and I was certainly going to do no worse than halve the match.

I stood over my ball, which was in a rather mossy lie. All I could see were rows of feet some two yards behind my ball – hundreds of spectators, some say thousands. This eager audience watched on in silence as I made a pig's ear of my pitch to the edge of the green. From there I ran it up to four feet and gently missed the putt well to the left of the hole. Turnesa, meanwhile, played a miserable chip and run and we ended up halving the hole in sixes, Turnesa winning our match by one hole. Meanwhile, Bernard Hunt, coming up behind, three-putted the last to only get a half point, so a Ryder Cup that had been ours for the taking turned to dust as we lost by a single point: 6-5, with one match halved. Much was written about the end result, and my collapse in particular. The fact my father was so well known did not, on this occasion, help my cause. The pain of those three holes stayed with me for a number of years.

Bernard Hunt and I were dropped for the matches in 1955. We felt it was some form of punishment doled out by the Ryder Cup committee. The matches that year were played in Palm Springs. Again, victory – 8-4, this time – for the United States, but the score-line doesn't tell the full story. Some magical golf was on display that year, played chiefly by Johnny Fallon and John Jacobs in the foursomes and by John in his single against Cary Middlecoff, America's best golfer at that time.

John told me that, as they shook hands at the end of the game, Middlecoff said to him, 'Well done – you've beaten me on one of my good days.' John never played in another Ryder Cup match, having realised instead that his true vocation was teaching, but he remembered that compliment all his life.

Next up: 1957, by which time I was back in favour and back in the team. The matches were played at Lindrick, a beautiful course in South Yorkshire, although they came close to never being played at all. Our PGA was then in severe financial difficulties, and if it hadn't been for Sir Stuart Goodwin (of Neepsend Steel fame), goodness knows what would have happened to the matches. I have a feeling they would have survived, somehow or another, but you never know.

The teams stayed that year at the Grand Hotel in Sheffield, a great mausoleum of a place whose best days were already two decades behind it. We did not do well in the foursomes, and the press (notably Desmond Hackett, the lead writer for the *Daily Express*, and Jack Wood, of the *Daily Mail*) had a field day. These writers went viral, as they say today, with articles criticising our lack of skill and fire. Desmond Hackett famously said he would eat his hat if the home team managed to fight back and claim victory. Jack Wood, on the other hand, said he would let himself be buried under two tons of compost – a polite way, I suppose, of saying horseshit.

Luckily for the British team (and unluckily for the country's leading golf correspondents), the golfing gods smiled down on us. We turned around our awful start and won the day 7-4, with one match halved. I say 'we,' of course, but the truth is that I didn't contribute one jot. Oh well. That didn't stop me from enjoying the jubilant scenes which accompanied our unlikely win.

Dai Rees, our captain, was carried shoulder-high around the clubhouse. Every man waved his trilby in the air while the ladies clutched their handbags and smiled benignly. The speeches were woefully boring, but nobody cared. The evening celebrations at the Grand Hotel went on and on. We must have drunk them out of house and home. We grew noisier and noisier as the minutes ticked by, while the Americans became more and more miserable. They couldn't wait to escape.

Two years later, the matches returned to the USA. The venue, again, was the Palm Springs area, then far from the golfing paradise it is today. Someone with influence in the United States somehow managed to get the matches played at a new club called Eldorado, which was technically in the Palm Desert. A staggering amount of development followed the tournament around the United States, and it seemed at times that the Ryder Cup had almost become a vehicle for selling real estate. Ryder Cup venues would be seen on American television and on various newsreels around the world; who knew, at the end of the day, how many plots of land, hotels, spas and all the rest would be built once the general public found out the delights of the Coachella Valley? Palm Springs today is but a dot on the map, although the valley itself runs for thirty odd miles, with well over one hundred golf courses. In fact, so many homes and golf courses have been built in the area that localised climate change has occurred over the last forty years. Humidity is off the charts – caused by course irrigation and the presence of thousands of swimming pools. I remember a fictitious book written some years ago, envisioning a situation where the Americans go to war with the Canadians over water rights. Could something like that ever happen? In some areas, the mighty Rio Grande river, once a raging torrent, is now nothing more than a shallow trout stream.

In happier news, I played well that year and had some good results. It was around this time that I struck up my partnership with Christy O'Connor. It was a joyous marriage, one that held for many years.

We still competed, and lost, under the banner of Great Britain, despite the participation of Irishmen like Christy. Indeed, there was at least one Irishman – from either the North or South – in every team between 1947 and 1977. However, it was not until the Muirfield matches in 1973 that our team underwent the official name change to become Great Britain and Ireland.

I played in all five of the 1960s matches. Although many of the matches were quite close – particularly those on home ground – the closest we got to a win was our half at Royal Birkdale in 1969. The blow-by-blow of that decade makes for rather miserable reading.

The swinging sixties teed off at Royal Lytham and St Annes in 1961, when the addition of a few new faces wasn't enough to balance out the presence of some rather jaded old campaigners. In 1963 we found ourselves in Atlanta, Georgia, the home of Bobby Jones. Looking back, this was one of my most enjoyable Ryder Cups – not only because I played very well but also because the hotel was excellent, the American hospitality bordering on outrageous. I soaked up the history of the East Lake Golf Club, where Bobby had played much of his golf, and I relished my victory over Arnold Palmer, then in his pomp, on the last green of the morning singles. Then, in the afternoon, I halved a titanic battle with Tony Lema, the rising star of American golf. The cheers of our travelling supporters were the soundtrack to a very enjoyable occasion, but despite my good performances, we ultimately lost.

On to 1965, then. Royal Birkdale was the venue, and once again, the Ryder Cup was looking peaky, financially speaking. This time it was Brian Park, northern businessman and club member, who saved the day, completing the trifecta of saviours who kept the Cup from ruin. Looking back, if it hadn't been for Robert Hudson in 1947, Sir Stuart Goodwin in 1957 and then Brian Park in 1965, the Ryder Cup really might have faded into history.

Financial difficulties sorted, it was on to the golf. The home team was captained by Harry Weetman, the Americans by the legend Byron Nelson – one of the greatest players ever to play the game. Birkdale is a superb venue, and it was here I had my best Ryder Cup ever, from a personal perspective, winning all but one match. Again, my partnership with Christy O'Connor ran like clockwork, and my two singles victories over reigning US Open champion Ken Venturi and the wonderfully gifted Billy Casper were extraordinary – exhilarating and enjoyable. But it was all for naught. The team lost, yet again.

In 1967 the matches were played at the relatively new Champions Club on the outskirts of Houston, Texas. The development had been put together by Jackie Burke and Jimmy Demaret. Their friends thought they had lost their senses when they bought hundreds of acres of swampland some thirty miles from downtown Houston, but this gamble made for a fascinating club in many ways.

I found out later that when they were putting together their idea of the perfect club, Burke and Demaret thought of all the courses they'd visited where the caddie master had worked his wonders; the waitresses had been efficient and attractive; the barman was never stumped, no matter what you ordered; the head greenkeeper was a mixture of ancient and modern; and his multi-talented staff all played golf to a good standard, loved the game and made the course their own particular baby. Burke and Demaret rolled together all these facets and produced a club in the image of everything they thought golf ought to be. And, my goodness, this new club was simply stunning! The clubhouse consisted of just two locker rooms and a central area, which contained dining and lounging space and a fine terrace, with comfortable chairs everywhere you looked. Colour bloomed, and fresh flowers dazzled. There was an abundance of parking space, the showers were powerful and we were furnished with dozens of white and fluffy Turkish towels. I'm almost crying with joy just thinking about it.

Ben Hogan was the American captain that year, while Dai Rees, for the umpteenth time, was our leader. How well I remember the formalities of the day before play began. I recall Dai standing at the microphone, brimming with confidence and boyish charm as he announced his team. He went on and on, luxuriating in each of our achievements, listing any and every accomplishment we had to our names. Occasionally, he made mention of glorious victories in tournaments which would have seemed very modest by American standards. Looking back, I can see Dai was trying his best to give us some gravitas, to convince his team that we were worthy of the litany of accolades he had bestowed upon us.

Dai eventually sat down, and Hogan approached the podium. He looked out upon the assembled crowd and let silence linger for a moment. Then he spread out his arms, gestured for his team to stand and uttered the immortal words: 'Ladies and Gentlemen, the finest golfers in the world.' There was no need for anything else. Dear old Dai's words sailed on the wind, all of those many achievements and endless accolades dwarfed by that simple declaration. No wonder I had the feeling we were a hole or two down before we got to the 1st tee.

Christy and I had a couple of ding-dong matches but we didn't claim any points, losing two and one in the morning to Arnold Palmer and Gardner Dickinson and again losing by the same score in the afternoon, this time to Bobby Nicholls and Johnny Pott. Billy Caspar beat me two and one in my first single before I managed to beat Gay Brewer, Masters champion, in the afternoon.

By now, the Ryder Cup was well and truly growing in scope and stature. The number of matches had increased, and there was already talk of bringing continental Europe into the fold, although that development was still a way off. And as for that year's matches, we lost. Again. But the trip proved to be a memorable one for reasons beside the golf.

Arnold Palmer, I recall, had just become the owner of a new aeroplane: a wee jet with not a propeller in sight. One afternoon, before the matches, he took several members of the press and a player or two up for a ride. He zoomed all over the course, showing off his acrobatic skills, but Captain Hogan was not impressed. Palmer eventually landed and returned to the clubhouse. I'm told Palmer asked Hogan what time he would be playing the next day. Hogan replied, 'How do you know I've picked you?' Retire a rather crestfallen Master Palmer.

Tony Jacklin was one of the passengers that day, along with George Will, Bobby Halsall (the professional at Royal Birkdale) and Jimmy Demaret. Tony, recalling his flight with Palmer, said they started with a very sedate pass over the course, 'so low we could recognise the players out practising.'

'Then,' he adds, 'without any warning, we were flying at 500ft and 400mph. He suddenly spun the plane upwards. Round and round we went, fearing for our lives. I remember George was wearing a pair of light grey trousers that were a darker grey below the belt. Eventually we landed, and at this point Arnold was very amused. But by the time we got back to the course, the local aviation officials were on the phone. Arnold's pilot was doing his best to deal with the situation. To Arnold's credit, he grabbed the phone and admitted he had been the one flying. There was quite a bit of grovelling going on, and in the end he was lucky not to lose his licence. Fellow Hall of Famer Jimmy Demaret helped him out there – he had friends in high places.'

Another lingering memory is of one of the practice days, which were then very different to today. Very few, if any, spectators watched us practice, although there were designated starting times for practice just in case any paying customers did turn up. On this particular, quiet afternoon, a couple of days before the matches were due to start, my caddie and I wandered out for a few holes in the company of the setting sun, only to find Doug Sanders, a close friend on the American team, doing the same thing. We teamed up and played the last few holes with a couple of balls each. It all ended with a laugh and a joke and cries of: 'Let's go for a beer!'

When Captain Hogan discovered what had transpired, he was not pleased. He told Doug that if he should be lucky enough to be named in another Ryder Cup team, he better not be so stupid as to play a couple of holes with the opposition before the off. How very different it all is now.

My final appearance in the Ryder Cup came at the end of that famous decade. We went back to Birkdale in 1969, when the American team was captained by the wonderful Sam Snead and the British by the delightfully fiery Eric Brown. I was only thirty-eight years of age, but I was going through a divorce at that time, which made life rather difficult for a number of people. My television work, however, was going quite well. There always seemed to be more of it – so much so that I was playing matches in the morning and having to be excused to do my television stints in the afternoon.

Although I was striking the ball as well as ever, my putting, for whatever reason, was abysmal. When speaking of such trials and tribulations, the concept of 'mind over matter' keeps popping up. Likewise Bobby Jones's wonderful remark in the late 1920s about the most important distance on any golf course being the six inches between one's ears. That, dear friends, is still true to this very day. There are so many wonderful-looking players, both men and women, who hit the ball majestically but have yet to learn how to play golf. The only game with similar traits is snooker. Attack or defend, choose your shot... these are the two of the most crucial aspects in these strangely alike sports.

Anyway, my lone single that year was against my dear friend Lee Trevino. He would be the first to say I played him off the course, but it was one of those days when my putting was truly awful. Lee won two and one.

I remember these matches vividly for a number of reasons, from Tony Jacklin's wonderful match with Jack Nicklaus (and that famous conceded putt of thirty-odd inches to halve the match and the tournament) to Brian Huggett's very emotional six-footer on the last green when he thought he had that to win the Cup itself. Honours were even, however, and so America retained the trophy. All in all, it seems a fair result, although Nicklaus was heavily criticised by some of his team and by many American writers for being too generous to Jacklin. They said he should have made him hole the putt to halve the match. There are cynics, too, who look at his concession another way. To many, by his gesture he would be a hero, a gentleman, a fine scholar and a unique member of the human race... but did he already know full well the score; did he realise in a flash that a halved match would result in America retaining the trophy and him gaining the plaudits without the need to risk anything; and was he conceited and confident enough to follow through with it? Of course, a halved match is not a victory, but it's not the end of the world. And it's certainly no bad thing when you can turn yourself into a sporting giant in the process, almost embodying the spirit of Olympia. It's not the winning that counts, as we're often told – it's the taking part.

ABOVE: Non-playing captain Henry Cotton meets his 1953 Ryder Cup squad at Wentworth

LEFT: Peter Alliss in new team kit for his Ryder Cup debut in 1953

RIGHT: Cartoonist Roy Ullyett looks ahead to the debuts of Peter Alliss and Bernard Hunt at the 1953 Ryder Cup

LEFT: The team that won the Ryder Cup at Lindrick in 1957. Back row (left to right): Harry Bradshaw, Peter Mills, Peter Alliss, Bernard, Hunt, Harry Weetman. Front Row (l to r): Max Faulkner, Eric Brown, Dai Rees, Ken Bousfield and Christy O'Connor

ABOVE: Peter Alliss and Christy O'Connor prepare to take on Don January and Ken Venturi in the foursomes at the 1965 Ryder Cup at Royal Birkdale, they won 5&4

ABOVE RIGHT: Dai Rees and the 1969 Ryder Cup team arrive in New York with the trophy that they had won in 1957

RIGHT: Lee Trevino and Gene Littler win 1 up against Alliss and Barnes in the 1969 Ryder Cup at Royal Birkdale

BELOW: Peter Alliss with Julius Boros and Gene Littler after he and Bernard Hunt had halved their match in the 1963 Ryder Cup in Atlanta

BOTTOM: The 1969 Ryder Cup team at Royal Birkdale

Do you really think, however, that all of that nonsense went through Nicklaus's mind in that pressurised split second? It's food for thought, of course, but only if you've got nothing else to do on a winter's evening and you're having a damn good argument in the corner of the bar. The only problem is that most golf clubs now shut up shop at about five in the afternoon in wintertime. There's no arguing in the corner as the clock ticks towards nine; those days have long gone. More's the pity.

The 1969 matches, as I said, marked the end of my involvement with the Ryder Cup as a player. Remarkably enough, the contest carried on without me. My relationship with the Cup changed then to that of a spectator, observer and commentator.

In 1971, the matches were played at Old Warson in Missouri. Eric Brown was our captain once again, with Jay Hebert – a great Louisianan gentleman of French descent – leading the USA. He and his brother Lionel both won the US PGA Championship and were, in the subdued terms of the day, a couple of 'characters.' Jay was a simple charmer, and Lionel was a tubby trumpet player of some note who enjoyed life and Cajun cooking to the nth degree. Meanwhile, we had a number of new players appearing for Britain: Peter Townsend, John Garner and Harry Bannerman to name but three. There was much to-ing and fro-ing, but at the end of it all, America triumphed by a margin of five points. Not the end of the world, but still another dispiriting loss.

In 1973 the matches came to Muirfield, the home of the Honourable Company of Edinburgh Golfers. Team Great Britain & Ireland got off to a good start, before slowly fading. The end result was a loss: 19-13.

This was the year I made my first and final Ryder Cup appearance as a referee – an experience which I found rather nerve-wracking. I do remember one of the team, who shall remain nameless, decided to try an oyster or two the night before the opening game. Yes, you've guessed it – it was nearly a question of 'taken suddenly at Muirfield Golf Club during a golfing holiday!' Not the best of preparations. From then on, I went to the matches purely as an onlooker working for various television companies.

For team GB&I, losing was, by now, a firmly entrenched habit – one we couldn't shake when the matches returned to America in 1975. That year the teams flew out to Laurel Valley, Arnold Palmer's club in Pennsylvania, where the final score was 21-11. That score is rather depressing on paper, but what it doesn't tell is an impressive feat by Brian Barnes, who had the honour/privilege/minor miracle (delete as appropriate) of beating Jack Nicklaus twice in one day.

In those days it was customary for the GB&I captain to lead the team for one home Cup and one away. The honour, in 1977, fell to Brian Huggett for the British and Irish, with Dow Finsterwald skippering the American side. The venue was Royal Lytham and St Annes, and it was here where Nick Faldo made his triumphant Ryder Cup debut – and how brilliantly he played in partnership with Peter Oosterhuis. The format then was five foursomes on day one, five four-balls on the second day and a final singles series of ten matches. This change of format made no difference. Again the final result made sorry reading, with the United States winning 12½-7½.

For some reason, Brian Huggett was never offered the captaincy for a second time. I was not privy to anything that went on in the meeting rooms before that decision was revealed, but I did hear that Huggett was unhappy about what he perceived as a lack of interest on the part of some senior players when it came to going back on the course to offer their support in the unfinished matches. This would have been very contrary to the American position; our cousins always appeared to take delight in rallying the troops on every occasion. What really happened? I don't know, but Brian Huggett was certainly swept under the Ryder Cup carpet and virtually forgotten. A shameful page in the history of the Cup, from the home point of view.

In 1979, the matches were played at The Greenbrier in White Sulphur Springs, West Virginia. September in that part of the world is quite spectacular, with its changing leaves and warm light – an artist's dream. America had as its captain Billy Casper, while John Jacobs was waving the flag for Europe – yes, Europe. After much discussion, this was the first time players from the continent were eligible to be selected. Two of Europe's finest, Antonio Garrido and Seve Ballesteros, joined the team, but the result was no different. Europe lost 17-11, and the much-heralded continental contingent won only a single point between them. It was an inauspicious omen, although bright moments came courtesy of Nick Faldo and Peter Oosterhuis, who continued their formidable partnership.

Much has already been written about the 1981 matches, played at Walton Heath in Surrey, but I'm going to go ahead and write a little more. John Jacobs was then in his second year of captaincy, while Dave Marr, former winner of the US PGA, was the man at America's helm. Many thought this was the strongest American team ever, with more Majors among them than the US army. Europe made a good start on the first day, and honours were very much even. But then, with the coming of the four-ball matches, the Americans wheeled out their heavy artillery and the golfing gods chose their champions. There was much grumbling behind the scenes, not least owing to the omission of Seve Ballesteros from Europe's team (the great Spaniard found himself dropped after an ill-advised interview). Jose Maria Canizares and Manuel Pinero represented continental Europe in his stead.

They played their part but the team lost heavily, 18½-9½. Faldo and Oosterhuis seemed to have lost much of their magic, although Faldo did manage to beat Johnny Miller in the singles by two and one. The weather was poor, and the atmosphere was almost non-existent, but then it's hard to clap enthusiastically with an umbrella in one's hands. Either way, the European 'experiment' was, by now, written in stone. Continental players would forever be an integral part of the Ryder Cup team, but this victory for inclusion didn't translate to victory against the Americans.

All that began to change in 1983, when the matches were played at the PGA National Golf Club in Palm Beach Gardens, Florida. The captains were Jack Nicklaus and Tony Jacklin. Faldo had found a new partner in Bernhard Langer, and as the Duke of Wellington reputedly said after a long hard day, 'It was a damn close-run thing,' or something like that… and so indeed it was. There were miracle shots on both sides, emotions ran high and the matches ebbed and flowed wonderfully. Lanny Wadkins produced a magical pitch at the final hole to halve his match with Jose Maria Canizares, while Seve Ballesteros should have won his match easily against Fuzzy Zoeller but had to produce perhaps the shot of the week to secure a half on the final hole, on which he hit a sensational 3-wood from a fairway bunker. So near and yet so far.

With another win chalked up for America, the away team's locker room carried an obvious odour of doom and gloom. Seve took it on himself to lift this ominous atmosphere. He said something along the lines of: 'Come on – this is the first time we've been so close. Next time we can do it!' And so it came to pass.

It happened at The Belfry on the Brabazon Course, and it happened over three extraordinary, magical September days in 1985. That year there were more continental players on view: Ballesteros, Pinero, Langer, Canizares and Rivero. I think it would be fair to say the result rocked the American team more than one could have imagined. Whether it was down to the home players having a better feel for the course, the very partisan crowd or the efforts of Lady Luck (or perhaps a combination of all three), Europe achieved a stellar victory. It was an historic win, and it was achieved, strangely enough, without the assistance of Nick Faldo, who, for a moment, seemed to have lost his magic touch. The celebrations went on long into the night, and that next morning – not too early – many a bleary eye opened to take in a new era in Ryder Cup history. Someone called for some hair of the dog over breakfast (or was it Fernet-Branca?) and uttered the immortal words: 'Enjoy it while you can, because in two years' time we've got to face those damned Yanks on their home soil. And, boy, will they be ready for us.' The time passed very quickly. The same could not be said for the hangovers.

Suddenly it was September 1987, and the US PGA had decided the matches would be played at the wondrous Muirfield Village Golf Club in Dublin, Ohio. Their captain, naturally, would be Jack Nicklaus – the man who designed the course and the co-owner of the club. Europe's captain was, once more, to be Tony Jacklin. I almost expected Jack to arrive on a white charger bedecked in a full suit of armour, gallantly leading his troops into battle. The setting was perfect… how could they fail? By now, the number of matches had been extended yet again, with foursomes in the morning and four-balls in the afternoon.

The Europeans got off to a flying start and were ahead at the end of the first day. On the second day, the morning foursomes were very close. It was much the same in the afternoon, so everything was still to play for on day three of the singles.

There were many memorable moments on that final day, including Ben Crenshaw's broken putter and Eamonn Darcy's downhill putt on the final green to beat him by one hole. Well done, Darcy! I swear everything moved except the putter head; I'm not sure he didn't even hit it with the shadow, but somehow, the ball wandered down the slope and disappeared. Europe won again, 15-13.

I was captain of the Professional Golfers Association that year, and rather like 1957, I confess we did slightly overdo our celebrations. Jose Maria Olazabal's magical two-step on the final green; Ken Brown's maniacal laugh, which could be heard several fairways distant; Europe's team celebrations with the travelling fans… wonderful, memorable moments.

In 1989, the Brabazon Course at the Belfry was the setting. It's a tournament which will probably be remembered for the number of matches that came to the final green; indeed, it was a tight affair, ending in a tie with fourteen points apiece. Since Europe was the holder, we retained the trophy. There seemed to be a few moments of petty behaviour, but on the whole, things went off very well.

It was very different in 1991, when the matches were played at the Ocean Course on Kiawah Island. Again there were one or two moments of hot headiness, and at times things became rather petty. The result was a one-point victory for the United States, but they appeared in danger of losing something more important. The sight of the US captain, Dave Stockton, being merrily dumped in the sea behind the 18th green was a memorable one. The only disappointing thing was that his team had won. On view for the first time was Paul Broadhurst, who had a superb Ryder Cup. Faldo's star was beginning to fade, and although the result was disappointing, I think in many ways it was a good thing the home team won. Many of the spectators were well-fuelled with alcohol, and as Langer's shortish putt on the last green slipped past the hole, I feared we might well have seen some fisticuffs had things turned out differently.

In 1993, once more the matches returned to the Belfry. This was a source of consternation in certain areas, and many questioned why the matches were played there so often. The answer has at least something to do with the fact that the PGA (who, you might say, owns the rights to the Ryder Cup) was based there. It helped also that the Belfry had a 300-room hotel, plenty of space for a tented village, lots of car parking, motorways passing within a few hundred yards of the front door and an international airport just a handful of miles away. Plus, it was located right in the middle of England, pretty well equidistant for any travelling

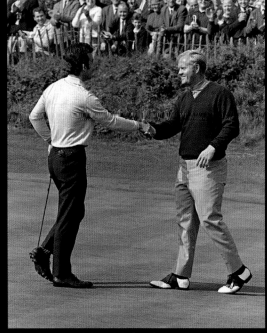

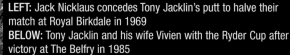

LEFT: Jack Nicklaus concedes Tony Jacklin's putt to halve their match at Royal Birkdale in 1969
BELOW: Tony Jacklin and his wife Vivien with the Ryder Cup after victory at The Belfry in 1985

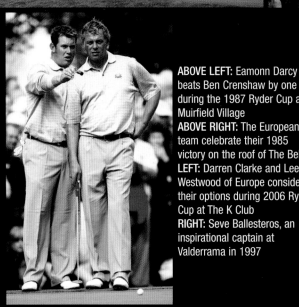

ABOVE LEFT: Eamonn Darcy beats Ben Crenshaw by one hole during the 1987 Ryder Cup at Muirfield Village
ABOVE RIGHT: The European team celebrate their 1985 victory on the roof of The Belfry
LEFT: Darren Clarke and Lee Westwood of Europe consider their options during 2006 Ryder Cup at The K Club
RIGHT: Seve Ballesteros, an inspirational captain at Valderrama in 1997

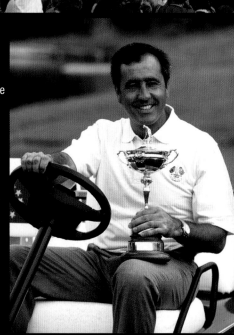

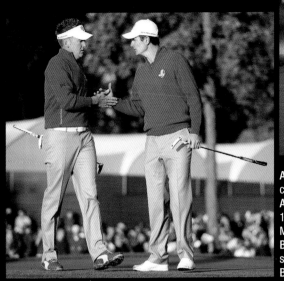

ABOVE LEFT: Ian Poulter and Justin Rose, a formidable combination at Medinah in 2012

ABOVE: Martin Kaymer sinks the match-winning putt on the 18th hole to retain the Ryder Cup on to complete the 'miracle at Medinah' in 2012

BELOW LEFT: Jamie Donaldson celebrates after his putt secured a win for Europe at Gleneagles in 2014

BELOW: Captains Corey Pavin and Colin Montgomerie before the 2010 Ryder Cup at Celtic Manor

BOTTOM: Dressed for the occasion – a lavish Gala at Versailles before the 2018 Ryder Cup

golfer. Merits of the Belfry aside, the home team had a lot going for them, but at the end of play, victory went to the US, 15-13.

Back to America in 1995 to play at the established Oak Hill Country Club in Rochester, New York. Once again, several niggles were reported, although I feel these were mainly driven by gossip and one or two over-enthusiastic journalists. Again, it was a close-run battle, with many matches going to the eighteenth. Two of the heroes, for me, were the Irishman Philip Walton and Nick Faldo, both of whom played very courageously with lots of character to win by one hole in the singles. Europe triumphed 14½-13½, leaving Lanny Wadkins, the US captain, crestfallen. European captain Bernard Gallacher, on the other hand, was elated. He suddenly looked twenty years younger. It had taken three tries, but he and his team had triumphed.

In 1997 the Ryder Cup was played for the first time *sur le continent.* The club was Valderrama in Sotogrande, southern Spain. After one or two colossal thunderstorms delayed the start, Europe carried the day 14½-13½. Europe's captain, Seve Ballesteros, was to many an enthusiastic delight and to others a mother hen with all the hormones flying in the wrong direction. I swear at moments there were five Seves out on the course simultaneously, running hither and thither, encouraging, cajoling, and advising non-stop. He later admitted he only slept for a couple of hours each night over that magical weekend, once waking his vice-captain, Miguel Angel Jimenez, in the middle of what was always going to be a short night's sleep to discuss the pairings for that morning's play. What an advert for those long-life batteries I'm sure he had digested. At the end of it all, Tom Kite, the US captain – bespectacled, serious, and never a match for Seve – was obviously disappointed but remained philosophical. The beat went on.

In 1999, at the Country Club in Brookline, Massachusetts, the scores were reversed. Captain Ben Crenshaw led his team to a remarkable comeback victory over Mark James and his men. This was, in many ways, a very unhappy Ryder Cup. Things happened both on and off the course which have never been spoken about since. Like how the European team returned from the prize presentation to find their locker room completely cleaned out of all memorabilia and souvenirs; everything had gone. I've spoken to Mark James on a number of occasions regarding this upsetting incident, but he's never come up with an answer as to how or why it happened. Of course, the matches should be hard-fought with no quarter given, but things went alarmingly far that year.

In 2002, the European team returned to the Belfry under Sam Torrance. For the United States, Curtis Strange took the leading role. These matches should have been played a year earlier, but the tragedy of the Twin Towers in September 2001 meant this Ryder Cup duel had to be rescheduled. At the end of the proceedings, three points separated the teams, the result going in Europe's favour. For me, there were some players who require special mention in the singles. Bernhard

Langer, Padraig Harrington, Thomas Bjorn, Niclas Fasth, Paul McGinley, Pierre Fulke and Phillip Price all deserve praise for their gutsy play. Particularly Price, who was playing in his only Ryder Cup. He beat Phil Mickelson, one of America's finest, three and two. It ended 15½ to Europe, 12½ to the USA.

One good thing came of that year's matches. Before the start of play, the captains got together in an effort to make sure there was no unnecessary unpleasantness or anything that would aggravate the crowd and lead to anything untoward. Their peacekeeping efforts worked a treat, and the right spirit was immediately reinstated. The attack on New York meant America once again had a genuine war to fight, and so the Ryder Cup no longer needed to be the substitute battle which, in many ways, it had become. Perspective had returned, and the great game was recognised for what it was: just a game, at the end of the day.

Back to the United States we all went in 2004, the tournament now taking place in even years. Hal Sutton captained the USA; Berhard Langer led the Europeans. The result was a crushing victory for Europe, 18½-9½. Such a victory on American soil would have been quite unthinkable just years ago, yet here we were. I felt very sorry for Sutton, who was criticised in the most horrible fashion for putting Phil Mickelson and Tiger Woods out together. They both played poorly and they were, frankly, humiliated. This told me a lot about Mickelson and Woods.

The whole episode made me think about how I would have approached a Ryder Cup match with Nick Faldo as my partner (you have probably gathered by now that we don't see eye to eye). I know I would have made absolutely certain that I was playing my heart out – if only to make sure he had no excuse to go away and tell the world how poorly I had performed. If he had anything about him, he would have done exactly the same. It makes me think, at the end of the day, that Woods and Mickelson could and should have been one of the most formidable combinations the game of golf has ever seen. But it was not to be. They both behaved in the most childish manner, their actions bordering on stupidity. For a time, I thought I was perhaps the only person in the world of golf who admired Hal Sutton for what I thought could have been a brilliant team selection. Sadly for Sutton, his grand gamble didn't work out.

Two years later, at the K Club outside Dublin, Captain Ian Woosnam was up against America's Tom Lehman. Again, it was a crushing victory to Europe: 18½-9½. The weather was (dare I say?) typically Irish; every day was 'soft,' a gentle rain.

These were very emotional times. Darren Clarke's wife, Heather, had died a few weeks earlier. Darren, in partnership with Lee Westwood, played magnificently, spurred on no doubt by memories close and dear. How great to see him celebrating with two, maybe three, pints of Guinness as a delighted Irish crowd urged him on during some wild, happy, Sunday-night revelry.

The Cup in 2008 was all rather topsy turvy. Valhalla in Louisville, Kentucky, was the venue. Nick Faldo was Europe's captain, while the delightful Paul Azinger led America. How well Azinger did. Faldo, however, never seemed a good fit. In fact, rather like Trevino's performance at the Belfry many years before, Faldo's captaincy was a disaster. Trevino had then seen no reason why he needed to advise his players on anything; they were all top professionals, and he supposed all they had to do was go out, play their game, and win. Faldo fell into the same trap. Evidently, it doesn't always work like that.

Some players need an arm round the shoulder; others need a sharp word, bordering on a bollocking, every now and then. One of my memories of Faldo at Valhalla was of him riding in a golf cart with his children and DJ Spoony, the whole posse driving hither and thither as if they were touring Disneyworld. His introductory speech, meanwhile, was bordering on pathetic, and his attempts at humour were non-existent. And so it seemed to go on and on, although the result (a victory for the USA by 16½-11½) was not as bad as it might have been. Thank goodness, some of his players had pride in their performance and fought to the very end, even though they had probably lost heart hours before.

And so on to Wales and Celtic Manor during the first week of October 2010. Colin Montgomerie for Europe, Corey Pavin for the USA. The weather was appalling – hour after hour of teeming rain. The course stood up to it remarkably well, although the trudging of the spectators created mudbaths alongside the fairways. Sou'westers, wellington boots and umbrellas were the order of the day – so much so that play had to go into extra time.

The result was down to one point: 14½-13½ in Europe's favour. For some reason, Colin Montgomerie did not seem a memorable captain, although his record in the matches as a player was magnificent. At the end of it all he was victorious, and that's all that really matters. If Faldo's team had managed to win, he too would have been hailed a hero instead of, to put it mildly, a grave disappointment.

And what can we say about 2012 that hasn't been said already? The Miracle of Medina, overseen by Captains Davis Love and Jose Maria Olazabal. Many wondrous things happened over these three days at the end of September. Ian Poulter became Europe's mascot, talisman, inspiration. How many times I heard the cry: 'Poulter, Poulter, he's our man! If he can't do it, no one can!' And, dammit, he did just that. He, Justin Rose, Francesco Molinari, Sergio Garcia, Rory McIlroy, Luke Donald, Lee Westwood and, of course, the man who holed the winning putt, Martin Kaymer... all were heroes on that magical Sunday when the golfing word stood still in disbelief at what was happening in Chicago. But happen it did. Down 6-10 at the start of the final singles matches, the Europeans needed an unprecedented 8½ points to win. A tall order under any circumstances, but to achieve such a mission on 'enemy territory' was as unlikely as it was glorious.

Next time out saw Gleneagles, and its wonderful facilities, chosen as the venue. The weather was unkind. The Scottish rain and gloom were not quite as dense as it had been in Wales, but it was still very late in the year, perhaps too late, to be playing events of this magnitude so far north. Paul McGinley captained Europe, and Tom Watson led the USA. Once again it proved that a great player does not necessarily make a great captain.

Phil Mickelson was very vocal in his criticism of Watson's captaincy. Watson, rather like Trevino and Faldo, seemed to be in the mindset of: 'You're among the top professionals in the world; I don't have to tell you anything; just go out and play.' But his lack of communication was obviously an error, resulting in a big win for Europe and adding more kudos to the life and style of one Paul McGinley. A good, though relatively modest, golfer, Paul was the ideal foursomes partner, a player in the mould of John Panton or Brian Waites. He was always on the fairway or the middle of the green, and he was a good long-range putter and a good companion. How remarkably his reputation has grown, both on and off the course. Tom Watson, on the other hand, seems to have lost a little bit of his magic, which is a great pity.

Next came 2016, which saw us at Hazeltine – a relatively new course, quite controversial in its day. When the US Open was first staged there in 1970, Dave Hill said all it lacked was 'eighty acres of corn and a few cows.' Hill finished second to Jacklin that year, although the course has improved a lot since then. Davis Love and Darren Clarke were the captains, by the way. Many thought Darren, with his larger than life personality, would carry the day. However, it wasn't to be; the United States won 17-11, a huge margin in modern times.

How different it would be two years on, when the matches were played at the Golf National, just outside Paris. The Dane Thomas Bjorn led the way, but it all appeared to be rather a struggle. Was he too demanding? There were rumours circulating that if he didn't pull his socks up (whatever that meant), he might lose his captaincy. How true that is I'm not sure, but something went on that I don't think will ever see the true light of day. The American captain that year was Jim Furyk, who always reminds me of Mr Punch, particularly when he takes off his hat. But he is a player who has made the very most of his talents.

Some observers worried about the matches going to France, and questions were asked. Would the spectators turn up in great numbers? Would they behave? Would the number of poodles on parade match those genteel ladies and gentlemen who would surely fail to appear if the sun wasn't shining?

They needn't have worried. The American team was crushed 17½-10½, and the Europeans ended up playing their hearts out. Were they competing with such pride for the flags of all their respective nations, the vision of a united Europe or Captain Bjorn? Who knows? Either way, the tournament was a massive success on all fronts. The only sticking point was the expenditure, which seemed way too high and might well be looked into in the years ahead. Is too much money spent on gifts? Do the wives and girlfriends really warrant as much as £20,000 worth of goodies? It's so easy to spend other people's money, and the players today are so delicate you'd think many of them were brought up on a diet of caviar, smoked salmon and truffles. Let's try to keep these matches within the realms of reality, I say, and do let's try to keep everyone's feet broadly tethered to the ground.

Since my playing days, the Ryder Cup has seen plenty of changes across the board. It now seems set forever that the teams will consist of twelve players and a captain, but there are regular discussions as to how many Captain's Picks there ought to be. The number of vice-captains is always another bone of contention, and questions are now being asked about the budget for the many gifts and other expenses lavished on wives, girlfriends and caddies. I only wonder what might be made of today's Ryder Cup by Messrs Hudson, Goodwin and Park – the three men who, at various points, saved the tournament's finances from collapsing into ruin. There can be no doubt that they would be astonished at the scale of global interest these matches encourage today.

––––––––––––

Now, I cannot leave this chapter without reference to my friend Peter Fry, a well known and respected figure in the West Country and a long time member of Came Down Golf Club in Dorset. Over the years, Peter has put together a whole host of information regarding the origins of the Ryder Cup. There is no doubt, he says, that Samuel Ryder paid regular visits to the Came Down Golf Club in the early 1920s. It was here where he met Ernest Whitcombe, who with his brothers, Charles and Reggie, was a stalwart of English golf in the '20s and '30s. Over the years, Peter has interviewed many of Samuel Ryder's descendants, and the points he makes about the cup's origins are exemplary and definitive. I like the way he describes Came Down golf Club as 'the birthplace of the Ryder Cup' and the Verulam Golf Club as 'the home of the Ryder Cup.'

Fry spent a lot of time with Ryder's eldest daughter, Margery, who confirmed all of his findings. However, by the time Fry had completed much of his detective work, it had already been established in many people's eyes that the Ryder Cup began and ended in St Albans through the good offices of Samuel Ryder the seed merchant.

During the 1920s, Ryder often visited Southern Africa in the search for new and interesting plants to provide more colour and choice for the gardener. With daughter Margery in tow, he wandered over dozens of gardens and experimental plots in an effort to find new varieties. And he certainly did just that. Probably his most famous was the 'Livingstone Daisy.' When he decided the time was right, he launched the flower as a hardy half-annual on the British market. It's still with us to this very day.

We know also that Ryder travelled into Rhodesia and Southern Rhodesia, where farming was king. He ended up buying the Matikas Cloof farm near Umtali for £4,000 in the summer of 1929. It was at an altitude of 4,000 feet and was close to the Mozambique border. Marjory and her husband, Leslie Claisen, continued to farm there for many years. Apart from growing seeds for Ryder's business, Marjory acquired a great reputation for caring for the sick, administering herbal remedies from the Ryder firm Health and Heather.

It's quite easy to see why much of Fry's work has remained in the shadows. The Ryder Cup has had its beginnings written about hundreds – nay, thousands – of times, so it's virtually impossible for a large part of it to be pushed to one side to make room for a whole new version of events. I think Fry has come to the conclusion that his information regarding the beginnings of the Ryder Cup will not become gospel any time soon, but in some circles he has been recognised as a great seeker of truth, insofar as he has tried to pinpoint the beginnings of this magical trophy.

At the end of the day, it's a bit of this and a bit of that. If it hadn't been for Samuel Ryder's holiday golf at Came Down Golf Club, where he met Ernest Whitcomb and admired his skill – even giving him some money to travel and play in the few tournaments where he made his reputation – the Ryder Cup may not have happened at all. That, of course, is just supposition, but we know that these things did happen in the mid-1920s. My father, Percy, although not able to play in the matches at that time, was very much there when it all happened.

Here I must add a final thought about the BBC's concession of live golf coverage to Sky, which controls the rights to the Ryder Cup. It seems that the BBC, despite being a multi-billion-pound business, seems not to have the money to compete with various other broadcasters from around the world.

There was a time, not so very long ago, when the BBC was the master of all it surveyed, respected throughout the world for the quality and integrity of its broadcasting. Working for the BBC had a special kudos; you felt you were somebody even if you were only a little way up the ladder. Over the years, commercial television has made huge inroads, and the combined power of advertising and media moguls has rocked the Corporation. Sometimes, one feels progress is a backward step. Older folk will know what I mean.

There's no doubt that over the years, some aspects of the BBC have not been run quite as well as they might. In my experience, most businesses fail from the top, and on reflection, some of the decisions made over the last few decades have been poor. One could say it all began with Harold Wilson, followed, years later, by Mrs Thatcher – or her advisers, who might have put words in her ear that the BBC was against her and her government. The organisation was getting too powerful, it must be brought to heel and so on. So it came to pass that one John Birt, now Lord Birt, was brought in to deflower the BBC.

Slowly but surely, the BBC's power has been eroded. This happened as the world of sport started growing almost beyond belief. I suppose it's only right and proper that those at the top of their particular tree should be rewarded. That's the society we live in, even if the wages of today's footballers have well-and-truly crossed the border into the obscene: £100,000, £200,000, £300,000-plus a week. A WEEK! And yet, there are very few complaints from the folk who go to watch, who might perhaps be struggling to make ends meet themselves. I wonder why that is? Much of the world of everyday business is run by the likes of Amazon, while High Street shops are disappearing. Only in small, out-of-the-way villages do the local butcher and baker survive. It is natural for times to change but, for some of us, it hasn't all changed for the better. *As ever, c'est la vie.*

The Best Ryder Cup Teams?

MY Ryder Cup playing days ended, of course, in 1969, after eight tournaments. These names represent, in my opinion, the best team we could have had at the time. That said, we were always a little bit thin on the ground when it came to the final four places.

Eric Brown tops my list, followed by Brian Huggett, Dai Rees, Howard Clark, Peter Oosterhuis, Neil Coles, Bernard Gallacher, Brian Barnes, Tony Jacklin and Christy O'Connor. Ten players made up the team back then. Of course there were others, including myself, who could well have made the cut, but the aforementioned all had great determination and always tried their very best.

Of the modern players, I've always thought this European team would take some beating: Colin Montgomerie, Ian Poulter, Nick Faldo, Sergio Garcia, Seve Ballesteros, Berhnard Langer, Jose Maria Olazabal, Justin Rose, Rory McIlroy, Martin Kaymer, Manuel Pinero and Lee Westwood.

Many superb players haven't made this selection. It's very difficult, but men like Paul McGinley, Miguel Angel Jiminez, Luke Donald, Padraig Harrington, Paul Lawrie, Maurice Bembridge, Sam Torrance, Thomas Levet and Graeme McDowell must forgive me.

As for the Americans, the 1981 Ryder Cup team was thought by many to be the best they ever assembled. They certainly had a lot of champions on their side. Over the years, however, I've been particularly impressed by some names that have now faded into history. Here's a selection for you: Larry Nelson, Lee Trevino, Tom Watson, Hale Irwin, Ray Floyd, Gene Littler, Dow Finsterwald, Billy Casper, Doug Sanders, Arnold Palmer, Jack Nicklaus, Cory Pavin, Sam Snead, Ben Hogan and Tony Lema. As for our modern era, those names are: Tiger Woods, Phil Mickelson, Jordan Speith, Dustin Johnson and an ever growing number gaining special notice even as I write.

FROM a backwater, almost niche, sporting event that the Americans routinely won, the Ryder Cup has grown into a global phenomenon. Ken Schofield, the European Tour boss, played a huge role in this transformation. His most significant legacy from his three decades in charge of the Tour is that he banged his head against the big door marked 'US Tour and the Majors' until finally he found a way through for European players. It is an achievement that is not celebrated enough.

It was Ken's stubborn, persistent negotiation which eventually meant more Europeans gained entry into the significant American weeks. Before his determined efforts, it was not unusual to witness, for example, a United States Open with no more than two or three Europeans participating. Gradually this changed, and Europe's finest became as well known in America as they were over here. This was a crucial factor in the growth of the Ryder Cup's popularity in the States and beyond.

George O'Grady took over the European Tour in 2004. He credits the great Ryder Cup victory of 1985 with enabling the Tour to expand the number of tournaments and argue for the ever greater inclusion of European players in significant American events. But if 1985 was when Europe's strategy first bore fruit, the seeds had surely been planted well before then.

'The younger generation grew up expecting to be able to win a Ryder Cup,' he says. 'That natural confidence, on top of real commitment by individual players, has led us where we are now with a Ryder Cup that always promises to be a close and enthralling match. A crucial factor was Tony Jacklin's decision that the players should receive no money for playing. Prior to this, players received £1,000 or £1,500. All sorts of things he changed. For example, when it was played here, the Americans got first choice of hotel rooms, and that stopped.'

I well remember the Ryder Cup in 1979, flying to Washington before heading on to The Greenbrier. The players and press were seated in the rear four rows of a standard British Airways plane. No turning left for any of us. Across the aisle from me sat Schofield, and behind him were players, wives and girlfriends, including Tony and Vivienne Jacklin. I happened to watch as, midway through the flight, Tony rose from his seat to head for the toilet. Unfortunately, a stewardess decided that this was the moment to wheel her cumbersome drinks trolley into his path. A short, rather sharp exchange followed, in which she refused to budge. A disgruntled Jacklin returned to his seat. Matters weren't helped when the same stewardess then accidentally – surely – spilled red wine over Tony's beige trousers. He was no longer disgruntled; he was livid. This may sound like a trivial incident, but for me, this was the moment the modern Ryder Cup was born. And its mission statement in Jacklin's head was straightforward: Never Again. Never again would Europe's team fly cattle class; never again would they wear cheap clothing; never again would these self-made men and their partners be treated as anything less than elite gladiators in a global sport. When he later agreed to become skipper, it was on these conditions that he accepted the job. The Europeans flew to Florida on Concorde in 1983; they draped cashmere around their shoulders and much else besides. They still lost – narrowly – but they did so in some style. And soon after, they started winning.

It is true that playing in the Ryder Cup brings indirect financial gain, while captaincy offers passage on a gravy train that continues for years afterwards, but the fact that no wages are paid for this hectic week resonates well with fans. The American players, however, receive a large amount of money either for their own charitable foundations or for a charity of their choice. It wasn't always this way, and I have no idea what this amount is now. However, I do know what it was and, indeed, how it came about.

During the US Open of 1999 at Pinehurst, in tranquil North Carolina, I blagged my way to a private interview with Tiger Woods. For half-an-hour we chatted about his game, his fame, what that year's Open Championship venue (Carnoustie) was like. He was friendly, relaxed and seemed to be enjoying himself, so I finally threw in the question I really wanted to ask. 'The Ryder Cup has become a really big deal these days,' I said. 'Do you think the players should be paid for turning up?'

Tiger leant on his club and thought for a few seconds. 'No,' he said. 'I don't think we should be paid personally, but I think it would be appropriate if we were to be given money for our charities and foundations.' When pressed, he said a figure in the region of $250,000 was what he had in mind.

I reported Tiger's comments in the Observer. *Then, that same autumn, at the Valderrama Club in Spain, the PGA of America proudly announced that members of the USA Ryder Cup team would, from now on, be given money for their various charities. How much? How about $250,000 each.*

GOING
CLUBBING
THE OLD WAY

PETER loved 'club life'; or rather, he loved what club life used to be. In his final years, he clung to what remained and regularly visited his club, Hindhead, in Surrey. In those days he no longer went to play, since, aside from the odd swish here and there, golf always asked too much of the body. No, instead Peter liked to sit in the corner, perhaps with an egg and chips, and talk to friends or indeed anyone who wanted to chat. Peter being Peter, everyone wanted to chat, and he never dined alone.

Peter loved club intrigue: the whingeing about the condition of this or that green, the bragging about so-and-so's longest drive, the gossip about who has fallen out with who. He was not the oldest member of Hindhead, although he must have been close, but he played his role to perfection by talking, observing, dispensing wisdom and wit, and generally enlivening proceedings on each and every one of his visits.

For Peter, the joy of golf was not only in playing but also in the social encounters that went along with it. After all, talking is what he did best (although he was very good at listening, too). An additional source of delight were the characters – men and women, members and staff – who inhabited these places. Critics of our sport often use the image of the club as a large implement with which to hit the game on its head (the other sort of club, if you will). In some cases they are right to do so, but as we stumble through this 21st century, the reassuring fact is that the majority of clubhouses are open, welcoming places. A small minority still clings to outdated mores, seeing membership of their establishment as confirmation that one is the 'right sort,' but as time passes, so will they. Club life, as remembered by Peter, may have been diluted and foreshortened, but for many golfers, the club remains at the heart of our great game. Peter, I know, wouldn't have it any other way.

THERE are not many people around today who will fully understand what I mean when I talk about 'club life'. In Europe, alongside myself, perhaps the only ones who would truly understand are the likes of Sandy Lyle, Tony Jacklin, Bernard Gallacher and Ian Poulter – plus a few others whose fathers or other close relatives had been involved in the game of golf.

Allow me to conduct quick recap of an earlier history lesson. Remember how, in 1972, the European golfing world changed forever? Our sport's professional ranks were split, and we ended up with two distinct bodies: the Professional

Golfers' Association and the newly-formed European Tour. Until then, golf professionals who played to the highest standard had to be attached to a golf club, and that meant running the shop, giving lessons, playing with members and visitors and conducting all the other duties which came with being a club professional. It was only when and if the situation arose that they would go off for a few days to test their skills in various tournaments and championships, and then it was straight back to the day job as soon as the final ball was holed. Needless to say, it was a different world back then.

I'm sure many of today's young players will also find it hard to believe that most of the courses used for tournament play were lacking proper practice facilities. As for the putting greens, they bore little, if any, resemblance to the greens out on the course. Everyone took their own practice balls back then, since there was no point in trying to hone your long irons by hitting a poor-quality club ball with a gaping slash on its face.

Around a dozen players used to practise all at once, hitting down a reasonably wide fairway with their faithful caddies positioned at various lengths to recover everything from a chip to a drive. Balls rained down like hailstones on these unfortunates, and many an argument began if – God forbid – a rival caddie picked up one of your few half-decent balls. Tempers could spike, and the disputes sometimes bordered on fisticuffs. I remember how the great Seve Ballesteros would turn maniacal if he thought an outsider had picked up one of his precious practice balls.

Just for a moment, compare those conditions with today's glorious facilities. Nowadays, it's standard to be provided with thousands of brand-new balls of various design. The ground conditions are almost always perfect, and the caddies can relax as they watch their man, or woman, hitting balls nonchalantly down the fairway for someone else to pick up. What bliss. How some of my old caddies – Joe Mamby, Liverpool Sid or Little Jim – would look on in awe if they were able to see even a glimpse of today's golfing scene.

But we're talking here about club life. Stocking the shop, giving lessons, taking in the green fees, repairing equipment and paying all the bills – these were the duties which governed the day-to-day life of an old-fashioned club professional. Rather like a good pub landlord, the pro could never get away with being off-colour. There was no time for headaches or gippy tummies, and part of the job involved meeting and greeting everyone in a cheery fashion and appearing as if one was happy to help – no matter one's true feelings.

There was, and still is to this day, a retaining fee for the professional. In days of yore, this money typically went towards paying the wages of an assistant – usually a sound investment, given how much work needed doing. In most cases, particularly during the summer, the shop was expected to be open no later than eight in the morning and to stay open until dark.

When I was stationed at Catterick, I used to take the bus to Leeds to stay with my friends the Kitchingmans, who were members at the Moortown Golf Club. My closest chums among that set worked at the Sand Moor Golf Club, which is next door to Moortown. I remember helping to clean off Saturday's clubs, ready for play on the Sunday. It was quite common to get through thirty or forty sets in one night. If we were lucky, we would be done by 10 p.m., when we would slip off to the Chained Bull just in time for last orders and a pint of mild and bitter or Tetley's Best. That's the way it was then. It took quite a few years before club professionals were even allowed to enter the clubhouse without an invitation, although you may, in the darker recesses of the golfing world, find one or two holdouts who still live in those far-off times.

Imagine having to do all the daily chores connected with the shop – on top of looking after the members' needs, giving lessons and playing a round when required – and then, at perhaps a day's notice, heading off in hope of winning the Open Championship! Just take Henry Cotton, who, even with all his great honours, was never anything other than a club professional. It wasn't so obvious back then that running a shop and competing in tournaments were distinctly different skills – and that this distinction necessitated a divide between those who ran the club and those who played for a living.

As these great changes were rippling through European golf, great changes were also occurring at the club level. One such change saw many clubs do away with the old rule that the professional wasn't allowed in the clubhouse uninvited. It seemed a big step forward at the time, but the repeal of this convention was not always a great success. This often proved true during the winter months, which always seem more like years 'oop north'. These northern winters typically saw a foot of snow, which would linger for three to six weeks a year. The pro, therefore, would often find himself on parade with not a lot to do, besides a spot of thumb twiddling and maybe a few repair jobs. But then some kindly member would pop his head through the door and ask, 'Fancy a coffee, or something stronger?'

Into the clubhouse they'd go; perhaps another couple of members would arrive, and suddenly you've got a snooker four-ball going. The coffees change to Whisky Macs and our poor old pro is now on a slippery, downhill path. But sooner or later somebody complains about something quite trivial, and the pro is likely to be the one condemned – often by the very people who had introduced him to morning snooker and Whisky Macs! Thereby he finds himself on thin ice. So you could produce an argument that in a way, those pros who were kept out of the clubhouse had the better of it. Whatever the cause, noble crusades don't always work out the way they're meant to.

And what of club secretaries then and now? In my youth, they were practically all ex-servicemen or financiers. Strangely enough, I never came across a warrant officer or a teller; at the very least, they were all captains or bank managers. Funny, that! But so many of them had a style, a presence, an aura, which invariably fitted the club they were at. Many wielded considerable power and influence, too. They would not be bullied; they were very confident of their being.

At Ferndown, where I grew up and basically learnt about golf, the secretary was one J C Beard. He was a wonderful character with two daughters who played splendid golf for Dorset. I'm sure if they had lived in a more fashionable county they might well have played for England.

Beard became very well known in the world of agronomy; he was a master grass-grower and a ruthless eliminator of weeds and weak blades. Verdone weed killer was his brainchild, and for many years it was accepted that J C Beard's tincture was the real McCoy if you wanted to improve your greens.

At the Parkstone Golf Club we had a wonderful secretary known as Daddy Bond. He was married to a delightfully eccentric Swedish lady who always called him 'Daddy' – so Daddy it had to be. A retired bank manager who lived in total chaos, he had an office half the size of a chicken shed, with room only for a very small desk, a single kitchen chair and a filing cabinet. There was paper, paper everywhere, and only he knew where anything could be found. He had a knack, in the midst of this whirlwind of paperwork, for laying his hands on exactly the right document in the wink of an eye.

I well remember a big golfing weekend held at Parkstone in conjunction with the Branksome Tower Hotel. A good sum of money was taken over the two days, and a posse of unlikely lads – scallywags, thieves, call them what you will – broke into Daddy's tiny office in search of the takings. The office looked onto the putting green, and these miscreants knocked a hole in the wall and dragged out Daddy's small but heavy safe. They carted the safe past the green and down the hill, where they had a car waiting. After driving to the far end of the course, they cracked the nut. What riches were inside? Nothing. Not one scrap of paper; it was just plain empty. Daddy, that delightful oddball, hadn't bothered with the safe; instead, he had put all the cash in two golf-ball boxes, held together with a large rubber band, and stuck them on a top shelf in plain sight. It was said that over £500 was stashed in those boxes. Not a fortune by today's standards, but in the late 1950s that was quite a bounty.

Ah, Ferndown and Parkstone – the two clubs where I learnt and honed my trade. The 1960s was the time to strut my stuff, and strut my stuff I did (quite successfully, I might add – and I had a great time doing it). At the end of the 1960s, with my best strutting behind me, I moved to Moor Allerton, a club halfway between Leeds and Harrogate. It was an entirely different world but one where my wife Jackie and I had some of our happiest moments.

Moor Allerton was a more hands-on club for the members, and there were half-a-dozen prominent personages who shaped the club very successfully. The course was the first Robert Trent Jones venture in Britain: twenty-seven holes on rather undulating ground with a number of mature trees. It had all the makings of a very successful modern club. Although we did hold tournaments there, we hosted not quite as many as I had hoped.

Now, I can't let the story of club life pass without mention of the secretaries at the Honourable Company of Edinburgh Golfers, better known as Muirfield, and of the Royal and Ancient at St Andrews. Captain Evans-Lombe was the first secretary I encountered at Muirfield. Circa 1945, he would arrive at the club on a bicycle big enough for a full-grown polar bear, with a pair of very powerful binoculars hanging round his neck and a forbidding look on his face. I think he must have been the original stern secretary, the man who set the pattern for those to follow. To most visitors, he was brusque, unhelpful and rather pompous. He was, in a way, a rather unsettling figure, but the members at the time didn't seem to mind as long as the course was in good condition and the caterers were on top of their game. Captain Evans-Lombe was followed by Captain Paddy Hanmer, a very eccentric ex-naval officer. He could be amazingly rude, and yet to some, including me, he was a delight.

It is difficult to write sensibly about the good Captain. Some might say he was bordering on insane, the way he made a habit of deterring visitors. 'Come back later when it's not so busy,' was one of his catchphrases – most often deployed when there were only three or four people out on the course.

A story is told of the year Tom Watson won the Open Championship on that splendid links. The tournament was over, and he and Jack Nicklaus, along with their wives and one or two others, were staying on at the Grey Walls Hotel, situated some twenty-five yards from the back of the 10th tee. One night after dinner (and, I suspect, one or two light refreshments), it was said that Watson and Nicklaus found a set of hickory-shafted clubs under the stairs. Picking up a handful of golf balls from God knows where, they set off to play the 10th and back down the 18th. Nicklaus, Watson, the ladies in their finery and high heeled shoes, and all of it taking place at ten o'clock at night with just enough daylight to see... how I wish I'd witnessed it.

The gallant Captain, meanwhile, was having dinner at a restaurant in Gullane when a messenger arrived, announcing that some players were out on the course. Worse, they were making quite a bit of noise and seemingly enjoying themselves. Knife and fork were quickly set down as the Captain made straight for the door, heading up the road and onto the course. The story goes that he approached Nicklaus and Watson in a rage. 'What the hell do you think you're doing?' he shouted. 'Who are you?'

To which Tom Watson replied: 'Paddy you know who we are. I've just won the Open Championship.'

'Never mind that,' said the Captain. 'Be in my office tomorrow morning at nine o'clock.'

I wouldn't know whether to laugh or cry. I'm told there was much gesticulating, but at the end of the day the three of them ended up either in the clubhouse or back at Grey Walls, where a couple of large ones settled everything down.

That Hanmer survived all those years was quite extraordinary. Despite (or perhaps because of) his cantankerousness, he became part of the fabric of the club. And rather like that pub in Fleet Street where the landlord was so rude, you felt that people went for a game at Muirfield in the hope of being insulted by the great man.

John Stirling, a dear friend and for many years the professional at Meon Valley in Hampshire, tells a great story about a visit to Muirfield in 1966. He had just qualified for that year's Open and came to Muirfield hoping to play a quiet practice round before the Championship got underway. He arrived at the club with a brand-new holdall and a new Burberry Mackintosh, his pride and joy, neatly folded over the bag. He left these treasured possessions outside the secretary's office, tapping lightly on Hanmer's door. No reply. He knocked again. No reply. A third time he knocked, a little louder this time. 'Come!' boomed the voice on the other side.

Hanmer was in no hurry to tear himself from the papers on his desk, but he eventually looked up and asked what Stirling wanted, speaking in that rude yet engaging manner that had always been his trademark.

'Well sir,' said Stirling. 'I've qualified for The Open and wondered if it would be possible to have a practice round.'

Hanmer looked at his watch and said quietly but firmly, 'It's half past eleven, a bad time. Come back at two and we'll fit you in somewhere.'

'Thank you, thank you,' said Stirling. He then backed deferentially out of the office, only to find the Captain's ageing black Labrador with his leg cocked, peeing all over that wonderful new Burberry raincoat and holdall.

'Did you go in and complain?' I asked, when Stirling told me that story.

'No,' he said. 'I was too afraid. I thought he might give me a bollocking for leaving my bag there.' Who can blame him? Nobody willingly opposed Hanmer; that's just how it was.

On to the Royal and Ancient Golf Club of St Andrews, assuredly the pinnacle of golf with its array of rule makers and adjudicators – they who shall be obeyed. They've had a wonderful collection of secretaries over the years, going through the obligatory colonels before the game grew and the need came for more modern management skills.

The great amateur Sir Michael Bonallack OBE might have been the last secretary to come – and I say this in fear and trepidation – from the ranks of golfers. He had been a glorious amateur golfer, and there was much to recommend him, but he was not a qualified accountant. Although the family had a very successful coach building business, Bonallack himself was not renowned as an all-guns-blazing businessman. Still, he carried off that position magnificently, much of the time aided by good, quiet common sense.

After Bonallack, Peter Dawson picked up the reins. He is a fine golfer and successful businessman. Dawson brought new style to the office, which was growing at an alarming rate. Money was flowing in and out, and agents and rights issues were becoming more and more important. Dawson retired in 2015 after sixteen very successful years in office. His successor is Martin Slumbers, a very good and knowledgeable golfer who is now taking the club ever forward. Not an easy task in these tricky times.

Of course, there have been many other wonderful secretaries over the years – individuals who have fostered both atmosphere and style at their various clubs. Being a club secretary today is like running a business, and the remit of a secretary includes handling wages, staff problems, greenkeeping, maintenance costs, members' complaints and a thousand other things. How different today's entrepreneurial and professional secretaries are from the captains and bank managers of fifty years ago.

There are many others besides secretaries who are involved in 'club life,' including stewards and stewardesses, greenkeepers and caddie masters. A few are engrained in my memory. Number one in my mental roll call would be Furly Davis, a man who turned up out of nowhere one day at Ferndown to have a talk with my father. This Mr Davis was very down at heel, but he was obviously an educated man. He had no money, and he was desperate for some sort of job at the club. Father, in his capacity as the professional, offered Furly the vacant position of caddie master.

In those days (I'm speaking now of 1938 or 1939), the caddie shed was as a big as a modern bungalow. The front third stored the members' clubs, while the rear was made up of benches and a stove for the use of the caddies. Somehow or other, Furly converted a couple of the shelves into a place to sleep and started spending his nights in the shed. He rigged up a couple of curtains to give him some privacy, and things just progressed from there.

Furly was certainly a character. He spoke at least three languages and routinely finished the *Times* crossword puzzle in under forty-five minutes. This was much to the chagrin of some of the members, who felt it was beneath their dignity to have to go to the caddie master, of all people, to ask the solution to 9 Down. As the weeks, months and years passed by, Furly grew in stature until he was very much an integral part of the club. Members often gifted him cigars, which he loved – and not only at Christmas. Then things really took off for dear old Furly.

One day, a gentleman by the name of Bill Tong arrived at the club with a rather strange-looking contraption. It was a frame of sorts, held up by a pair of wheels which had obviously been taken from a child's bicycle.

'What have we here?' asked my father, having been presented with this novel invention.

'This,' said Mr Tong, 'is the future. I call it a golf trolley. You rest your bag on these two cradles, top and bottom, do up these straps here to hold the bag in place, and off you go.'

My father looked long and hard, and then he started pushing the thing up and down, wheeling it around his shop.

'I can see a club like this having a few of my trolleys to rent,' continued Mr Tong. 'You'd save the members all the aggravation of carrying a bag, forever lifting it up and down – particularly in wet weather. With a trolley, your members would also be able to carry waterproofs and anything else they might need.' (All this was long before the days when everyone went on to the golf course with four litres of water, two bananas and a couple of chocolate bars as a matter of course.)

'How much are you selling them for?' my father asked.

'Four pounds each,' said Mr Tong.

'And what do you think they would rent for, per round?'

Mr Tong came up with the answer of 1/6d – seven-and-a-half pence in today's money.

Father gave it some thought, but in the end he told Mr Tong it wasn't for him. At that moment, Furly Davis entered the Pro Shop and saw what was going on. He asked Father if he could talk to Mr Tong about his invention. Father assented, and that was the genesis of the golf trolley not only at Ferndown but in the whole Bournemouth area. Within a few weeks, Furly had purchased four trolleys, a fleet which quickly doubled in size and soon doubled again. He charged 2/6d – twelve-and-a-half-pence – and did rather nicely out of the whole affair, thank you very much. All this was to the small annoyance of my father, who was far too kind to relieve the caddie master of his newfound wealth but probably felt he should have taken advantage of this gap in the market when he had the chance.

Sunningdale Golf Club, meanwhile, had a magnificent caddie master by the name of Jimmy Sheridan, and he ran that side of the golfing operation quite magnificently. He was a formidable-looking figure, tall and straight-backed with a deep and mellifluous Scottish accent. His son was for many years at Denham Golf Club, where he gained a wonderful reputation not only for being a first-class club pro, encouraging both young and old alike, but for becoming, for want of a better word, the club's general factotum. After his retirement, he still continued to go the club to help with the starting and any other golfing activities that needed a hand. I'm not sure if it's still there, but for many years a portrait of Sheridan Snr hung in the members' bar at Sunningdale – an honour bestowed on very few.

In the '60s and '70s, a club like Sunningdale would have had twenty or thirty caddies descending most weekends in search of work. This was at a time when the members' children would also come to the golf club to earn their pocket money by carrying bags, pulling trolleys and the like. Those days have gone now, although I have no idea why. Perhaps pocket money now comes too easily?

Gleneagles was another grand meeting place for caddies eagerly looking for work, and work they got. Lucrative work, too, but only for a short season. It was not uncommon for some of the caddies there to cash in by completing two rounds a day, carrying two sets of clubs – the golfing equivalent of going halfway up Mount Everest.

There was a time when almost every club in Great Britain had some form of caddie facility, but these are sadly now all gone. Likewise the artisan section. I can remember when many clubs, both grand and not so grand, had an artisan membership. These too are dying out for various reasons, nearly always connected with money. Personally, I hope some of the (dare I say?) grander clubs will continue with this tradition.

And what of the stewards? Long ago, the ideal set up was thought to be a husband and wife, with perhaps a daughter or two, working as a unit at a club. If they were good and the club was sensible, they stayed there for years. It's difficult now for new members to appreciate that there was a time not so long ago when golf clubs had to be open to sell alcohol during pub hours. In many cases, that meant being open from 11:00 a.m. to 3:00 p.m. and opening again from 6:00 p.m. to 10:30 p.m. This worked as long as you had staff in situ, and with the coming of television, even if the club wasn't busy, the steward could always sit quietly in the bar area watching TV with his bowl of soup, bemoaning the fact that nobody had turned up that particular evening. Nowadays, with so many clubs franchising their catering arrangements, a great number of clubs close early, particularly in the winter. I find it rather a sad sight when I pass by a golf club at seven o'clock on a winter's night and see not a light burning. And how I long for the days of a really good steward and stewardess, for a fine team could really add a certain charm.

I must tell you of two stewards who I will never forget. The first is Micky Flynn, who, for so many years as a steward-cum-general-manager, was effectively the driving force behind Sunningdale Golf Club. The place virtually opened and shut according to his whims. I remember how he'd take the members' bets whenever races were on, and everything around him ran like clockwork. Whether this particular clock told the right time didn't really matter, since almost everyone was happy.

And then there's Mr Holly of Royal St George's. Harry Carpenter, a dear friend and much respected fellow commentator, always said Mr Holly frightened the life

ABOVE: Peter Alliss with his first family, Gary and Carol
ABOVE RIGHT: Early golf trolleys much in evidence during practice for the Women's National Golf Tournament at The Berkshire in 1961
RIGHT: Ferndown Golf Club in 1938

ABOVE LEFT: Peter Alliss and Dai Rees are guests of London Scottish Golf Club for the club's centenary in 1965
ABOVE: Chatting in the car park at Moortown
LEFT: Douglas 'Daddy' Bond, secretary at Parkstone for many years
RIGHT: JC Beard long-serving secretary of Ferndown Golf Club

ABOVE: Jackie Alliss with baby Simon at his christening at Moor Allerton. Godfathers Bruce Forsyth, Henry Longhurst and Cliff Michelmore encourage a golfing future
ABOVE RIGHT: Peter Alliss with younger son Henry
RIGHT: In the garden with daughter Sara
LEFT: With Dave Thomas, former professional golfer and Peters' first partner in the designing of golf courses

ABOVE: Michael Bonallack (back second from left) with his successful Walker Cup team in 1971
ABOVE RIGHT: Clive Clark and Peter Alliss formed a long-term association as broadcasters and golf course designers
RIGHT: Paddy Hanmer on the look-out for inappropriate behaviour at Muirfield in 1984

out of him. It was said that Mr Holly had served in the Kenya Rifles or some such African regiment and had reached a pretty high rank. Incidentally, some claimed this rank placed him higher than many of the members. Either way, I remember Harry and I were in the club one day before an Open Championship when a member came in and shouted, 'Holly! Two club gin and tonics, quick as you can.'

Harry was mortified. 'I could no more call him "Holly" than jump off the Empire State Building,' he said, and he never did. Great respect was shown between the two but never any great warmth – just a hint of fear on Harry's side.

Then, of course, there are the greenkeepers, those custodians of the turf. My earliest encounters with these men came at Ferndown. How well I remember Jim Bracher, who used to let me ride on the mudguard of his tractor while cutting the fairways. I can still smell that wonderful cut grass, accented with a touch of diesel. Sheer magic – but not one for the health and safety experts.

Jim Dean was the boss, the head greenkeeper at Ferndown. He was a wonderfully solid and staid man of the soil. I remember how half a dozen of Jim's men would arrive on their bicycles every morning. I can picture them cycling down the side of the 18th fairway to the greenkeepers' sheds, hidden away by the 2nd green (where they remain to this day).

For some reason, Scotland has always produced wonderful greenkeepers. They still have a magic touch today, even though many are overpowered by modern rules and regulations on what they can and cannot use to get rid of the dreaded leather jackets, better known as daddy longlegs. I've not known many bad greenkeepers, although even the best have accidents – a leaking mower, perhaps, or a home-brewed fertiliser which burns the green to a cinder.

I salute all those men and women who work so hard to keep their clubs running and the members happy. Some years ago, there were over 2,000 golf clubs registered in the British Isles. There has been much to-ing and fro-ing with the passing of time; many clubs have disappeared, but others have returned or risen in their place. In all, I'd say the club scene is relatively healthy, numbers wise. But just imagine a club with an excellent secretary, a wonderful steward and stewardess, a superb greenkeeper and a professional who gives credit. Sheer bliss! And even more so if the clubhouse is well designed. In my experience, there aren't many architects who have a feel for the perfect clubhouse; I've known only a dozen or so in my life, and their names will remain a secret.

What, then, of the professionals? In all my time in golf, I have met very few professionals who have been poor at their job, although obviously there have been one or two over the years. Some were a tad grumpy, some ran a poorly stocked shop, some weren't particularly good teachers and a couple didn't possess a golf game worth bragging about – but these were few and far between, and even pros have their cons. It would be impossible to mention every one at every club I've visited over my seventy-odd years of golfing travels, but some stand out like beacons of professionalism and skill.

There's Ian Marchbank, for so many years at the Gleneagles Hotel; Bob Jamieson, resident at Turnberry long before President Trump and his collaborators spun their golden web; and Andrew Reynolds, down there in Deal on the Kentish coast – dare I say a huge fish in a relatively small pond. All three, in their different ways, were geniuses at running a Pro Shop. They tended to all the visitors' and members' needs and mentored many young men and women to get on as professional golfers at the highest level. Although Bob and Ian had reputations for being rather canny as far as money was concerned, they brought together a wonderful array of staff, all of them talented and destined for successes of their own. The same could be said of Andrew Reynolds, although he wasn't quite so careful with his money. In fact, he's been known to buy a round of drinks!

I'm both privileged and fortunate to be an Honorary Member of over thirty clubs, the nearest of which is Hindhead, which is less than a mile from my front door in Surrey. Although I can no longer play, I visit the club to meet with friends three or four times a month when possible and to talk about all things golf. Those conversations regarding the running of the club have always been fascinating, even if, on occasion, common sense can seem to wash away in a torrent of petty jealousies.

The advance of women in business, sport, golf, politics and all the rest of it has been terrific and welcome. But this wonderful social change has led, on occasion, to moments of unrest – particularly as far as the diehards are concerned. You know the type, I'm sure: those men who still live in the age of plus fours and trilby hats and who refuse to surrender their image of the little woman slaving away in the kitchen out back. On the whole, however, good sense usually prevails.

Speaking of good sense, how about this? I call it the Alliss System, designed for the aged golfer. I've been trying to popularise it but have not yet succeeded as well as I might. You can think of it as legalised cheating, and so what? If you're just playing in your own little circle for a pound or two, or to decide who buys the first round of drinks, why not go to the most forward tee and then, if you're on the fairway after your drive, tee it up? If you're in a greenside bunker, it doesn't matter if your clubhead touches the sand. And be generous, if sensible, on the green when giving a putt. A couple of my friends – who are over eighty, I hasten to add – were about to give up the game before they tried the Alliss System. And, I daresay, it has revolutionised their golfing lives. It's rather like playing tennis and letting the ball bounce a couple of times before trying to flick it back over the net. If you're looking for exercise, try it my way. The correct score doesn't even enter the equation; just have fun and keep moving – that's the game.

After all, the joy of playing golf is about more than just the golf itself. Take the halfway hut – at many clubs, an institution, and in some cases, a very memorable one. Sunningdale, Wentworth and the new Centurion Club near St Albans are at the very top of the tree, as far as culinary delights are concerned. These are joined by other wondrous places far too numerous to mention. Sometimes a halfway hut is so good there's not even any need to bother with the second nine.

Although golf on the continent is not yet for the masses, every continental clubhouse I have visited over the years has been quite magical. I've never quite worked out the source of the magic, and perhaps it's a combination of the architecture, the foreign flowers in huge vases, the bowls of oranges, a wisp of garlic emanating from the kitchen and, in years gone by, the distinctive waft of Gauloises.

Incidentally, I've long thought there should be a new list of the 100 best golf clubs in the UK but concerning only those built since 1960. We have many wonderful young clubs, but only occasionally do any get into the top 100. That strikes me as quite unfair on those who provided the finances and the others who prepared the plans and oversaw the construction. Here, of course, I should declare an interest, as I've helped to design over fifty courses in my time. The Belfry is the best known, but there have been many others – some of which I believe are really good, although I doubt they are ever properly looked at when it comes to compiling the top-100 lists. Instead, we get the same courses listed year in, year out, with perhaps six or eight new names if we're lucky. I don't think that's right. Just as I don't think it's right that the Old Course is forever towards the top. For me, St Andrews is like the Taj Mahal or the pyramids – it's historic, iconic, a one-off. If anyone tried to build a course like it now, they would be laughed out of town and would have to find another job. Like everyone else, I think it's wonderful, but it should not be judged against other courses today. It's simply in a different category and there it should stay: splendid, ancient and alone.

You need knowledge, imagination and a talented and passionate workforce to create a golf course. But most of all, you need money. Generally speaking, the grander your plans, and the more brilliant you wish a course to be, then the more money you need to hit the target. I don't think we – Dave Thomas, my first partner, and Clive Clark, my second – ever had much more than a million pounds (and we often had much less) to construct our courses. In the mid-seventies, when Turnberry was chosen to host its first Open – the one that gave us the glorious 'Duel in the Sun' between Tom Watson and Jack Nicklaus – Dave and I were asked by the R&A to make some changes. We did a lot of rebunkering, among other things, but we also suggested a new par 3 across to the lighthouse, thus eliminating the par 4 ninth, a semi-blind tee shot to a hogsback fairway and a poor, though difficult, hole. At the time, the R&A said no to our plans; they didn't have enough money for that. Now this new hole has been constructed by the Trump people, who definitely have the money. But imagination and expertise without the funding is unfortunately not enough. For the Turnberry job, Dave and I put our fee (about £20,000) into the budget to pay for extra work which the R&A might never even have known about. The money mattered less than doing a good job. After all, a great golf club is worth every penny, and if I haven't convinced you of that already during this chapter then I doubt anyone ever will.

Aha, I hear you say, but what about the members? Well, I've only been attached to three clubs in my golfing life, but through my various travels I have met an incredible number of extremely interesting people from all walks of life, and so many of them have enriched my time on this Earth. It's hard – indeed, dear friends, it's virtually impossible – to mention more than a few of the people who have crossed my path over the years and brought such pleasure into my life.

Perhaps I was too young during my years at Ferndown to take in even a sniff of fame and fortune. Joe Davis, the snooker player; Gordon Richards, winner of the Derby in 1953; Len Hutton, the great Yorkshire cricketer; and Fred Perry all visited Ferndown during my formative years. How was I to know they were famous? These men all knew my father, and they were all very relaxed and had a pleasant time, with the exception of Joe Davis, who my father said was the worst putter he'd ever seen.

Parkstone Golf Club, my second home, was quite different. We were often visited during the summer season by showbusiness personalities: Jimmy Tarbuck; Max Bygraves, who lived for many years in a beautiful house perched right on the West Cliff overlooking the bay; and Lady Docker, who many of you will remember from the halcyon (or should that be vulgar?) days of ostentation. Harry Redknapp and Graeme Souness are recent residents of the Sandbanks area, along with a number of other sporting and business personalities.

I moved to my third home, Moor Allerton, in 1970. I was coming to the end of a divorce which had taken its toll on many, but Moor Allerton was a very welcoming place. It was here where Jackie and I spent ten very happy years, although even these were shot through with times of great sadness. Much of this centres on our daughter, Victoria, who was born with very severe complications and died aged ten.

We were supported through this period by a host of friends, including Ronnie Sumrie of Sumrie Clothes fame. Then there were Marshall and Irwin Bellow, whose company imported Pfaff sewing machines from Germany. Irwin always took an interest in local politics, and he went on to join to Mrs Thatcher's government. Marshall, on the other hand, stayed on to run the business, and how magnificently he did that. Marshall and his wife Carol were a great help and comfort to Jackie and I when we arrived in Leeds, and to this day they are as staunch as ever. True friends.

The Moor Allerton Golf Club of today is very different from those days in 1970. Back then it was predominantly a Jewish club – in fact, it was one of the oldest such clubs in the world. Now it's a grand mixture of all sorts, and how well it's working. A lot has been achieved there without sacrificing the club's great heart. Just ask the legendary Geoffrey Boycott, who is a member and true supporter.

At all the other clubs I've only been a visitor, so I've not been able to observe too much for too long. Still, there have been occasions when something rather magical has happened. I remember, for example, a day at Royal St George's, where we were playing the British Masters. I walked into the bar and out called a cheery voice: 'Ah Peter, come and join me for a pint.' It was Wing Commander Stanford Tuck, who was sitting at a small table by the window and nursing half a pint. Stanford Tuck – one of the heroes of the Battle of Britain! And there I was sipping a pint and chatting away with someone who, in different times, might have been one of Lord Nelson's closest companions. All taken for granted, I'm afraid, as indeed was the case when I met another RAF fighter ace: Group Captain Douglas Bader, who was an amazing man. Apart from being a war hero, and regardless of walking on what he called his 'tin legs,' he could drive racing cars, had been down to 7 at golf and had braved the Cresta Run. Deep inside, however, he possessed one of the strangest mixtures of traits ever to be shaken together. Heroically admirable, of course, but not the easiest chap to get on with.

So many great characters from so many golf clubs. Take Ireland, where every visit is an experience, North or South. Royal Dublin, Portmarnock, Lahinch, Ballybunion, County Down, Royal Portrush, Portstewart… and on, and on. It makes me stop and think: what a wonderful life I'm having. At moments like this, when putting a book together, the urge is to continue. This, however, is impossible, so I'll just say 'thank you' to all those people who have contributed to my world and, indeed, to the world of golf. You have all been quite magnificent.

PETER'S reminiscences about club life remind me of a conversation I once had with the secretary of one of England's most prestigious clubs. 'I love my job,' he told me, 'but it would be absolutely perfect if only we didn't have any members.' For today's secretaries, it is no longer enough to merely have a commanding air and a brisk, upright walk. Now the secretary needs to possess genuine business acumen on top of imagination, people-skills and an awareness of proper book-keeping. It helps if they also quite like the game, although they shouldn't expect to play much golf.

As Peter has pointed out, Muirfield's Paddy Hanmer was a legendary figure. My own dealings with Hanmer started so well that I was rather disappointed. Booted, suited and ready for a fight, I arrived one morning, and as I entered the club, Hanmer exited.

'Morning,' I said, hoping to be told my tie was inappropriately knotted. Maybe he would have barked something like that, but before he could answer, the middle button on my blazer popped off the jacket and dropped at Hanmer's feet.

'Right,' he said. 'Give me your blazer; I'll get that sorted. Go on in and get a drink.'

I did just that, the only bloke in shirtsleeves. Ten minutes later, one of those mumsy Scottish ladies appeared at my side with my mended blazer. When Hanmer walked into the bar ten minutes later, I tried to buy him a drink. He refused rather brusquely and my hopes of a belated confrontation soared, only to immediately dip when he ordered a couple of whiskies and handed one to me. As ever, one should take as one finds.

By the way, Peter's observations of the jealousy with which professionals guarded their practice balls is spot on, and this was still the case as recently as the early eighties. Peter Coleman – for many years Bernhard Langer's right-hand man – once told me of the time he stepped in to caddie for Seve Ballesteros in Switzerland. At the end of his week's labours, Seve handed Peter a fistful of dollars – short of what had been agreed. When Peter complained to the Spaniard, Seve said it was because he'd counted his practice balls and half-a-dozen were missing. 'Your job was to pick up all the balls on the range when we practice, and you didn't,' he said. Even by Seve's standards, this was on the mean side of ridiculous. But to his credit, Peter just smiled, perhaps a little tightly, and walked away, never to return to that particular bag.

Clive Clark, Peter's business partner, fellow broadcaster and friend, writes:
Many of Peter's close friends would attest to the fact that he was generous and kind. Moreover, though, Peter was unique.

I remember how, as a successful teenage amateur, I qualified for a few of the PGA Tour events in Britain. I was a mad-keen golfer, and I was eager to improve my game by watching the professionals at work. Having finished a round, I would return to the course specifically to observe Peter. I thought he had a very strong long game and a great golf swing. It didn't matter whether it was a 3-iron or a 3-wood, the ball always fizzed towards its target. After I turned professional in 1965, I was fortunate to play a number of rounds with him.

Years later, I was even more fortunate to find myself working alongside him. We spent eighteen years as BBC colleagues, commentating on the sport we both love. What a great privilege and honour to work with the greatest golf commentator the world has ever seen. You talk about knowledge of the game, hilarious and spontaneous wit, a melodious voice and great timing... that's Peter, a man who was always destined to be an extraordinary broadcaster. He really was the finest there has ever been.

I remember once we were invited Down Under to work on the Australian Open. At our first production meeting with the Aussie team, we discovered that Australia had gone metric. The executive producer insisted we could not talk about yards, feet or inches in our commentary. This was totally foreign to Peter, who had always believed golf went hand-in-hand with British imperial measurements. But Peter had his ways of handling things. In this instance, the first player to appear on the screen was the great Peter Thomson. Cue Alliss: 'Here's Peter Thomson, who is a splendid two under par on the 5th hole and has a putt of 12 paces.' None of that metric stuff for Peter!

His elegance, wit and style lit up hundreds of thousands of TV screens around the world. A further example of his sharp humour came during the third round of the 2002 Open Championship at Muirfield, when Tiger Woods was nearly blown off the course by gale-force winds and was clearly not going to break 80. Peter summed it up succinctly with the comment: 'Tiger's on his way to not breaking 80 today, which – for the gallery – is like going to see Pavarotti when he has laryngitis.'

In the late 1980s, Peter and I formed a golf course design partnership which rapidly became the top design company in Europe. We thoroughly enjoyed this new way of working and designed twenty-two courses, many of which won top awards. I have so many stories from our time together, but I will share just one more.

I remember asking Peter what was the finest shot he had ever seen. He said, 'I was playing in the Ryder Cup at Eldorado in Indian Wells in 1959, and I was one down playing the 18th hole in a singles match against Jay Hebert. The last hole is a par 5 with a frightening amount of water guarding the green. I blistered a 3-wood to within six yards of the pin.'

I said to Peter, 'So is that the finest golf shot you've ever seen?'

'No,' he said. 'Jay was a few yards ahead of me and proceeded to hit a fat 2-iron into the lake. Now that was the finest golf shot I've ever seen!'

Bruce Critchley, fellow broadcaster and friend, on the joy of working with Peter: Before 1980, Peter and I knew one another – but not well. Henry Longhurst had died a year or two earlier, and in 1979 a chance encounter led to an audition with the BBC. The second half of my working life would be as a broadcaster and journalist, after twenty years in construction. It's not hard to work out which was the more enjoyable, and Peter was the one responsible for that.

I spent a dozen years working with Peter, followed by another thirty listening to him broadcast with others. With a microphone, Peter was first and foremost an entertainer – a sporting Terry Wogan with golf as his canvas. Each day's play was an opportunity to amuse, educate and wander mentally and verbally wherever his thoughts took him. He was blessed with the ability (given to very few) to crystallize those thoughts into witty opinions, with his pauses and timings always spot on. A great observer, both with ear and eye, he would have learnt much from working with Henry Longhurst; he already had – or had acquired – the same linguistic skills, the same antennae for the absurd, the ability to recognise balloons of pomposity and the verbal pins with which to prick them.

In many ways, Peter was the easiest to co-commentate with; he did his thing but left plenty of room to fill in the nuts and bolts of what was happening on the golf course. Such was the force of his personality, his clear popularity with his audience, that many who worked with him fell into the trap of believing the Peter Alliss way was the only way to do it, but of course, nobody else had his gifts of observation.

I have one regret from our time together at the BBC. Back then, there was no culture of conversation in commentary. Apart from The Open, there were few long spells of golf on TV; golf had to fit in between other sports, so often it was just an hour here and an hour there. Our one attempt at 'chatting' was jumped on by the producer. 'Stick to your allotted hole and shut up when we tell you.' That was the way it had always been done, and innovation was frowned upon.

Peter was the master of the impromptu, unplanned story. One year at Ferndown, on a sunny afternoon lunching between broadcasts, I opined that in today's sporting world there was no room for the Great Corinthian, no chance for someone gifted in several fields to excel and reach the top in more than one. Peter demurred and went on to lay before us a scenario where some mythical character – a mix of Bobby Jones, Ted Dexter, Steve Redgrave and Tim Henman – would go through his year doing great deeds; rowing in the Boat Race one early April morning; riding in the Grand National in the afternoon; opening the batting for England at Lords (scoring a ton before lunch); getting well into the second week of Wimbledon (only losing in the fifth set to Pete Sampras); finishing well in The Open despite having to fly his private aircraft from Leuchars on the Friday afternoon to pick his mother up from Fairoaks... and so on. Those listening wished they had a tape recorder handy to catch this drop of sporting gold! The most amazing thing was that he had made up the whole story on the spot, an entire monologue concocted on the hoof.

Peter had a great ability to entertain those who had little or no interest in golf – those who maybe tuned in for The Open and nothing else. He deployed many turns of phrase that would induce a smile and keep the itinerant viewer listening in. One example came when Jose Maria Olazabal was new on the scene, back when there was quite a debate about how to pronounce his surname. It even merited an article in a Sunday newspaper. That day, Peter summed it up by saying you could only pronounce Olazabal properly if you had 'the soft lower jaw of a good gun dog.'

Nearly forty years ago now, Peter and I started the Grand Match – an annual contest between past Walker Cup and Ryder Cup players. I eventually became too busy to be part of the organization, but Peter and Jackie kept it going until very recently. Back in 1985, and before a Senior Tour got going in Europe, old pros had little or no competitive contest in which to take part. Peter noticed that we amateurs still had club and county matches and, if you went to the right schools, The Halford Hewitt and wanted something similar. The Grand Match became a rare opportunity for old Ryder Cuppers to get booted and spurred once more.

Of many memorable moments, two stand out for me. A year or two in, I invited America's Clark Mackenzie to play. Long a scratch golfer, Clark had never played in the Walker Cup, but his grandfather Henry Fownes (creator of Oakmont Golf Club) had helped start the Walker Cup with Herbert Walker, grandfather and great-grandfather of the Presidents Bush, respectively. As such, Clark definitely merited an invitation and even brought a collection of matching shirts so each side would have its own uniform. To this day, the pros wear blue, the amateurs yellow. My fondest memory from The Grand Match is partnering Clark to (a rare) victory over Peter and Dave Marr.

Another special pleasure came when I got Laddie Lucas to play, aged seventy-one, in an early Grand Match. On the evening before, he spoke at our dinner and recalled a time when, as an RAF fighter pilot, he had been 'shot up' over France. 'I thought I could make it,' he said, 'though not back to base. Of course, I could have "stepped out," but I knew that coastline of England well, particularly its golf courses – my father had been secretary of Princes – and I thought I could land there. I came in over St George's, aimed for the 18th fairway at Princes, over-shot that – over-shot the 12th too – and finally ended up out of bounds at the 7th.' It's a story I have never forgotten.

Neither will I forget Peter. During out chats, we sometimes aired our thoughts and concerns about getting old and eventually passing on. We both agreed that death held no great fears, but a decrepit old age and becoming a burden to those who have to look after you was a nightmare. Of Peter's passing – having worked on the Masters just three weeks before and, after lunch one day, just not being able to make it upstairs to rest – I like to believe his way of going was one of the best 'rounds' of his life.

SWINGING AND DANCING WITH THE STARS

WHEREVER you find celebrities, you'll find golf courses. And with the advent of 'celebrity golf' as a format, it is clear that golf is now the sport of choice among the glitterati.

Golf enjoys an obvious appeal for film stars, who are barred from playing contact sports or engaging in even vaguely dangerous pastimes by risk-averse studios. The old game has emerged over the past decades as a relatively harmless alternative and a mostly safe way to pass the time without running the risk of a serious (and expensive) injury. The same holds true for today's elite athletes, many of whom choose to relax on the golf course. Here, a footballer can exercise and have fun with only a minimal chance that they'll hurt themselves and ruin their season. A further appeal lies in the seclusion; many celebrities have turned to golf over the years as a means of putting distance between themselves and the media circus which tends to follow them.

Bing Crosby said once that he loved the peace of the course and the challenge of the game. Golf, he believed, can serve as an antidote to life in the public eye. Of course, he died in 1977 on a golf course: La Moraleja outside Madrid. He collapsed from a heart attack at the end of a match, having played well to win against three friends. He was reportedly laughing and joking as he walked away from the eighteenth hole. If you have to go, and you do, then what a way to say goodbye.

Peter's own jousts with fame, as he confirms in this chapter, became more frequent as he added other TV and media adventures to his 'day job' as a golf commentator. The irony now is that while he remained at heart a professional golfer, many people think of him only as a bloke who appeared on the television. To them, Peter Alliss is another such celebrity, not a former (and much lauded) player. I'm happy to confirm that this thought always made him smile, if a little wryly.

THROUGHOUT my childhood, I often found myself in the vicinity of golf stars, but it wasn't until 1954 that I first came into contact with famous people from outside that milieu. I spent two months on the west coast of America that year, playing in a series of eight events. A group of us, including John Jacobs, ended up travelling in convoy with Peter Thomson, his then-wife Lois and their young daughter. Thomson drove his luxurious Jaguar Mark VII, while the rest of us made do with a hire car.

We arrived in Los Angeles on New Year's Eve, and off we set for Palm Springs, a journey of just under three hours. I was delighted when we arrived at the

Thunderbird Golf Club. It was a true oasis back then, with just a handful of houses dotted around. We were allocated a delightful property some 400 yards from the entrance to the golf club. Only later did we find out that the house belonged to Frank Sinatra, although we never set eyes on him.

That first night we enjoyed vibrant celebrations at the club, with Harry James and his band providing the music. Harry, arguably the world's greatest trumpet player, was the husband of Betty Grable, the forces pin-up girl during the war. In attendance was Lucille Ball and her husband Desi Arnaz. Phil Harris, the actor, singer and comedian, was part of the cabaret, and over there was Esther Williams and her husband Ben Gage, who was a huge man but fleet of foot. John and I found ourselves sitting at their table.

We were a few drinks in when Vic Gezzi, an Italian-American golf pro of some note, came over and asked Esther to dance. She assented, and there followed a show-stopping moment as the pair whirled around the floor. Eventually, they returned to the table, and Gezzi remarked to Ben, 'We've either got to sit around or find a motel room!' Cue much laughter and another round of drinks. Then Esther took my hand, looked into my eyes and said, 'Peter, let's dance.' Now, even in my prime I was no Dan Dailey. A hug and shuffle was more my style, but Esther was very energetic. She was a magnificent specimen of womanhood, standing at about 5ft 8in, and everywhere you touched she was as solid as a rock, a real athlete.

Many of you may not remember Esther Williams, but she was a great actress and a sporting marvel. She starred in many films where her incredible swimming talent could be put to some use. She was quite brilliant, and I never was able to work out how she managed to smile underwater without a single bubble escaping her mouth. To this day I still don't know her secret, although clearly she could hold her breath for several minutes at a time. Aquatic skills aside, dancing with this beautiful film star was my introduction to the world of celebrity – and quite an introduction it was, too! I still tingle at the memory.

I recall that day when I was approached by Ray Lakeland and offered my first job with the BBC. I knew from the first moment that I was onto something good, but I had no idea that I would embark on such a wild journey into the world of celebrity – or that I would end up spending so much time with so many stars.

From 1961 until 1973, I was working for the BBC as a commentator, covering various golf tournaments. One year we did seventeen events, including trips to the United States for their Open and Amateur Championships, plus other special events like the Curtis Cup and Walker Cup matches. It was all so new and exciting then, and although the United States seemed to win most of those early events, they were played in an atmosphere of friendly competition which we in Britain at that time rather took for granted. It was not the winning that counted, it was the taking part... you know the sort of delicious nonsense. Then my life changed.

Towards the end of 1973 I received a letter from Brian Cowgill, Controller of BBC One, asking if I would attend a meeting at Television Centre in Shepherd's Bush. I spent the train journey wondering what this meeting might be about. Even after I arrived – indeed, even as I was in the lift to the sixth floor – I had no idea what Mr Cowgill wanted to talk to me about. Then the doors pinged open and there he was in all his glory: the great Mr Cowgill, the guv'nor. He was someone, they said, who could make strong men weep.

But there were to be no tears today; in fact, I found Brian rather charming. Having exchanged the usual pleasantries, he said an idea had come up: a golf series filmed at the Gleneagles and Turnberry courses, where two well-known professionals would partner a pair of celebrities in a spot of friendly competition. The matches would be filmed over six days, with the results of those efforts to be shown around Christmas. Naturally, I was interested.

And so I was passed on to Bill Cotton, then the BBC's Head of Light Entertainment. He told me this new format might even end up running for a few years, if everything worked out. Well, in the end, *Pro-Celebrity Golf* ran for fourteen years, over which period we produced 140 programmes to be enjoyed by an audience of golfers and non-golfers alike. We featured a formidable glut of professionals: Arnold Palmer, Gary Player, Johnny Miller, Greg Norman, Tony Jacklin, Peter Oosterhuis, Fuzzy Zoeller, Tom Weiskopf, Lee Trevino, Ben Crenshaw and the ever-charismatic Seve Ballesteros. What a fantastic line-up. It makes me wonder what it would cost to gather such a high-quality roster in this day and age. Too much, is the probable answer.

As for the amateurs, this firmament of stars was no less impressive. There was the actor Jack Lemmon – an absolutely delightful chap, but he was going through a period of drinking more than heavily, and there were times when I wondered how he kept going. The same could be said for his fellow film star George C Scott, who walked a very thin line between being pleasant when sober and nasty when drunk. He had a couple of serious disputes with Burt Lancaster when the pair came to discuss the size of their respective bedrooms. George thought he ought to have the prize suite, but it turned out he was a few inches short. He expressed his displeasure by ripping some telephones from their sockets and throwing them out of the window.

Alice Cooper, meanwhile, arrived in typical rockstar style but never made it to the first tee, having been done in beforehand by some fine Scottish wine. He was, nonetheless, a devotee of the game, and he went on to give up alcohol and play off a mean handicap.

Howard Keel, of acting and singing fame, was a sheer delight. He was a member of the Bel Air Country Club in Los Angeles, and in later life he became chairman of the greens committee there. I like to think he livened up meetings by bursting occasionally into song: "The corn is as high…" But possibly not.

Meanwhile, Robert Stack, star of *The Untouchables*, liked to tell us all that his was one of the first families to settle California in the early 1700s.

Dick Martin, of *Rowan & Martin's Laugh In*, came along, as did Dennis Morgan, Phil Harris, Fred MacMurray, Telly Savalas, David Soul and *Mission Impossible*'s Greg Morris. They were joined, of course, by the usual home suspects: Bruce Forsyth, Jimmy Tarbuck, Terry Wogan, Christopher Lee, Max Bygraves, Henry Cooper, Ronnie Corbett, Charlie Drake, Alan Price, Hurricane Higgins, Geoff Lewis, James Hunt, Jackie Stewart, Peter Cook, Kenny Lynch and, inevitably, James Bond himself – Sean Connery. The roll call goes on and on, and in all truth, every one of them had a touch of magic about them, even though one or two got rather grumpy if their golf was off colour. But this is certainly not a charge that could be levelled against one of our star guests, Bing Crosby.

Over the years, one or two unattractive articles have been penned about Crosby, on subjects ranging from his family commitments to his carefulness with his many millions of dollars. But to us, during the filming of that BBC series, he was a sheer delight – kind, gentle and amusing. Rather like Sam Snead; when he took his hat off, the man disappeared – but we all loved him. That was 1976, and it seems like only the day before yesterday.

One of my abiding behind-the-scenes memories of *Pro-Celebrity Golf* is from that same year. We were in the brand-new sauna at the Gleneagles Hotel, and Bing had come from America to lead a star-studded field of global celebrities against Britain's homegrown stars. It was quite a year, but I digress... back to the sauna. The previous day, around eight of us had arranged to play, and a few pounds had been put into the kitty. However, we woke up to atrocious weather, so we called off our little game. As we'd all over-imbibed the night before, we thought perhaps an hour in the sauna would kill or cure – and it would definitely pass some time while the weather was dreary.

Picture the scene: a double tier of wooden benches and, in the corner, a stack of red-hot stones, beside which was a bucketload of scented water and a wooden ladle. Sitting alongside the stones and holding the ladle was Sean Connery, 007. Also present: Bruce Forsyth; Jimmy Tarbuck; Kenny Lynch; the jockey Geoff Lewis; yours truly; and a couple of Bruce's friends. The hotel provided white towels too small to fit around your waist, so they were duly laid down and sat upon. Connery was controlling the heat, and he insisted on regularly adding more water to the coals. Every time he did, huge clouds of steam rose into the air, and the temperature spiked. For a moment, you could hardly breathe. There followed, each time, a round of moaning and groaning, and we took it in turns to ask the eternal question, 'Why do we do it?' Somebody broke wind, and it proved to be the heavy variety, hanging in the air like a storm cloud. That was when Tarbuck noticed through the glass door the approaching form of Eric Sykes.

Tarbuck shook himself out of his stupor and said, 'When Eric comes in, don't say a word.' Sykes was, by then, profoundly deaf, so this had the potential to be a highly effective – if slightly mean – jest.

Sykes entered cheerfully through the fog of steam. 'Hello, hello everyone,' he said. 'What a day. Pity it's been rained off.' He took off his towel, exposing his lilywhite frame, and sat down on the bottom bench. He was probably the thinnest man I'd ever seen in my life, and I'm quite sure you could have played his ribs like a xylophone. He tried to engage everyone in conversation, but none of his remarks was met with a response.

'What chance do you think the rain will stop?'

'Maybe we can play a few holes this evening.'

'One thing I do know, you need a good local caddie round here. Reading the greens is so difficult.'

Nobody answered, nobody looked up, nobody smiled. Connery reached for the ladle, and up came the obligatory plume of steam. The moaning and groaning went on, and another fart was unleashed into the humid air. Silence reigned for a couple of minutes, during which you could literally hear the sweat dripping on the floor. Oh, the heat! The oppression! Connery insisted on yet more punishment, and the mercury rose amid another cloud of steam. Then the evil silence was broken as poor old Eric uttered the immortal words: 'Does anyone know what time this train gets into Calcutta?'

We couldn't ignore him for a second longer; all of us fell about laughing. Some of us laughed so hard we had to step out for some fresh air. Since then, that question has become a catchphrase to be deployed during awkward silences and at opportune moments, and the hilarity of that occasion has stayed with me ever since.

But back to the course. Throughout the *Pro-Celebrity* series, we encouraged our professionals to offer some advice to their partners. We felt some expert tuition would pad out the programme and thought it could be informative for our audience. This led to a classic moment on the 17th hole on the King's Course, where Greg Norman was partnering Alex Higgins. Higgins was having a poor day; he was keen but not very good and had pulled his tee shot left, up into the broom and heather. My producer said it would be a good idea if we asked Greg to go over and give him a tip or two, which he did willingly. Alex, however, was in no mood for help, and they almost came to blows. Everyone calmed down just enough to get the match finished, but you could see that Higgins was a very volatile character.

On another occasion we were in the ballroom: Sean Connery, Bruce Forsyth, Jimmy Tarbuck, Eric Sykes and a few hangers-on. We were just messing about – singing and dancing and having a good time. Until, that was, Tarbuck noticed movement in the wings. He pulled back the curtain with a flourish and revealed a small man wearing a warehouseman's coat. I admit strong drink had been taken, and Tarbuck, in a gentle way, pulled the fellow to the stage and asked him if he cared to join in with our sing-song.

'Oh, no, no, sir,' was the reply. But Tarbuck insisted, and I confess now that the scene had a touch of goading about it. This gentle soul was on the verge of being shown up, and he probably felt he couldn't really decline.

'What will you sing?' asked Tarbuck. He refused to take nothing for an answer.

"Rose of Tralee," the wee man eventually said. Silence descended, and a few cynical smiles cropped up in expectation. Bruce Forsyth helpfully struck the first notes, and suddenly a crystal clear tenor's voice rang out around the ballroom. Mouths dropped open, and soon our man had finished a sparkling rendition to tumultuous applause and sheepish grins. In later years, that episode reminded me of the impact of Susan Boyle on an audience.

Gleneagles was the backdrop to many other good times and hilarious moments, both on and off-camera. I grew to know the place well. Over the years, the hotel has had a few different managers. They were all unique, but one who springs to mind is John Bannatyne. Now there was a man of rare patience and diplomacy. He discharged his duties magnificently throughout his many years of service, and the most amazing thing was that he somehow always managed to remain calm, even when all hell was breaking loose or when one of our prima donnas was demanding the impossible.

Yes, there were a few disappointments among the celebrities. George C Scott, Burt Lancaster, Alice Cooper and one or two others never quite lived up to their billing. The pros, however, were uniformly magnificent, and they all played their part brilliantly. Peter Oosterhuis is one I remember with great affection. His ongoing struggle with dementia is a source of much sadness.

Of the celebrities, the most competitive were definitely the Formula One drivers. I'm thinking of Jackie Stewart, Nigel Mansell and James Hunt. The speed demons were followed closely by tennis players and jockeys, who were generally good golfers. I like to think that the fusion of these lively characters, all of them very talented in their own ways, made for wonderful television. I know I had a fantastic time filming with the BBC, which was the home of *Pro-Celebrity Golf* from 1974 to 1988. After the BBC called time on the show, the format was swiftly picked up by ITV. Tony Jacklin fronted the new series, but it lasted only a few years in this guise.

One of our great moments – although it didn't seem too great at the time – centred on the Canadian actor Leslie Nielsen, then one of the most recognisable and funniest faces in the world of cinema. Picture the scene: it was 7:42 a.m., and I was finishing breakfast when one of our stage managers, a man named Harry Coventry, rushed over. He was obviously disturbed by something or another.

'It's Leslie Nielsen,' Harry said. 'He can't play.'

'What's the matter with him?' I asked.

Harry took a deep breath. 'I mean he can't play.'

'Well what's happened, for goodness sake? Does he have a cold? Has he fallen down the stairs?'

'Nothing's the matter with him, but I'm telling you – he can't play! I've just been watching him on the practice ground and I think that's the first time he's ever held a golf club.'

'You must be mistaken,' I said. 'We'll be able to fudge it, anyway. We'll make it work.'

Off we all went that same morning to the short 8th hole on the Kings Course. It was Leslie Nielsen and Charlie Drake with Peter Oosterhuis and Fuzzy Zoeller. The professionals drove first and found the green. Next up was wee Charlie Drake, out with his 4-wood. He gave it a whack and found the front of the green; cue loud cheering from the 150-odd spectators, who were made to look and sound like thousands when the programme came out. Up stepped Leslie. Now for the moment of truth.

As Leslie positioned himself for his tee shot, the first warning sign manifested itself. It was his grip, which could only be described as unorthodox. Still, he gamely swung and gamely missed the ball by at least a foot. He swung again, and again, and maybe even again – all with the same result. Growing some five yards in front of the tee was some tall grass, and on his fourth or fifth try he eventually clipped the ball with just enough power to send it rolling off the tee and into that grass. I can remember, very clearly, the producer's voice in my ear.

'Let's move on. Peter, you'll have to tell the viewers Leslie had a couple more shots and took no further interest in the hole.'

The hole played out and we moved across to the 11th, a long par 3. The pros played beautifully onto the green, while Charlie Drake, again, unleashed his trusty 4-wood, knocking his ball up to the front of the green. Leslie, too, was given a 4-wood by his caddie. He looked almost dangerous, holding it more like an axe than a golf club. What followed was a suitably vicious swing. This time, he caught the ball, and although his shot rose barely eight feet off the ground, it sailed forward on a low and flat trajectory right into the front bunker. A sigh of relief could be heard from miles around, and it seemed we were off.

Only, we weren't.

Cut to Leslie, feet rooted in the sand, swinging at least six or seven times and missing every time. Then, as if by a miracle, he at last caught the ball. It went flying out of the bunker, over the heads of the spectators at the back of the green... and into the forest behind the 12th tee.

Again, a voice in my ear advised me to wrap it up and move on. I did as I was told and we soon advanced to the 12th. Three drives sailed away, and then, amid much anticipation, it was Leslie's turn. I can see it all now as if I'm looking back down that fairway: a man leaning forward with his hands clasped atop his umbrella, trying to get a better view amid a throng of spectators all craning to see the action, or the lack thereof. Leslie, meanwhile, swung wildly. He connected with the ball, which flew off at around ninety miles per hour, low and hard to the right. There was a loud crack and a yelp from the unfortunate gentleman who had been hit and whose thumb had grown to four times its normal size in a matter of seconds.

Pandemonium reigned. Once again, the producer's voice came through, informing me the match was off. 'Tell 'em what you like. You'll think of something,' he said. There we were a mile from the hotel: all those spectators plus two professionals, one 15-handicapper and a total novice. How to tactfully call off our match and get them all back to the clubhouse? That was the question.

Well, I thought up a wonderful excuse for calling it a day. The large transformer supplying all the power had broken down, and they'd had to send for a replacement from Glasgow. It would take a few hours to come, so there was no chance of finishing our match. Job done.

I walked back with Jimmy Tarbuck. We had one of those colourful conversations, lamenting the day's events. We made our point with every swear word known to man. Tarbuck even came out with a couple I had never heard before (I won't repeat them here, but rest assured, they were very descriptive). When we got back to the foyer, Jimmy and I were met with a wall of frosty stares – and for good reason.

Unbeknown to me, my microphone had never been switched off. This meant our entire conversation had been picked up and piped through the various television sets in the hotel, the public rooms, the Pro Shop and the café. Some charming blue-rinsed ladies had heard it all, but they didn't understand at least seventy-five per cent of the swearing, thank God, so all was not completely lost.

That evening I approached Leslie Nielsen, the man of the moment. I asked, with all the tact I could muster, how he had ended up here at the Gleneagles Hotel. He told me he had been having a very pleasant lunch at the Bel Air Country Club when he was approached by a gentleman who asked if he liked golf.

'I certainly do,' Leslie replied. 'Why do you ask?'

'We're making a golf programme for British television,' said the stranger, evidently a booker or producer or some other BBC bod. 'If you agree to take part, we can put you on a plane with your wife or companion, fly you first class to New York, send you by Concorde to London and transfer you to a BA flight to Glasgow, where a limousine will pick you up from the airport and sweep you to the hotel. There you can stay for a week, and all expenses – and I mean all expenses – will be paid.'

Naturally, Leslie was interested. 'That's for me!' he replied.

Having heard his side of the story, I said to Leslie, as gently as I could, 'But Leslie, you can't play!'

He smiled and said, 'Nobody asked me if I could play.' End of story. Although, in this case, there is a happy postscript. Some years later, Leslie released a video called *Bad Golf Made Easier*, which did very well. I wasn't surprised, given he was such an expert at bad golf.

I enjoyed so many memorable nights during the making of those programmes. There's not enough paper in the world to write them all down, but I do remember one or two special occasions. The first was when Jackie and I found ourselves with Peter Cook and his charming plus-one in the grand drawing room at the Gleneagles Hotel, where three or four ancient musicians were doing their best on the piano, drums, bass and an accordion almost as big as the man playing it.

Cook's companion that night was a stunning black girl, who he introduced as his niece. She had the most glorious figure and moved ever so sensuously, like a panther. She seemed to be wearing only three articles of clothing, two of which were shoes, and although the music was slightly antiquated, she insisted on standing at the edge of the floor gyrating very slowly while everyone in the room – hotel guests, waiters, musicians, the lot – watched open-mouthed. When she eventually returned to our table, Cook produced a small box made of tin. He opened it, and to me, it looked like he'd been collecting half-smoked cigarettes, no more than an inch-and-a-half long, from outside the hotel's front door. He offered them around, but only his delightful companion accepted. He produced his lighter, and the pair lit up. They inhaled deeply. Moments later, and with knowing smiles on their faces, they seemed to have arrived in a world of their own. She returned to the dance floor and produced another magnificent series of moves – the kind that sent many an observer scarpering off in search of a cold shower.

The next morning, Cook arrived on the first tee of the King's Course dressed, inexplicably, in full riding kit. One of the local caddies followed closely behind, carrying a goldfish bowl with a single fish swimming round and round in circles. Cook announced that he would referee that morning's match, which saw cricketer Ted Dexter and Formula One star James Hunt against professionals Crenshaw and Trevino. My producer suggested I interview our ever-eccentric referee to ask him how he saw the day progressing. Cook instead used his interview to solemnly announce to the watching world that the goldfish was Abe Ginsberg, his golfing coach and literary agent, who was on his first visit to Scotland.

So there we were on the first tee, with James Hunt's dog, surely the biggest Alsatian ever bred, sitting alongside the goldfish bowl where Abe was swimming his slow laps and taking in the view of the King's Course. It was a moment of pure, surreal hilarity, but that was Peter Cook for you. Before he destroyed his own reputation through the demon drink, and whilst things were relatively normal, he was a delight.

As with many of these programmes, the events of *Pro-Celebrity Golf* were largely unscripted. The same was true of the nights in the hotel ballroom, where

ABOVE: An early brush with celebrity in 1965, with Eric Sykes and Hattie Jacques in the TV programme *Sykes and a Golfer*
ABOVE RIGHT: Playing golf with Gary Sobers in South Africa

ABOVE: Filming at Walton Heath in 1972 with Jackie Stewart, Lee Trevino, Sean Connery and Max Faulkner
Pro-Celebrity Golf with (above left) Gareth Edwards and Terry Wogan: (left) Ray Reardon and Alex Higgins and (below) Dick Martin, of *Rowan and Martin's Laugh In*, Ed 'Stewpot' Stewart, Charlie Drake and Peter Oosterhuis
BELOW LEFT: With Ted Dexter at Sunningdale

RIGHT: With the crew filming *Golf in the Sun* for British Airways in Tobago and (above) relaxing afterwards with Christopher Lee

ABOVE: Terry Wogan, Jimmy Tarbuck and Johnny Mathis at Moor Park in 1981
LEFT: There was always much Waterford Crystal on offer for competitors at *Pro-Celebrity Golf* – Tony Jacklin and Sean Connery examine the prizes
BELOW LEFT: Peter Alliss receives an Honorary Doctorate from St Andrews University in 2005 supported by Bruce Forsyth
BELOW: A regular feature of Christmas was a specially created card from Ronnie Corbett

Bruce Forsyth would position himself at the piano and sing with Howard Keel and Kenny Lynch – with the occasional interruption by the actor Dennis Morgan, who insisted on performing excerpts from *Tales from the Vienna Woods*. All of this usually took place while Dennis was mightily, cheerfully drunk. He told me later that his prime reason for visiting the UK was to lecture on the evils that can befall you if you take to the bottle, although I never quite worked out his connection in that department. I also recall sitting next to Christopher Lee in the magnificent dining room and hearing him order just a bowl of peas and a spoon with which to eat them. That was lunch. No wonder he kept his 6ft 4 frame in such beautiful condition, or perhaps it was thanks to his spirited wife, Birgit. She was, dare I say, quite a handful – maybe even two!

Turnberry was the venue on quite a few occasions, but more often than not, we filmed at Gleneagles. I think this was mainly because the golf course was gentler and the hotel slightly easier to get to from Glasgow Airport. On one occasion, my daughter Sara, who was about seven at the time, came rushing over to my wife. She was brimming with excitement, for she had shared a lift with Howard Keel. 'Mummy, mummy!' she cried. 'I've just come down in the lift with Miss Ellie's husband!' – shades of *Dallas*.

All in all, *Pro-Celebrity Golf* enjoyed a wonderful fourteen years on prime-time television, and I enjoyed a wonderful fourteen years making the show and making memories. And there were more shows – and more memories – yet to come.

We were a few years into the successful run of *Pro-Celebrity* when Bob Abrahams, a famed BBC producer, came to me suggesting a new television programme: *Around with Alliss*. We completed thirty-six programmes, each introduced by a delightful piece of jolly, cascading piano music, and again, we were blessed with a wonderful range of interesting guests for me to chat with and play against. Among them was racehorse owner Vernon Sangster, who was just beginning his early battles for prominence with Sheik Mohammed. He told me he was bound to lose in the end because the Sheik's bank account was bigger than his, but he promised to give him a good run for his money. I found it interesting that he kept many horses in New Zealand, where he said the air was so fresh and the grass so lush.

Then there was the actor Tom Courtenay, now Sir Tom, of course; Dame Kiri Te Kanawa; and the comedian Harry Secombe, with whom I had the pleasure of playing a few holes on the New Course at Sunningdale. On only the second hole, Harry's trousers split while he was bending to pick up the ball. We managed to complete the programme, but by the end, he was considerably out of breath – and not just because he had been desperately holding his pants together. He told me that a doctor friend later watched his episode and, upon hearing his heavy, uneven breathing, suggested a check up, which came just in time. Harry lost at least six stone and, as sometimes happens, with that loss he also shed a little bit of his personality. That was according to his lovely wife, Moira.

We had also as a guest a man I greatly admired: Jimmy Hill, footballer, pundit and much else besides – and, not least, a man who did so much for his profession. For me, he had four great claims to fame, starting with the new wage structure he negotiated for the players while chair of the Professional Footballers' Association. This was the first time players began to earn decent money (although, mind you, many think they've now gone too far down that road). Jimmy also campaigned for, and secured, the points system still used in the beautiful game today: three for a win and one for a draw. He achieved the giddy title of Head of Sport for London Weekend Television, going on to become Deputy Controller of Programmes, and he also introduced an all-seater stadium at Coventry. These achievements came alongside all the things he did to spread the gospel of football worldwide. He was a remarkable man, certainly ahead of his time, and although he was admired and respected by those in the know, I still feel his contribution to sport is rather underrated. Not, however, in my house.

Time now for a confession. *Around with Alliss* was the only golf show where we 'cheated.' Why? Well, the programme had to last for twenty-eight minutes, and in that time we could only play three holes each. Our games either finished all square, or with me or my opponent winning by one hole. It was important that each episode was engineered in a way that there was something to play for on the final hole. The worry was that if one of us was already two up with one to play, some viewers might lose interest.

I remember another memorable guest in the form of Hugh Scanlon, the trade union leader who almost single-handedly, I was assured, brought down the Ted Heath government. Scanlon loathed Arthur Scargill and what he was doing to the coal miners. Scanlon wanted a good day's work for a good day's pay, but he stressed that it was essential the workers stuck to their end of the bargain and put in that good day. He and I sat long into the night in front of a roaring fire in a delightful hotel in Moretonhampstead, in Dartmoor. I came to the conclusion he was a Labour wet and I was a Tory wet. I was struck by how fair-minded he was, and he reminded me that business problems were usually created at the top of the tree and not at the roots. I've never forgotten that.

In all, I was joined for some very pleasant walking and talking by a huge variety of the day's celebrities from the worlds of showbiz, sport, and beyond. We had the likes of Liz Hoad, model and keen golfer, and Buzzer Hadingham, former chairman of Slazenger and then the head honcho at Wimbledon. These luminaries were joined by Kenny Dalglish and Bobby Charlton of football fame; Gareth Edwards from the world of rugby; Jackie Stewart and Nigel Mansell from Formula One; Jim Watt, one of Scotland's finest pugilists; John Conteh, former WBC light-heavyweight champion; tennis great Lew Hoad; Ted Dexter, again, with Colin Cowdrey and Ian Botham (what a cricketing threesome!); and, not forgetting our ladies, Helen Wogan and Pauline Tarbuck – and what tales they had to tell. It made for a magnificent cast, a regular all-sorts of characters, styles and personalities. And a special mention for Norman Wisdom, who brought tears to all our eyes with vivid descriptions of his struggles in early life.

Special, also, is my memory of Andrew Barlow, who, at twenty-nine, was then Britain's youngest recipient of a heart transplant. He came to Woburn in April 1980 to take part in the programme, and from the moment we met, I knew he was not long for this world. The fact is that Andrew had already made up his mind that he was not going to make old bones, so he decided to live life to the full. For him this meant smoking, drinking, dancing – the lot. Sadly, he was right in his diagnosis of his own life chances, and he died two years later. I found him such a nice, courageous young man and was greatly saddened that he should be taken at such a young age.

I look back today on the many years I spent making those shows, which ran for rather longer than anyone expected, and I feel immensely fortunate. I know some of those programmes are still spoken of today with a great deal of fondness, and they are certainly remembered by me with enormous warmth, appreciation and gratitude for the opportunities they afforded.

Naturally, all these television appearances led to other things. I appeared on *Desert Island Discs, Any Questions, Blankety Blank, A Question of Sport* and *This Is Your Life*, as well as sitting down with Michael Parkinson and Terry Wogan for two very enjoyable interviews. Fancy all that happening to a boy who left school at fourteen and went into golf with the sole ambition of making a half-decent living.

Many of the events of my life have been totally unexpected. I never went out seeking a life as a broadcaster, but somehow it happened. I'm no statistician, but I've always prided myself on my observational qualities; hopefully, somewhere along the line, I've served as a source of interest and pleasure for a few. What I know for certain is that it has all been enormous fun, and if one can make one's living while having some fun, then there indeed is one of the core secrets of a happy life.

LIKE most sportswriters, I've had my own run-ins with a share of the famous crew, and I have played with some as well. However, as Peter's rich and varied recollections make clear, golfing with celebrities is not without its potential pitfalls.

I remember a certain Stage Golfing Society day which saw me partnered by James Bolam and another actor whom I didn't recognise and whose name I didn't properly catch. I knew he was called Ian, but that was about it. Halfway round I was whingeing about the endless repeats of Dad's Army which seemed to clog the airwaves at the time and which I had never thought to be particularly good. That was when Bolam asked if I'd been properly introduced to our other player. It was Ian Lavender, Private Pike himself. Thankfully, I think Ian took my faux pas in good part, although we haven't played together since. A coincidence, I'm sure, but that's celebrity golf for you.

THE
PETER ALLISS
HALL OF FAME

MANY sports have undergone revolutions in the past few decades. The first, and most obvious, change is surely the soaring remuneration of elite athletes. The second, however, has come slightly more subtly, although its effects are no less profound. I'm talking about the quality of today's playing surfaces and the standard of modern sporting equipment.

The conditioning of present-day golf courses, even at less prestigious clubs, is exceptional. More often than not, lies on fairways are perfect, while greens offer a smooth consistency that would have been inconceivable to the professionals of fifty or sixty years ago. Older footage, even at Augusta, shows most players rap-putting, rather than pursuing the silky-smooth movement we see today. Plus, as Peter has already pointed out, practice facilities were often more of a challenge than the course itself. Factor in the huge technological improvement in equipment – clubs, too, but especially balls – and you would expect scoring averages for the better players to have improved significantly. Research shows this is exactly what has happened.

This point is proven by a study of all the seventy-two-hole rounds played from the 1960s through to the 2000s on the PGA Tour (a total of 2,558 tournaments). There is a slow, steady improvement in scores throughout the earlier three decades. Then comes a marked improvement in the 1990s and an even more drastic uptick in the 2000s. By 2010, the average four-round score was five shots better than it had been in the heyday of Nicklaus, Palmer and Players. This is some improvement, and while player fitness and equipment advances have played significant roles in this progress, I respectfully submit to the jury that the wonderful conditioning of most courses remains the biggest factor. Quite what the next big leap forward will be remains a mystery.

Meanwhile, consider this: at the time of writing, there have been twelve sub-60 rounds recorded on the PGA Tour. The first was by Al Geiberger in 1977, the second by Chip Beck in 1991 and the third by David Duval in 1999. The other nine have come in the last decade or so, including the Tour's only round of 58 – an achievement notched by Jim Furyk in 2016. This extraordinary spurt in low scoring dramatically underlines the progress of player, course and equipment. If this progress continues, then it could well be that by the middle of this century, the Grand Slam events will be won by scores in the region of 30 under par. That's not golf – that's a turkey shoot. Maybe, instead of making courses ever longer, superintendents should counter this trend by reintroducing some of the old, rather dishevelled bits of the fields Nicklaus and his pals used to joust on. Just a thought.

AS far as conditions are concerned, to draw comparisons between the professional golfer of yesteryear and the professional golfer of today is to compare an old Dunlop 65 ball with the latest Titleist. I've already discoursed on the state of practice facilities, but let me just remind you that in the 1950s and 1960s, those that did exist were often on the far side of not very good. Traipsing around dodgy facilities and making sure your balls found their way back to you was the order of the day. Professionals back then didn't have contracted caddies – much less managers – and the burden of making travel and logistical arrangements was solely theirs to bear. Years ago, the done thing was for pros to contact in advance the club where the next tournament was being played. The pro would enquire if the professional there could arrange for one of the members – an artisan or whoever – to be their caddie for the week. Local knowledge was considered to be of tremendous importance.

I'm sure this hardly ever happens today, in an age when players talk often about the 'team' that surrounds them. Indeed, it's much the same with tennis professionals. In golf, one gets used to hearing players refer sequentially to their personal swing coach, physio, trainer, financial adviser, chauffeur, hairdresser, dietician and mind coach. The list meanders on and on. Perhaps they also ought to employ someone to mop their fevered brow and be done with it.

Watching the US PGA Championship in 2019, I was interested to see how many people were standing at the back of the practice ground 'just looking on.' There was Pete Cowan, and over there was one of Butch Harmon's sons, while Denis Pugh and several others were all present and looking very professorial: arms crossed, chins stroked, saying nothing. What do you say, as a coach, if your player is hitting the ball beautifully? I suppose you might continually utter the usual banalities: 'That's good... keep it going... just like that... perfect.' But when a shot wanders off right or left, do you stay back or jump in with an immediate suggestion or solution? I often wonder, also, how these coaches/advisors/analysts are paid.

I promise I'm not here just to criticise the new generation, but I can't help sharing a few observations about the old game's newest developments. My two great dislikes, especially in the modern game, are slow play and spitting. Both are easily rectified, if the spirit is willing.

Perhaps the biggest problem is that players today hit too many practice balls. Let's take the most difficult club in the bag: the driver. Say you're hitting the ball well; you go to the practice ground, and your first three or four sail away on the perfect trajectory, getting on for 300 yards. Then, after ten or twelve drives, one ball veers off-course. You can – and I stress you really can – put too much thought into that one misdirected shot, and then you find that your brain is suddenly and needlessly cluttered with all sorts of possible remedies, some going back to the days of hickory. By all means, if you've identified a fault, think about what you wish to do to correct it, and then practice a little with that in mind. But

I mean it when I say 'a little.' You will learn more from hitting twenty practice balls in the right frame of mind than from thumping 100 down the range in a mindless frenzy.

All shots from 120 yards come under a different category. Chipping, pitching and bunker play require imagination and touch. Some have it, and some don't. Others manage to develop these twin traits halfway, and many never even get close. However, if you listen to many of today's television commentators, you could be led to believe that the players are firing sniper rifles – not hitting a golf ball side-on with half a dozen factors to be taken into account before the club is even out of the bag. Golf remains a game of extremely fine margins, and anything can interfere with any player at any time. In truth, this is what makes the game interesting and so difficult to forecast.

Anyway, I think practice rounds take too long today – and that's in spite of professionals playing less golf than they did in my day. Because the practice facilities were often so poor, we used to go straight to the course, and we used to play briskly. It was considered a cardinal sin to take longer than three hours for a two-ball over eighteen holes. But next time you're watching golf on TV, take note of just how long some players like to linger on the tee before they inevitably select their driver. Dammit, the hole's over 480 yards away, and nine times out of ten a driver is the only conceivable club for the job! What's the hold up? What's there to discuss? Yet despite the seemingly simple arithmetic of the situation, player and caddie will often deliberate for a minute or two before finally giving in and surrendering to the obvious. Then watch them carve the ball into deep rough anyway.

One other thought is that the game's rule-makers, the USGA and the R&A, have allowed the players to lean on too many artificial aids. In doing so, the authorities have undermined the natural skills which were once central to the game of golf. Things like judging distances from the fairway and reading the greens were all part of learning to be a better player. And not only have modern innovations reduced the need for natural skill, they have also played their own part in slowing down the game. But again, I get on my favourite hobby horse and say the pace of play will not change until the players themselves decide enough is enough. George Duncan, who won the Open Championship in 1920, wrote a book on putting called *Miss 'Em Quick*. I'm not suggesting we adopt that specific method, but somewhere between there and today's approach I believe we'll find the sweet spot.

I've said it already, but it bears repeating: sport has changed so much in recent decades that it has become impossible to compare different generations of players. Just for a moment, try to imagine those tournaments from the mid-1950s to the late 1960s, and ask yourself how you think today's stars would cope. Surely, it's an impossible ask. And this is true for almost all sports, not just golf.

Those of you who can, think back to those grainy pictures of Fred Perry winning the Wimbledon Tennis Championships in the mid-1930s: how he moved, the tactics he employed, the speed of service, the equipment and the condition of the court. Try to liken that to today. It's impossible – the fact is, it was what it was and it is what it is. It's why comparing then and now on any subject is, to a large extent, a waste of time, although this sort of thing is arguably the ideal conversation topic for a long winter evening at the club.

Golf is so wonderful, of course, because there are all these fundamental principles regarding technique, grip, takeaway, follow-through and so on, but there are so many different ways of achieving these. The different styles of so many successful – and some truly great – golfers have always fascinated me, which is why one finds oneself so drawn to weighing the titans of our sport against one another, even if such an endeavour is impossible or pointless. There are many players whom I have admired hugely over the years, and while 'great' is a much abused adjective these days, I'd like to flog it some more. So, how about this: rather than pitting the greats against one another, I'll simply share with you the names in my personal Peter Alliss Hall of Fame…

MEN

JACK NICKLAUS

YOU have to believe that every possible superlative has already been written about Jack Nicklaus's glittering career. His record is truly remarkable, including his sheer number of victories at the highest level and his tally of second and third finishes. And beside his record-breaking professional success, he raised a large family with his wife Barbara and managed to keep it all together. My grandmother used to say you've got to live closer than next door to know what a person is like, and she's right – so we know only a little about the home life, stresses and strains of the Nicklaus family. But they did it all with no great scandals or indulgences, and for that they should be praised to the rooftops.

Nicklaus deserves praise also for his special quality of level-headedness, shared with so many of the greats. He rarely, if ever, did stupid things out on the golf course. When caution was needed, that's the way he played. When the situation called for a more daring approach, he was up to the task. He has also built up a magnificent golf course design and construction business, and although there are a number of very talented golfing architects out there, I don't believe there is anybody better.

Take Muirfield Village, on the outskirts of Columbus, Ohio. Rather like Augusta, this development had some early teething problems – in this case with cash-flow, weather conditions and drumming up interest. Both developments, however, have since grown and prospered in their own ways. The Nicklaus family and their friends, suppliers and investors should certainly all be proud of the way things have worked out.

Jack has now passed eighty years of age, and by that point the body isn't what it used to be. In the early days, we used to read of the massive Jack Nicklaus smashing the ball higher and further than it had ever been smashed before. Now, on his occasional trips out for a few holes, he looks not much bigger than Gary Player. How can that be? Age might not wither a man but it makes him smaller.

It has been a delight and an honour to share a great number of years with Jack and Barbara. They are remarkable people. However much time has reduced Jack physically, his stature within this game has remained huge. Truly, he is a giant.

TOM WATSON

There are not many players who can maintain a pretty much identical golf swing over thirty years, but Tom Watson is one of them. He can still give it a full pivot, take the club back to the horizontal and swing through with the grace, charm and power of a young 'un! He was a bit of a slow starter, but when it all began to click for Tom, the trickle became a torrent.

His dominance of our Championship, particularly in Scotland, was a thing of joy and wonder. And he did it all with half a smile on his face, as if he was carrying around the course an amusing secret which he was not yet ready to share with us.

There was a time when he had too much hair and wore caps that were too small and which, in all honesty, looked rather silly. Somehow, he managed to keep them on even in a stiff breeze, and I often wondered how he did it. But joking aside, it has been my pleasure to watch Tom strike the ball so purely for so many years. He is also a truly superb putter, particularly from ten feet and in.

Tom had his personal problems, of course; he developed a taste for fine wine and scotch, and for a period, he over-indulged. Whether this resulted in some of his marital problems I know not, but there was a period when Tom did not have a happy home environment – although that was long ago. Over the last ten years he has been a stalwart of the Champions (previously Seniors) Tour, and although the Watson flame does not burn quite so brightly these days, he will always be remembered as one of the game's greats.

GARY PLAYER

It may sound rather foolish, but I've never felt Gary Player received the accolades he deserved. Perhaps it's because he was always so busy telling us how many miles he had travelled, how many tournaments he'd played in and won, how he wanted to be known as the finest player the world had ever seen and so on that others felt they did not need to add to the Player promotion party. He did, however, genuinely compete everywhere, from New Zealand and Australia through to Japan, Europe, South Africa and the USA.

Gary and his wife Vivienne managed to raise a large family even though a tremendous amount of travel was involved. However did they find the time and the solitude to have a bit of slap and tickle? Who knows, but they did and they prospered, rather like the Nicklauses. The common denominator? Two wonderful, forgiving wives.

ARNOLD PALMER

The same could be said of Arnold Palmer. In his late first wife Winnie he had found a perfect partner (although they weren't as prolific as the Nicklauses and the Players, managing only two children – both girls). I wonder if Arnold would have enjoyed having a son, but sons of very famous fathers invariably find life a struggle. Many doors are opened, but the expectation of success is so feverish that it can be a terrible burden. Oh, these famous sons may have the trappings – money, cars, property, all things material – but many feel they didn't earn it, that it was passed down. You could say good luck, get on with it, and that would be a fair assessment, but for someone of a delicate nature it can be hard.

Anyway, Arnold took professional golf to another level. His bludgeoning, gung-ho style of play went wonderfully with his 'ordinary guy' image and good looks – all of which dovetailed perfectly with the growth of golf on American television in the fifties and sixties. It was a natural fit, and a star was born.

TONY JACKLIN

Fifty years have passed since Tony Jacklin became Britain's golfing hero. I've known Tony since his teenage years and have always enjoyed his company, although he does complain a bit too much on occasion, blaming everyone but himself if things haven't gone perfectly.

So much has been written about his various movements, the buying of houses, the moving to Jersey for tax reasons, taking up residence in Florida, joining forces on occasion with Jack Nicklaus and his organisation… and all in all, he's been okay. He's certainly been blessed with two superb wives. His first love was Vivien, the pride of Belfast. She was a girl with both feet firmly on the ground, and she wore the mantle of his fame with ease, discretion and undying love. She was taken from us far too young, dying in Spain when Tony was attached to the Valderrama Golf Club. His second wife Astrid is a strikingly attractive woman who has kept him going steadily in the right direction. I've rather lost track of their children, but I hope and pray they're all okay and doing well.

GREG NORMAN

I remember the first time I ever set eyes on the 'Golden Bomber.' It was at the Downfield Golf Club on the outskirts of Dundee, where I was filming *Play Better Golf.* Norman was being chaperoned by Guy Wolstenholme, who had made his home in Australia and had been given the task of looking after this new wunderkind. It didn't take long for Norman to establish himself as a star, although in the end, many critics wrote that his potential had been unfulfilled. I agree. Given his talent, Norman could and should have won more. Two Open Championships is pretty good, but really he should have had at least half a dozen big ones.

On a couple of occasions he was robbed. On other occasions there was a bit of self-destruction going on, but still, Greg Norman should be remembered as someone who was a great figure in the game. His looks, his build, his clothes, his personality and that wonderful hat... it was all part of the package. After his failure at Augusta, people wrote of a lack of nerve and a weakness of character. I never saw it that way, though; I had seen him win under the most trying conditions, sailing through majestically.

As his playing days were coming to an end, he went into various business ventures. All his businesses appear to have been a great success, although sadly the same could not be said of his marriages. Perhaps that's one of the dangers of a life in golf – particularly in days gone by when wives stayed at home and brought up the children while their menfolk were out on the road trying to make a living.

SEVERIANO BALLESTEROS

European golf owes a great debt to Severiano Ballesteros, for no one captured the public imagination quite like he did. In doing so, he not only created a wonderful career for himself, but he also accelerated the growth of the European Tour like no one else before or since. In that sense, he was our Tiger Woods, drawing in not just golf fans but many others who had paid scant attention to the old game before he strode so memorably on to the scene – and, importantly, on to our television screens.

To suggest Seve was photogenic would be to underplay his looks, his charisma, his charm and his wonderful swagger. On top of these qualities, he communicated naturally with the paying customers and made them feel important – which, of course, they are.

His sense of fun and mischief and his ability, in a second language, to be both amusing and profound marked him out from the rest. He was different from the others; he knew it, they knew it and we certainly knew it.

I loved watching him play – loved commentating on his audacity and artistry – although I never quite understood why he could not consistently drive the ball straight off a tee. Not least because he certainly could do everything else! No one, surely, has ever been better at recovery shots. Seve often hit the ball into the sorts of places that men and women who play the game for fun at their clubs are only too familiar with: into bushes, behind trees, on to the wrong fairway. While the club player would groan and suspect they were in the middle of the worst round of their lives, Seve would spot an audacious escape route and conjure up some more magic to find a way to get back on track.

He was indeed a magician, with a surgeon's hands and a lion's heart – and possibly he was even braver than that. We commentators loved him for the same reasons as the public. He thrilled us too, and even on his bad days he always gave us something to talk about and to marvel at. Like all great players, he was a naturally great competitor, and he told me once that whatever score he signed for was always the very best he could have achieved that day. Like everyone, he could be disappointed with his score, but I do believe he was never disappointed with the effort he put into any day's play.

Who could forget his great, swashbuckling triumphs in Ryder Cups and his victories at the Masters and the Open Championship? I'm thinking especially of his victory at St Andrews in 1984, when he holed that final winning putt and then danced that jig of rapturous delight. If ever a man was almost literally beside himself with joy, that was the moment and the image that endures.

When Seve smiled, even sunny days got brighter, but when he was angry or upset it was perhaps advisable to stay clear. He died in 2011, a victim of brain cancer taken far too young. I spent time with him for a BBC programme as he recuperated from treatment at his home in Pedrena. He looked like he had been through a tough fight, but he was still full of charm and mischief.

At one point, he put on his reading glasses, taking these folding spectacles from his pocket. I had never seen such a pair and told him I liked the look of them. Straight away, he insisted I have them. I still do. They are among my most treasured possessions, and every time I put them on, I think of the one and only Seve.

NICK FALDO

Without doubt, Nick Faldo is one of Britain's finest ever golfers. You have to go back to the great triumvirate to discover players with similar records, and that was well over 100 years ago. What a legacy to have won three Open Championships and three Masters, all in slightly different ways. It would be too simple to say he was gifted two or three of them, for that is true of most people who have won a handful of Majors.

It's only now, at my great age, that I realise how apt is the old saying: 'You never remember who came second.' This generally holds true, although it is not 100 per cent accurate. I'm thinking now of Doug Sanders – his failure at St Andrews to secure his par at the last hole fifty years ago – and of Tom Watson at Turnberry in 2009. It was there, after he'd hit his second shot to the 72nd, that I announced to the watching world, 'He's won the Open Championship.' But no. His ball, which had looked so perfect in mid-air, pitched halfway up the green, took a firm bounce and ran into thickish grass. From there he took an untidy three shots, ending up tied with Stuart Cink. The play-off was a huge anti-climax, with all the sympathy flowing through to Watson. Cink, like a number of players before him, never truly received the praise afforded to a Championship winner.

As for Faldo, he only took up golf in his mid-teens, so it's remarkable how quickly he nailed down the art of hitting consistently. It's on record that he loved hitting golf balls and was never bored. You could say he was well suited to the life of a lonely competitor. He enjoyed a great deal of early success and then decided he could do even better, finding a little-known teacher in David Leadbetter, with whom he set off into unknown territory. The fact that their system worked is a credit to them both, and over a ten-year period, they were supreme.

In 1988 Faldo tied with Curtis Strange for the US Open, and the play-off was a great battle. After eighteen holes of cut and thrust, Strange claimed his second consecutive US Open. Faldo rarely featured again in their Championship, and I've often wondered why. I thought with his game and mental capacity, the USGA's set-up would be right up his street. He had more success in the US PGA Championship, finishing second, third and fourth in 1992, 1993 and 1994 respectively. And then his game appeared to desert him.

Curtis Strange believes the problem started when the huge hitters arrived on the scene. Out of nowhere, Faldo was routinely finding himself thirty or forty yards behind off the tee. In Strange's own words: 'Faldo ended up like a man with only one golf ball left in his bag.' Make of that what you will.

Faldo is a sort of Jekyll-and-Hyde character, seemingly enjoying a great relationship with his children and other young people while not boasting a great deal of success in the marital stakes (or, indeed, in any of his female relationships). The same could also be said of another one of our greats, Colin Montgomerie, who I liken to James Mason.

Look at it this way: James Mason was a fabulous actor, appearing in many films of the highest quality. In fact, I don't think he ever played a role poorly. In golfing terms, he never went over 74, and yet he never received an Oscar in recognition of his fine work. I'm sure Montgomerie feels that way about the lack of Major trophies on his mantelpiece; so near and yet so far. He had a couple of chances – good chances, too – but failed like Devon Loch in sight of the winning post. We've no need to feel sorry for him, though. Even though he's had a couple of expensive divorces, I'm sure there's still a few bob in the kitty.

But back to Faldo, who has forged a very good career with CBS Television in the United States. His television delivery is not for me, but he obviously has friends in the right places who value his contributions. I wish him well, although perhaps he should examine the way he comes over on screen. We could probably do with less umm-ing and aah-ing and waving of hands – oh, those huge hands, quite the biggest I've ever seen. But whatever one's opinion of Faldo, nobody in British golf has had a more successful career, so well done. Once again, no hard feelings!

PHIL MICKELSON

September 1991 was the first time I set eyes on Phil Mickelson. It was the occasion of the Walker Cup matches, which were played that year at Portmarnock on the outskirts of Dublin. Mickelson arrived in a blaze of glory as an immensely talented youngster – one who played the game left-handed, no less (which, for reasons I know not, always creates a bit of a stir). I suppose golf is just one of those sports where the left-handers always seem strangely elegant, with something slightly different about them. Mickelson was no exception.

He had a very good series that year, winning all but one of his matches. But he also left a sour taste. He had the effrontery to tell the folks back home that Ireland was okay, but he'd been there for a few days now and had not seen one attractive woman. Well, I can tell you now: hackles were raised. Mickelson, evidently, has a rather rude streak, and over his career he has issued several near-vitriolic outbursts, ranging from the qualities of various Ryder Cup captains to criticisms of the USGA.

These outbursts were more than slightly surprising at the time, because from day one Mickelson had presented himself as the face of innocence, one for whom butter wouldn't melt. Yet over the years, he has acquired a reputation for being a substantial gambler and dabbler on the stock market. In fact, a few years ago he was fined for insider trading, something I've never quite understood. What's the difference in being given a stock market tip and being privy to inside information? But that's another story.

On the course, however, Mickelson has always been an entertaining player to watch. He plays golf in the mode of Arnold Palmer, Seve Ballesteros and perhaps Bubba Watson. Devil may care, go for broke, let the cards fall where they may; and if it doesn't come off this week, there's always the next. The permanent picture I have of Mickelson is of his gentle, smiling face, with him tipping his hat a dozen times a hole, fulfilling every autograph hunter's needs and generally setting himself up as the one the public loves. Deep down, however, I'm sure there lies a very steely core, which springs to life occasionally when his game or life is under strain. A prolific winner but also a regular loser, he has always been good value to watch. He is also someone who displays more courtesy than most but who, on occasion, fires off the odd rocket. He remains, in middle age, a great addition to the world of professional golf.

TIGER WOODS

Are there any new words to say about Tiger Woods? The dramas in his personal life, his injuries and various recoveries, his mindset… all has already been so well documented that it's hard to know what more I can add.

His victory at Augusta in 2019, then. Let's go with that. In many ways, it was amazing. Of course, one must realise he was helped along the way by those players who made crucial mistakes over the last six holes, opening the door for Tiger and his final round 70 – a score which was good without being earth-shattering. On the other hand, bearing in mind his physical and mental situation, this fifteenth Major win was a stunning victory, won very much against the odds. What a talent.

ERNIE ELS

Probably one of the most talented all-round sportsmen in the world, some say Ernie Els could have been a first-class cricketer, rugby player or tennis star. He might even have excelled at swimming. Thankfully for us, he settled on golf. Although he has four Major victories to his name, he's rather in the Greg Norman Club and is one of those players who didn't quite fulfil his enormous potential.

After much early success in South Africa, Ernie moved his family to England. They lived, for a long time, on the Wentworth Estate, before moving to Florida. Apparently, the main impetus for this move was the fact that his son Ben was autistic; the USA supposedly offered a superior environment for Ben and the rest of the family. Ernie was, at first, greatly affected by his son's condition. As his wife, Liezl, told the *New York Times*: 'It was hard for him. I think he just wanted to know were we in any way responsible for what had happened to Ben? He was like, "I'm supposed to take care of this family – where did I mess up?"'

At one point, Ernie, like a number before him, did go through a difficult patch and turned to drink for solace. After a short but very unhappy period, he shook off that malaise. I now wonder if we will see him on the Champions Tour? I'm sure we will. His languid power should bring in more than a few dollars as he saunters into older age.

More significantly, the story of Ernie's family life has a very happy ending. Having raised millions of dollars on top of their own substantial backing, Ernie and Liezl founded the Els Center of Excellence, a superb school in Florida for autistic children. The Els Center is a beacon for so many, and today it is an even more significant legacy than Ernie's outstanding golf career.

Liezl's Times interview concludes with her saying, 'Ernie's relationship with Ben has gone from "What am I going to do with this kid?" to "When can I spend time with him again?" It's been a beautiful evolution.' What a happy and touching conclusion to what must have been a difficult time for this formidable family.

PADRAIG HARRINGTON

Here is a man who is very nearly on the edge of being forgotten, which is ridiculously unfair. Padraig Harrington's three Major victories in the space of a couple of years was a remarkable achievement. But then he decided to change things around, and only he will know why.

Harrington was forever experimenting with his swing, always developing new thoughts about the game. That was what made him so unique. For a period, however, he was more than just an eccentric; he was a wonderfully gutsy player, and he did most of it with a smile on his face. As I write this, I shall be very interested to see how he gets on as captain of the European Ryder Cup team. Paul McGinley, our last Irish Ryder Cup captain, did a superb job, thinking of every possible way he could make his players feel at ease. I hope some of the McGinley magic will rub off on Harrington, but remember, at the end of the day, it's the players who win matches – not the captain.

THE NEWCOMERS

From 2010 to 2019, a large number of players have caught my eye. Many swing the club superbly, but they have not yet learnt how to compete, or indeed play, and make far too many elementary mistakes under pressure. It's easy to criticise, but if you're going to be consistently successful you have to overcome your own fears. Very few can, and these are the ones who get to the top of the tree and stay there for a long while. Look back over golfing history and you'll see the ones I mean: Bobby Jones, Walter Hagen, Gene Sarazen, Ben Hogan and Byron Nelson, up to Palmer, Nicklaus and Player, then on to the domination of Tiger Woods and coming right up to date with Brooks Koepka. I don't know why, but I get the feeling some of the media have not taken to Koepka, which doesn't make any sense. He hits the ball magnificently, appears to have a good golfing brain and could well go on to be an enormous credit to the game of golf, even if he does spit too much for my liking. I often wonder what he chews: gum or tobacco? But no matter, he's good to watch.

Another player to catch my eye is Matt Wallace, who cuts a powerful figure. He has a very fine swing, and is rather reminiscent of McIlroy. In a recent interview he said his team – yes, his 'team,' whoever they are and whatever they do – is working on one or two of his weaker points. I'd say his chief weakness appears to be his hot-headedness. Wallace is one of the most talented players I've seen for a few years, but he seems ready to flare up at any moment. This is something he is trying to address, although he wouldn't be the first hot-head to make his mark on the golfing scene.

Incidentally, these sort of characters have always been around. Ky Laffoon, a relatively well-known American pro in the 1940s, once tied his putter to the back of his car and dragged the bastard all the way across Florida to teach it a lesson. Tommy 'Thunder' Bolt, winner of the US Open in 1958, was deliciously elegant and eccentric – and a renowned club thrower. I saw him once giving some young players lessons in how to throw their clubs properly. ('Always throw them flat, not end on – that way, they could break. And always throw in the direction you're walking. You don't want the ignominy of having to walk back and pick up your favourite 7-iron.') Wallace isn't quite at that level, but there was a period when he wasn't a million miles away. And the truth is that if you can hit the ball consistently and you've learned the strategy, the last part of the jigsaw is controlling your mind and your temper. Believe me, this focus and self-control is of equal importance to anything else you might be working on. If today's up-and-comers can get that into their heads, there's no telling how far they'll go. Maybe some of them will join these other great names in my own personal Hall of Fame.

RORY MCILROY

A majestic striker of the ball, I've never seen Rory McIlroy off balance when driving. When you take into account the power he generates, that is remarkable. I wonder what the next five years will hold for this golfing genius and whether he'll get tired of the negative press. As far as I can see, his main failing is judging the correct distance from 150 yards in.

There's definitely something wrong there, but I don't know whether he's too bold, trying to be cavalier, or if he simply has a natural chink in his golfing armour. His mistakes are glaring and yet simple. What help does he need? Can he work it out for himself? Should his caddie have a greater influence? Only he knows the answer, but an answer he must find – otherwise he will never totally fulfil his huge talent. These words may sound rather strange, but if McIlroy retired now, his record would still be formidable. Remember, Bobby Jones retired at thirty, but that was many years ago.

When playing well, McIlroy is a joy to watch. When out of top gear, he looks vulnerable and naïve. Time to look in the mirror, Rory, and find the answer. He must have done precisely that before playing in the 2019 Canadian Open, which he won in fine style. More importantly, he did so in a carefree sort of way, swinging with freedom. He came close to winning with a 59 in the last round (when his 61 set a course record), and to my eye, he did so well because he went out and just played golf without allowing his mind to become too cluttered with this thought and that. This, on top of his terrific talent, was the secret of his early, bludgeoning success, and this same mindset will likely propel him to whatever triumphs await.

JORDAN SPIETH

Here's a player who burst onto the scene like a breath of fresh air, heralded to the sky by the media and spectators alike. His boyish charm flooded the fairways, and the golfing world soon knew that a new hero had been discovered. He took off at an astonishing rate, although nothing he did was extra-special except from his putting. It looked, for a while, as if he was in league with the devil, holing putts from eight, ten, twelve yards in extraordinary, routine fashion. Many felt this would go on forever, as it had years before with the great Bobby Locke and New Zealand's Sir Bob Charles, the Open Champion in 1963.

Perhaps inevitably, Spieth's magical caravan ground almost to a halt at the Masters in 2016. He seemed to suffer a meltdown at the short 12th – as many have done before. He fought back manfully, but the damage, seemingly, had been done. For a couple of years, he wasn't the same player, then came 2019 and the signs of a recovery. It doesn't look as if he is going to repeat his former glories, but who knows? Although I've never spoken to Spieth, I have watched him at close quarters and always felt, beneath the boyish charm, that there was a steely core and not a particularly nice character ready to emerge. The odd verbal exchange with his caddie, a sharp word or two to a spectator, the look given to a television interviewer… all tell a story from beneath the surface, which is why I've always felt that his nature has a nasty side trying to escape. And although he has putted magnificently many times, I must confess I don't particularly care for his methods, particularly from within a range of four or five feet.

DUSTIN JOHNSON

DJ, on the other hand, is a very different character. He lopes through life like the easy-going sheriff of some hick town from many years ago. He's had a number of personal problems over the years, but with his marriage he seems to have put them all behind them. He may be the world number one at the time of writing, but on a couple of occasions he has been found wanting at the crucial moment. He was robbed of a Major title through, what seemed to me, a dreadful rules decision, but his recovery from all those dramas now seems complete. He has his own particular style, and he is certainly a good watch. I'm sure he'll go a long way in the years to come.

WOMEN

THE world of women's professional golf really began in 1940s America with the advent of the WPGA Tour, a limited circuit with an even more limited roster of players. The Tour lasted just a few years before it disbanded in 1948. By then, however, just before my sixteenth birthday, I had already begun to take a serious interest in the women's game.

Nearly all the best players in the world at that time were American, and although a fairly large number of women were already playing in the amateur game, women professionals were rare. But when a new professional circuit for women, the LPGA Tour, began in America in 1950, the profile of the women's game increased. Of course, the Americans were fortunate in having a handful of genuinely great players; Patty Berg, Louise Suggs and Babe Zaharias were among the thirteen pioneers who formed the LPGA and got the ball rolling. I watched their early struggles with great interest, and over the last fifty years, I've marvelled at the development of the women's game worldwide.

Lady Heathcote Amery and Enid Wilson are two of Britain's finest, although I never saw them play. My early memories were of Jean Donald, Mrs Anderson, Wanda Morgan and Jessie Valentine, but back then, professional women's golf in Britain and Europe was very small-fry. Gradually, things began to change as excellent players emerged from the continent, with France, Italy, Spain, Sweden and Germany supplying many of the game's stars. I shall always remember the Frenchwoman Catherine Lacoste, of the great clothing family, going to America as an amateur and winning the US Women's Open Championship – a quite phenomenal feat. Most of the really good players in Europe, however, remained in Europe, where they built their own reputations.

Then came the creation of the Ladies European Tour, of which I was the very proud first president. Soon after, a burst of talent appeared from Sweden. Several of these players visited Britain, but they didn't stay long before moving on to the USA, where the pickings were much richer.

For years, American women dominated their golfing scene. But then, like the genie escaping from the lamp, players arrived from Asia and Mexico. From England, meanwhile, came Laura Davies. And who will ever forget the emergence of that smiling American Nancy Lopez – or Mexico's Lorena Ochoa? Then there was Karrie Webb from Australia and Annika Sörenstam from Sweden – plus so many others who lit up the sport.

There is one woman, however, who I will always remember above all others. I'm talking about somebody very, very special: Babe Zaharias. She excelled initially at basketball, then track and field, before settling on golf. She was also a fine singer and recorded several records. Oh, and she played the harmonica rather well. What a woman, and what a shame that we met only briefly, back when I was eighteen.

Born in 1915, Zaharias made her fame when she established world records at the 1932 Olympics in Los Angeles. She won two golds and a silver in the eighty-metre hurdles, javelin and high jump. On giving up athletics, she turned to golf, winning the US Women's Amateur in 1946. For a handful of years, she ruled the world of women's golf, winning ten Majors on the pro tour. She was voted Female Athlete of the Year in 1932, 1945, 1946, 1947 and 1950. In 1949, she was acclaimed the greatest female athlete of the half century.

Zaharias was, I believe, among *the* first – if not actually the first – woman to hold the post of head professional at a golf club. Her husband was George Zaharias, an all-star wrestler, and what an impressive pair they made! I am also advised that, on occasion, The Babe could be rather relaxed – cavalier, even – where the rules of the game are concerned. Whatever the validity of this charge, there can be no doubting her supreme ability in so many different sports. She died of colon cancer aged forty-five. They certainly don't make 'em like her anymore.

Many other female golfers have impressed me greatly over more recent years, and now I'd like to mention some of these tigresses of the game for you to consider.

LAURA DAVIES

Laura Davies has, for so many years, been an inspirational figure. She is an enormously successful player and still capable of great things, despite now being in her mid-fifties. She lives in West Byfleet, where she enjoys a splendid house – complete with a football pitch in the back garden. It is said she has a room with several television sets, where she watches all sorts of sports simultaneously, keeping track of multiple games at once and having the odd wager here and there.

MICKEY WALKER

A great English golfer, Mickey Walker was one of the first women to hold the position of head professional. It was at the Warren Golf Club in Essex, a busy club with a large membership, so it was quite a bold step to offer her the job – and, indeed, it was bold of her to take on the challenge. She captained the European Solheim Cup team four times and coached the Curtis Cup team on three occasions. She went on to do television work, becoming a great figure in women's golf.

CATRIONA MATTHEW

Catriona Matthew captained the Solheim Cup team in 2019, when the matches were played at the Gleneagles Hotel in her Scottish homeland. In her play, Catriona reminds me in many ways of Luke Donald: she's accurate and not too powerful, but with good straight hitting and a sound short game. That's the way she's always played, and it has brought her much success. Too many players, men and women, decide somewhere along the line that things must change – sometimes, it seems, for the sake of change. I must hit the ball further, they think, or I must learn to fade it right, draw it left, et cetera. Most of them have disappeared with hardly a trace or have gone back to being journeywomen.

JULIE INKSTER

Captain of the American Solheim Cup team for the third time in 2019, Julie Inkster is remarkable. Her longevity in the game and her ability to concentrate have propelled her into legendary status. She has been a consistent winner in the United States for many years, and her record in team golf is also excellent. She's a tough cookie, though, so don't be fooled by all those smiley-faced interviews she has given over the years. When the bell rings, the lips close into a hard, thin line, the eyes go steely and she becomes ready to challenge anything or anyone. That's her style. She's a great asset to women's golf and proof that you can raise a family and still compete at the highest level.

LYDIA KO

A golfing phenomenon, Korean-born Lydia Ko studied in New Zealand, where she developed her skills at an incredible speed. Before she even turned twenty-one, she had already established herself in the world of women's golf. By the time she was twenty-five, she had won practically everything of note, but then things began to change.

It started with Ko's look. She jettisoned her glasses, found contact lenses, and went for a new hairstyle – perhaps, and who knows, she found a new love? But whatever the reason, suddenly her game went off the boil. As of 2019, she has not figured very often, and when I think of how easy she made it look a few years ago, I wonder what has changed. Has she followed the road of Martin Kaymer, who won two Major championships and then decided that if he was to win at Augusta he needed to learn a different way of playing? A number of pros have certainly thought that way in the past.

IN the last couple of decades, building on the exceptional Americans who founded it, an influx of talented players from all over the world has brought new and exciting talent to the LPGA Tour. Many of these players came from the Far East, particularly South Korea and Thailand. These Asian players certainly took well to life in the States – so well, in fact, that the newcomers swamped the American players who, for so long, had dominated the sport. America enjoys its winners, male or female, and I get the feeling the public lost a lot of interest when the majority of winners started coming from outside the USA. However, with the passing of time, the golfing public has got used to the charm and elegance of these players from far-away countries, and I'm happy to observe that interest in the Women's Tour has been rejuvenated.

The position of women in other sporting activities has always been of great interest. Over the past few years, great strides have been made with regard to prize money. I very much doubt that most women's sports will ever become as rich as the men's, although aims to introduce financial parity are very noble. It is very obvious to me that there are certain sporting activities in which women are unable to compete with men on a level basis. In football, rugby, boxing and cricket, women have their own skills and reach their own levels, and certainly there's nothing wrong with that. But why is it so few women are able to compete with our top snooker and darts players? These two activities do not seem to require great physical strength. It is interesting, also, to note that a full hospitality ticket for the Men's Wimbledon Tennis Final in 2019 cost hundreds of pounds more than a ticket for the Women's Final. Could that be purely because the Women's Final is over three sets instead of five? I don't know the answer, but there is a difference – whether you like to admit it or not.

THE PETER ALLISS HALL OF FAME

On the American men's professional golfing circuit, the first prize every week is now invariably over $1,000,000. On the Champions Tour, the first prize is about half that, and on the Women's Tour it's slightly less, so there is a difference over the whole scale of events. I'm sure the winners don't complain, and whatever way you look at it, it's a wonderful way to earn a living.

As I write, the European Tour appears, superficially at least, to be reasonably healthy, as far as the professionals are concerned, although the ongoing exodus to America by Europe's biggest stars remains a problem that may never be solved. I note, however, that perhaps some of the excellent work carried out over many years by the former chief executives, Ken Schofield and George O'Grady, is being set aside in an attempt to face up to the changes in public expectation which have evolved in line with modern life. Large sums of money are being spent one way or another, and I hope the required results are in the offing. Change, of course, is necessary in all walks of life, and the need to keep fresh generations involved is vital. The present boss, Keith Pelley, was brought in from a high-flying media rights role in Canada to carry out something of a revolution, and he and his team are certainly trying to do just that. It is far from an easy task, and I wish them much luck in their endeavours.

At the club level, meanwhile, golf is going through a strange period. A lot of people are giving up their memberships, maybe because of their financial situation or because of competing demands on their time. Will they ever return? Is membership becoming too expensive, despite the efforts of many clubs to offer more flexible, cheaper ways to be a member and play this great game? How will it all end?

I don't know what lies in store, but I have a feeling that golf will somehow survive. Let's hope so.

PETER has known, watched and played with many good players, but his roll call of honour makes clear just how good one must become to join the pantheon of 'the greats.' So what is it that separates the excellent player from the very good one? Many of us have been ambitious to some extent, chasing a dream and working hard for it, but how many of us have really aspired to become the best in the world at any given craft? I suggest not many, and further, I suggest that the majority of men or women who have ever harboured such aspirations are likely to be delusional.

Yet this is exactly what the world's elite golfers have done and continue to do. At some point, as technique blossomed on top of natural talent, a coterie of players decided that it would not be enough to merely be among the very best... they wanted to actually be The Best. It is this extraordinary self-confidence on top of an unnatural, if impressive, drive that moves them forward and upward and away from the pack. This superman/woman gene is visible in all sports, but it is most obvious in the old game – if only because golf, by its nature, offers greater longevity on the highest plateaux.

These elite players are not like the rest of us. Not only are they immeasurably superior at the game, but they are hard-wired in a different fashion. They are obsessed with the pursuit of success, with winning and proving themselves to themselves over and over again. This, as Peter suspects, does not necessarily make them nice people, but it does make them champions.

Ken Schofield, former executive director of the European Tour, remembers Peter Alliss: I first saw Peter play on a cold, wet and windy autumnal day at Gleneagles in 1958. He was then twenty-seven years of age, striding the fairways of the King's Course like a golfing Adonis. Years later, I told him of the impression he had made – and of course, Peter just smiled. Within a month of that day at Gleneagles, Peter embarked on a blistering run of form, winning three successive National Open titles in Portugal, Spain and Italy – a quite superb and unique achievement. Those titles, and the many others he won in Europe and around the world, reflected his standing as one of the very best British golfers of his generation. Peter's involvement in eight Ryder Cup matches is further proof of his magnificent talent.

Then, of course, he transitioned into broadcasting. He stared off with his friend and mentor Henry Longhurst on BBC television, becoming Britain's undisputed 'Voice of Golf.' Then, later on, he joined ABC television in the United States, working alongside the superb David Marr and Judy Rankin.

Despite the demands of all those broadcasting commitments, charitable causes remained at the forefront of Peter and Jackie's busy life together. Through their joint efforts they have raised millions for so many worthwhile charities, led by Peter's strong support for disabled children through his powered-wheelchair access program.

Peter Alliss touched everyone in the game of golf – firstly as a fine player and then as a master broadcaster. But more importantly, he touched millions from all walks of life with his wit, humour and his desire to help others. It is a privilege to have known Peter and an even greater honour to have been his friend. Those of us who knew him recognise our good fortune. Truly, we were blessed beyond belief.

THERE'S SOMETHING ON MY CHEST, DOC!

THIS will most probably be my last book. Bearing that in mind (and hopefully without sounding too arrogant), I thought I would pass on to you some of the thoughts that have run through my mind over the last seventy-odd years. I have always loved to think and talk about golf, but even I must admit that our time on Earth is about more than just the old game. As such, I have developed some hypotheses over the years about life itself and how it affects us all. There have been so many changes in my lifetime that it's quite difficult to know where to start, but here goes. Here's a hotchpotch of miscellaneous thoughts, a potpourri, a rush of blood… call it what you will.

As I write, we are embroiled in the Brexit saga and the selection of our next Prime Minister. I have come to realise over the years that politics has never been – and never will be – easy. I was warned many moons ago never to discuss politics, religion or marriage. If you wish to retain friendships and family unity, that advice holds true today. But I am now going to ignore much of my own advice by going ahead and discoursing on it all anyway.

When I was in my late teens and early twenties, I wasn't all that interested in politics, although my father bought three newspapers every day: the *Daily Mirror,* the *Daily Mail* and the *News Chronicle.* Between them, these publications covered three different points of view: Labour, Tory and Liberal. Father always enjoyed reading the same news story in each of these newspapers; he was interested to note the spin they all employed to convey, or obscure, the same basic facts while promoting their respective political outlooks. So it was my father who introduced me to newspapers, and the habit of reading them has remained with me all my life. It both worries and saddens me that one day, in perhaps not that many years, there won't be any printed newspapers left. It'll all come through on your phone or your iPad or your home computer, and I don't really see any fun in that. I suppose it would be better than nothing, although we would all lose access to those happy accidents that so often occur while leafing through a newspaper. I'm speaking of that small piece buried on page eleven that one stumbles upon quite by chance and actually finds to be the most interesting and thought-provoking story of all.

Perhaps because of my large appetite for news, I used to believe that in order to be a politician, you had to be clever. Certainly, I thought, you had to be cleverer than the rank and file, and that's how you got to Westminster. You went there to look after us, to make sure the world we lived in was the very best you could make it. I suppose there's still a little truth in that – but not too much.

With the passing of the years I have taken much more of an interest in daily politics. It is amazing just how much the population has been squeezed on all sorts of tax schemes to allow the country to continue to compete with the 'big boys.' I wonder how much longer you can keep squeezing the relatively affluent middle classes, those earning around £80,000 a year. Of course, if you're on £30,000 or less, you might well think such an income signifies great wealth, but does it really? Consider your fairly typical family of four looking to enjoy a pleasant house, a couple of cars and perhaps one or two family holidays a year; after tax has been paid, these hard-working parents are left with much less than a fortune. Even holidays at home are very expensive, and if you go self-catering all that means is that Mum or Dad, or both, will spend most of their time cooking and cleaning up. A holiday for some, perhaps, but certainly not for all.

During my lifetime, I have always been encouraged to save money, to tuck some away. All of us have been cajoled – bombarded, even – into doing this through newspapers, radio and television; the message has always been that it is an urgent necessity to save money and that it would be imprudent not to do so. I'm sure you have heeded that message and put aside money for everything from holidays to funerals, but consider this: if you are frugal and save well, what is your reward at the end of it all? Well, in the final accounting, the government only takes more of your savings. That's how you are paid back for your sound financial management. I am, of course, talking about the inheritance tax, which, to me, is one of the most insidious of fiscal interventions. At one time there was talk of removing that particular tax, but as ever, it all ended up as hot air.

Meanwhile, houses are becoming ever more expensive, and the same goes for cars. Likewise, the cost of running these vehicles ticks ever upwards, while the price of food and drink scarcely ever goes down. I have great friends in Norfolk whose families were, for many years, at the centre of the turkey industry, maybe half a step behind Bernard Matthews. Many of these once thriving poultry farmers have now gone out of business, due mostly to cheaper imports from the continent. So in this rare case where food has become cheaper for consumers, it's British farmers who have lost out.

Farming in general appears to be in crisis. Apparently, thousands of gallons of milk are poured down the drain every day. Farmers are paid to do nothing with their land, while fishermen find it hard to thrive because great vessels from Spain, Germany, Russia and wherever else have come through and virtually swept up the lot with no regard for the rules. Our noble fishermen seem to be the only ones who do things by the book, and they're worse off for it.

Meanwhile, the influx of giant supermarkets has, in one way, been a great blessing, but at the same time these giants have played a role in the demise of the small shopkeeper. You also can't help but point at least one finger of blame at supermarkets for the huge rise in obesity among the young. Sometimes, I feel we could do with a whole new political system (I'm not thinking of the Brexit Party) looking at things from a new angle, sweeping with a very new brush and giving Britain and its people an entirely different look at life and the world.

Great Britain is just over half a thousand miles long, and yet wherever you are in the country you're never more than eighty miles from the sea. So how can it be that many of our children have never set foot on a beach – one in five, would you believe? It is extraordinary and rather sad, I think. Is getting there the problem? Before Dr Beeching and his axe, all those years ago, we had a rail system that was, perhaps, the envy of the world. But then someone in power decided to do away with all those lines than ran through the countryside – the ones giving access to pretty well everywhere. Against this backdrop of rail dismemberment, do we really need to spend billions on a new railway to get us to Manchester half an hour quicker? With the many technical advances we've seen in recent years, plenty of people are now able to work from home, so do our politicians really believe people are going to travel from Crewe to London every day to go to work? Rather than spending a fortune on HS2, why not just improve the systems we have?

And what about the problems around Stonehenge? The dreaded A303… I've travelled on it dozens of times, and for they last sixty years, at least, they've been talking of a bypass – or even a tunnel. I wonder why nobody has gone to the landowner a few hundred yards on the south side, paid him double – no, treble – compensation, and made a simple cutting. The old road could be kept open for local traffic, and a couple of bridges could be made so farm machinery could travel to-and-fro. The whole job could be completed in double-quick time and at a relatively low cost, or is that too simple a solution?

Meanwhile, the Scottish Nationalists are always banging on about home rule and how they'd like to shake off the yoke that's entrapped them for so many years. They boast of the way their National Health Service is run (mostly with English money), but they seem to forget their country holds just over five million people while England is home to more than fifty-five million. It doesn't take Albert Einstein to realise that looking after five million is a damn sight easier and cheaper than looking after fifty-five million. Wales, on the other hand, has a similar population to Scotland but is often criticised for the manner in which its own NHS is run. Why?

Now think of our great open spaces – Dartmoor, the New Forest, the South Downs, Epping Forest, the Chilterns, the Derbyshire and Yorkshire Dales, the Lake District, Mid Wales, North Yorkshire and much of Northumberland and Cumbria – and you can see there are hundreds of thousands of acres of open land. When you consider that, it's a miracle we manage to fit so many people into our sceptred isle.

These are the kind of thoughts that have been cultivated by my willing exposure (perhaps overexposure) to the cut and thrust of Parliament. But quite aside from the policy debates, one of the fascinations of watching Parliament TV is the various fashions on view. Labour members often appear to have been dressed by a committee. It helps if they have a strong accent, preferably northern. It seems Conservatives, on the other hand, have been told to either wear their favourite suit (albeit one that hasn't been to the cleaners for a year) or fall back on blue-and-white pinstripes with a white shirt and club tie. The Liberal Democrats, as ever, flounder somewhere in-between. The same generally seems to apply to the women. Somehow, the Conservatives manage to look slightly better groomed, but to my eye, it seems as if they're all trying to make an effort to ape the looks most popular among their constituents.

Allow me, briefly, to switch the channel and move away from Parliament TV. At the other end of the spectrum, you'll find one of the most popular programmes on television these days. I'm talking about *Love Island,* a dating show featuring quite a large number of young boys and girls. All are handsome or beautiful, and many of them have clearly gone to great lengths to stand out from the crowd. Of course, this is not a phenomenon unique to those *Love Island* contestants, but many seem to have spent their savings enhancing their bodies: improving their teeth; indulging in manicures, pedicures and regular visits to expensive hairdressing salons; and wearing fashionable clothes in an effort to look special. Very few, however, seem to have invested even a shred of time and effort into improving their vocabulary or simple grammar, let alone working on the timbre of their voice.

The most handsome young man or beautiful young woman will look superb right up until the mouth is opened, at which point the listener is met with an onslaught of weird noises that deaden the brain. I can assure you, like, this isn't a matter of snobbery but if, like, you're going to try to make a living, like, projecting yourself, like, through television, film, or theatre, it's not, like, ridiculous to make an effort at, like, communicating clearly. How much I dislike the unnecessary use of the word 'like' to punctuate sentences (if you hadn't guessed that already). Plus, inevitably, those who watch these shows must endure a cascade of 'we done good;' 'they come down;' and so on. On and on they go – individuals who, in some cases, earn hundreds of thousands of pounds a year but are unable to cobble together a decent sentence. At these times, I always remember the famous line from *My Fair Lady* that poses the question: 'Why can't the English teach their children how to speak?' You tell me, guv.

Music has always played a big part in my life, although there is one realm in which I've never been involved, the truly high-brow, the Beethovens and the Brahms. For me it's Vivaldi and Strauss and the lighter end of the classics. I love singers who can sing in tune and the classical balladeers of thirty or forty years ago: Frank Sinatra, Dean Martin, Al Martino, Dickie Valentine, Matt Monro, Johnny

Mathis, Tom Jones and Alan Price. And what of the ladies? It's all about Dusty Springfield, Lulu, Shirley Bassey and Barbra Streisand. And then there are the big bands: Ted Heath and Jack Parnell. There's really nothing like a twenty-piece swing band to get your feet tapping. It's all quite superb.

As for today's comedians, to me they are no longer funny. Jimmy Carr, Frankie Boyle and their ilk – plus some female comedians who aren't a million miles behind – continue to get away with their foul jokes and crude language, and nobody seems to mind. Why is that? I don't feel I've lost my sense of humour, and although I'll hold my hands up and confess that I have not moved with the times, I must admit I'm quite grateful for that particular small mercy.

Over the years, I've enjoyed watching my share of cookery programmes on TV, although today I fear we're overrun with them. I particularly enjoy James Martin (who, incidentally, is a mean golfer off a rather suspect handicap) and his weekend programmes. Saturday Morning always ends with a celebrity getting a dish specially prepared for them, but before they tuck in, the conversation inevitably turns to the accompaniment. James returns from the fridge brandishing a bottle and announces that he found this one in Majestic Wine. It's a 'cheeky little New Zealand number and it's only £7.99 a pop.' The top chefs gather, swill it round and give it a good old sniff. Then they have a taste and then invariably proclaim its worth. 'What a beauty!' they say. Then I think: how is it that when we go to these famous restaurants there's never a bottle of wine on the list for under £50? I know they have high expenses, but it does look rather foolish seeing restaurant wine prices after a cohort of top chefs have told us, that same morning, just how much they enjoyed their £7.99 bottle!

Incidentally, how many of you remember when there were pig swill bins allocated to every restaurant? This was back in the war days, when uneaten food was taken away and fed to the porkers. I don't remember any great epidemics, but these days the high priests of health and safety say, 'No, you can't do that!' The pig industry has suffered greatly due to proper feed being so expensive.

And that's not the only way in which we seem to have made a pig's ear out of things. In recent years, we have seen a surge of knife crimes, with dozens of young people murdered for no reason whatsoever. Take a bit of gang warfare, add a few religious differences and throw in the fact that the victim was wearing the wrong colour scarf... you end up with a recipe for a murder, as senseless as it all is. In my world, the young would be instilled with discipline – maybe even fear. Nobody rode a bicycle on the pavement when I was but a lad for fear of being caught by the local bobby. Now pedestrians share the pavement with cyclists who ring their bells and shout obscenities to clear the poor foot soldiers out of the way.

On a lighter note, I'm sure we all laughed over the years at *Yes Minister* and *Yes Prime Minister*. Although these shows were written years ago, they're as fresh today as they ever were, and they ring oh-so true. My earlier recollections of radio humour were *Hancock's Half Hour, Round the Horn, The Goon Show* and *Beyond Our Ken*. How I remember laughing along with Ken Dodd and Tommy Handley. Meanwhile, early black-and-white television saw me enthralled by American sitcoms: *The Beverley Hillbillies, Hogan's Heroes* and, of course, *Sergeant Bilko*. More recently, I've revelled in *Everybody Loves Raymond, Two and a Half Men* and *Friends*, while on the older home front I have been delighted by *Steptoe And Son, Last of the Summer Wine, Hi De Hi, Dad's Army* and, of course, *Porridge*. That's my kind of humour. Sadly, it seems to be a dying art.

One thing that is certainly not dying out is the mobile phone. Almost all children over the age of seven seem to have one. In many cases, I fear this privilege is abused, with too many hours spent playing games, sending messages or with the user somehow finding their way into trouble. And by the way, I don't believe in homework. I think all school work should be done at school. Whether that means altering school hours I know not, but it is clearly not the way to go for children to come home tired (to parents who are also tired) and to have to do an hour or more of studying. Finish it all at school, say I. And yes, I realise I have ended a sentence with a first person singular nominative-case personal pronoun, but do I care?

Despite various governments telling us our education system is now so much better than it was, I'm not convinced. The softly-softly approach in many schools has clearly not worked, leading to unruly behaviour, bad language and, in a small number of cases, assaults on the teachers. The Scottish education system was the envy of the world when I was a boy, but recently I have read troubling reports of falling literacy rates north of the border. How could that possibly be? Even the remotest Scottish islands once had wonderful village schools; there were perhaps only a few pupils, but all of them would leave with the ability to read and write and with a good working knowledge of many things. It is disgraceful that anyone should leave school illiterate.

As for my own continued education, I learnt a lot about television by watching Jack Hargreaves, the presenter of *Out of Town*, a country programme produced by Southern TV from Southampton. Meanwhile, Cliff Michelmore, David Jacobs and Terry Wogan were all friends from whom I picked up a few tricks of the trade. One trick I learnt is that men should never show any leg when being interviewed on television. That was a favourite line of David Jacobs. He should have told Mr Johnson. Long socks – that's the answer, Boris!

As for golf, I've already said how the last seventy years have seen many great improvements, from the standard of equipment to the condition of the flora, fauna and all things that grow. But do you know what else has improved beyond all recognition? The caddies.

Caddies, of course, have been around for several hundreds of years. In the early days – in fact, right up to the 1970s – the good ones were able to read the line on the greens, and given a couple of holes, they could hand their man the right club nine times out of ten, particularly on their home course. Things began to change in the 1960s, with Phil Rogers (who tied with Bob Charles at the 1963 Open Championship at Royal Lytham and St Anne's) and, later, Jack Nicklaus. Their caddies worked out the yardages step by step, and so began the sophisticated systems in use today.

However, it's a shame to see that the R&A and the USGA have let things go as far as they have – too far, I believe. Now you can even get a diagram of the green slopes showing yardages to the inch. Mistakes are still made, but the addition of these crutches has taken away much of the game's skill. I have already marvelled at those players, like Bobby Locke and Peter Thomson, who were innately superb at judging distances and reading the greens. But the days of those great golfers are gone, and such natural gifts have been rendered obsolete by a system of almost legalised cheating. Many important skills have been taken away from the player who could judge distance with his eye or read a green after a few seconds' observation.

Jimmy Dickenson, Tip Anderson, Jackie Lee, Alfie Fyles, Dave Musgrove… all were superb caddies from the 1970s right up to 2000. The majority of caddies in ye olden days were rather like rogues and vagabonds, or else waifs and strays. Many a caddy was even chased around the country's golf courses by an irate wife or the DHSS! Over the last twenty years, however, the Yorkshireman Billy Foster, Phil 'Wobbly' Morbey and the New Zealander Steve Williams have been three of the very best. Williams, in particular, may not have been the sweetest of companions, but he was a wonderful caddie and a huge driving force behind the success of Tiger Woods.

Today's caddies are very well educated. Many possess university degrees, and the majority are witty, amusing, knowledgeable and good companions. I'm told on reliable authority that at one of the tournaments in the Arab Emirates at the back end of 2017, Justin Rose's caddie was handed a cheque for $1,000,000. It might even have been pounds! It's all very different from the days of my caddie, Jimmy Cousins, who was with me for eight years and whom I paid £10 a week from the Sunningdale Foursomes in March to the Gleneagles Foursomes in October, whether there was a tournament that week or not. If we had a good year, he got a bonus. Now, that's not quite as good as a cheque for a million, but it did put food on the table.

Speaking of great names within our sport, Tommy Horton was a great contributor to the world of professional golf. For many years, he was attached to the Royal Jersey Golf Club, and he was someone who spent quite a bit of time on various committees, always hard at work promoting the game. He and I spoke many times about the possibility of getting either the PGA or the European Tour to provide funds to make a video showcasing various aspects of golf. He suggested I would be involved alongside John Jacobs, Pete Cowan, Ken Schofield, George O'Grady, Michael Bonallack, a smattering of Ryder Cup captains and others who, over the years, have been involved in running our wonderful game – including the manufacturers of clubs and the creative minds behind the country's greatest Pro Shops. Tommy wanted us to share our thoughts on the myriad subjects that make up our game, and he was eager to get it done before it was too late. Sadly, we're already on the verge of that. Neil Coles, Brian Huggett, Brian Waites and myself are getting ever closer to that telegram celebrating our 100th birthday (if we should be so lucky), and by then the thoughts and mysteries of a bygone life in golf will be lost. It's all rather unfortunate, bordering on sad. A dream that Tommy never saw fulfilled.

As for tennis, I have a question regarding Wimbledon. Why do the powers that be put up with all the shrieking and grunting? I propose that they should give the players a year to stop and then, at the end of their twelve-months' notice, if they haven't found a way of playing without making those various bodily noises, the worst offenders should lose a point. I guarantee there wouldn't be too many grunters left on view. A few may be disgruntled, perhaps, but to hell with them!

I've never been a fanatical football fan, probably because my formative years were spent in Ferndown, six miles north of Bournemouth. For many years, Bournemouth were in the 3rd Division South. The nearest decent football was to be found in Southampton, where the team flitted between the 3rd South and the 2nd Division. A little further east was Portsmouth, one of England's premier teams up until the mid-1950s. The fanaticism of many fans I find both fascinating and worrying, along with the amount of destruction caused by many so-called supporters over the years. To burn a lovingly and painstakingly collected bonfire of memorabilia, for instance, because one does not agree with the current direction of the management is something which will always seem baffling to me.

I sometimes wonder if sport as we know it today will continue. Is everything becoming too expensive? Can the fans be continually charged more and more to attend various matches and competitions? And what about the perpetual increase in the cost of sporting memorabilia and the rise in player wages? Will the bubble ever burst? You would think it must. But mind you, I've been thinking that for twenty-five years, and so far, said bubble remains very much intact. Many of us would dearly miss our sport of choice if it didn't exist, but the world would keep turning and life would go on. Life would be a bit more dull, a bit boring, maybe, but it wouldn't be the end of civilisation. Just a thought.

Here's another. Many years ago, I was lunching at Langan's, that delightful eatery in London, with Eric Sykes and another great friend, John Humphries, who was the last of the big private bookmakers to sell up and retire. For no real reason, Eric Sykes, a man of gentle humour and a sheer delight as a companion, suddenly said, 'Isn't it a pity we're living through an ugly period?'

'What are you referring to?' I asked.

'Well, take fashion,' Eric replied. 'It's dull, ugly and everyone's wearing black or navy blue. The films are all about death, illness, or destruction. And we don't have stars any more, only a few meteorites who flash across the sky and disappear before you've learnt how to spell their names.'

I think we're going through another ugly period, but this time it's haircuts. I blame it all on the Premier League footballers. I'm told the poorest players in the league make around £30,000 a week, while the real stars earn more than ten times that amount. Good luck to them, but who suddenly thought it a good idea that we should all have haircuts like the one I got on 17th June 1949 at the Padgate Camp on the Wirral, the day I joined the RAF Regiment? Talk about short back and sides – it was almost down to the bare bone with just a wee tuft on the top, all done in just one minute. But it was free! How anyone now pays £60, £80 – £100, even – for such a dreadful haircut is beyond my comprehension. In my opinion, no man should have a haircut shorter than George Clooney's, and if you're going to dye your hair then don't colour it brown, especially if you're going on television, where the camera always shows it up and makes you look ridiculous… shades of Paul McCartney and Tom Jones. Thank goodness both of them have seen the light and become mature, handsome gentlemen. A belated bravo to both.

While we're on the subject, I confess I've been very fortunate over the years to be financially successful, although I like to think I've been reasonably sensible with my money. I've not indulged the Alliss family with a boat or a stable of racehorses, and I've not been a great gambler, although I have spent more than I should have on motor cars and, dare I say, education. We all want to give our children a better education than we had ourselves, and that's certainly been true in my case. Moyles Court, Milton Abbey, Bedford College, St Edmunds, Cranleigh and Charterhouse are all schools attended by the Alliss children, although how I managed to pay for all that and clear a mortgage is still beyond me.

Today's broader educational outlook does concern me. Some people are horrified if you say too many young people are going on to university, but I might just go ahead and say it anyway. I don't want to deny anyone the opportunity, but is higher education a good idea in every case? Wasn't it better when parents were called in to see the headteacher to be informed that their child was a good worker and an excellent member of the school but not particularly academic? These were the children who had skills in other departments, be it woodworking, electrical engineering, domestic science, gardening or one of many other subjects. It seems pointless to me to go to university and graduate with a third-class degree just for the sake of it, especially if you have accrued a small fortune of debt to be there.

My father, a Yorkshireman, was in the Argyll and Sutherland Highlanders during the Great War, so I've always felt a genuine Scottish connection. My father also travelled extensively as a golf pro and, as a consequence, had a much broader outlook on life than many. This attitude was swiftly passed on to me. When I was young, I saw no divisions within our country, and I had already seen quite a lot of this Green and Pleasant Land by a relatively young age. Now, however, we're continually told of the dreaded 'north-south divide.'

It is a familiar refrain to claim the north is starved of investment, yet it was not so long ago that ninety per cent of Britain's wealth was to be found north of Watford. Of course, London has always been London, a world of banking, insurance and money men. But for the most part, the rest of the south once consisted of farmland and various tea rooms selling Cornish pasties or Devonshire cream teas. Torquay was part of the English Riviera, Bournemouth with its chines and pine trees was fabulous for those with a weak chest, St Leonards and Bognor were genteel watering holes and Brighton – dear old Brighton – was a fun place where pretty well anything was okay. In the north, meanwhile, they made things. Birmingham was one of the great centres of industry. Likewise, Leeds-Bradford had the woollen industry, while Manchester, Oldham, Rochdale and the rest were the home of cotton. Coal was king both in the north and in Wales. All these places were doing well until the advent of nylon and cheaper cloth from abroad.

Our shipbuilding industry was the envy of the world, too, and our steelworks flourished. And then, over the years and for a variety of reasons, it all began to drain away. Whose fault? Trade unions? The bosses? Labour costs? Did those steel workers in the Far East really work their guts out for a handful of rice? I doubt it, but it was suggested they did.

So the story of the recent past has been, for many, a tale of disappointment and decline. Few of these disappointments, however, will ever match my own sorrow at the demise of sport on the BBC. I know the powers that be are always ready to wave a dossier extolling the BBC's jam-packed agenda, consisting of athletics, rugby sevens, snooker and some football (particularly women's football, a sport for which interest is very much on the rise). Sadly, however, there is little or no room in the BBC schedule for cricket, horse racing, Formula One and golf – and there is certainly nothing even close to a full men's football schedule. There is no darts, either, but you may find one or two other bits and pieces that have crept in – probably because the rights were going cheap.

I do miss the golf, although I have to salute Sky for providing a most fantastic golfing offering. Sometimes they show as many as three or four events in one day. From Thursday to Sunday, for forty-odd weeks a year, there's golf from somewhere. Often, there are repeats on Mondays and Tuesdays as well. It is wonderful, the effort that goes in and the gizmos they utilise – all to make the viewers happy.

I'm often asked if I have ever been approached by Sky to work for them. The answer is no, because my many commitments the BBC were always more than enough to keep me busy and interested. In that capacity I have worked with wonderful people and made great friendships over the years. We really have been the happiest of teams, although nowadays we are very much the poor relation. No attractive commentary positions for the likes of us – just a simple Portakabin, which, believe it or not, does the trick.

Sky employs a myriad of commentators, some of whom I enjoy and some of whom I find tedious (but then, many have said that about me). With the retirement of Howard Clark and the slowing down of Bruce Critchley, they have lost two experienced, knowledgeable voices. Very few of the present commentators have had any great success for any length of time at the top of the golfing tree, although there are always exceptions. The American Rich Beam, a US PGA champion, is both knowledgeable and entertaining; the Australian Wayne Riley brings an air of mischief and knowledge from the fairways; Richard Boxall's entertaining style has developed well over the years; and Tim Barter has become an accomplished interviewer. Meanwhile, Robert Lee and Nick Dougherty have both developed into excellent presenters.

There are one or two others, but they leave no lasting impression. The main issue is that these others lack a sense of timing, so they're always playing catch up. Too often, they seem to talk without looking at the screen. This means they never know when the picture has moved on, rendering their comments, in the last second or two, completely irrelevant. It's a bad trait and the serial offenders should be given more direction. Here's some free advice: always keep your eye on that damn screen! It really is so important. I liken it to being driven in a car by someone who insists on looking at you and talking at the same time, oblivious to whatever might appear in the road ahead. For all my grumpiness, I do enjoy Sky and what it provides, although it's getting very expensive compared to the relatively modest fee asked by the BBC. The license fee, of course, includes not only television but all the radio stations, which are worth the price of admission alone as far as I'm concerned.

Finally (and please forgive me), I just can't leave this chapter without referring once again to the enigma that is Gary Player. I've always had the greatest admiration for him, even if his overstated recollections have worn rather thin. In the excellent series *Chronicles of a Champion Golfer* on Sky, he recites in fulsome tones his early life. Tragically, his mother died when he was very young, leaving his father alone to raise three children, Gary among them. He tells us he used to come home from school to an empty, dark house, where he cooked his own meals and washed and ironed his own clothes.

I'm not sure this rings totally true. His father managed a gold mine, his sister went to boarding school and when he got married to Vivienne Vervey (the daughter of a well-known golf professional), he married in a full morning suit with all the trimmings... hardly the trappings of lingering impoverishment. It makes me wonder why he continues to pontificate about those ancient times. Is he looking for sympathy, admiration or what? He probably thinks everyone who can remember those far-off days is dead. It's certainly not enough to detract from his wonderful career, but it does tell us something, and that is perhaps something only a psychiatrist with the right key could unlock. I'll leave it there and go to take my medication. Oh, modern medicine truly is a wonder. (Well, there's got to be something I like about today, hasn't there?)

Just before I pop that pill... those who have known me for many years may be wondering why, to this point, there has been no mention of Joan, my first wife. Well, fifty years on from the divorce, the repercussions still linger along with some natural regret, although my marriage was over and my subsequent marriage to my darling Jackie has been life-enhancing for me – a great joy. I could not have achieved what little I have without her love, support and encouragement.

A RETURN TO PORTRUSH

FOR Peter, The Open's return to Portrush was an emotional experience – one that encouraged reflection as well as anticipation. Flash back to 1951 and you'll find Peter at this majestic course, playing in one of his first Opens at the ripe old age of twenty. The halfway cut proved a bridge too far, but for an up-and-comer like Peter, it was a delight just to have taken part.

Now, sixty-eight years on, The Open was finally back at Portrush, and Peter was no longer a budding professional but an eighty-eight year-old doyen of the game. On the first day of this 2019 Championship, I was lucky enough to join Peter in the Portakabin where he and his co-commentators would spend long hours peering at TV monitors and talking through the day's events.

There is nothing glamorous about this rather cramped set-up, parked for the week in front of the clubhouse. Imagine the Apollo 11 space module but without the views. As a general rule, the four commentators sharing the cabin were: Peter, Ken Brown, Andrew Cotter and a new voice from America, Ned Michaels, the former PGA professional. Peter and his colleagues commentate here in the knowledge that most of what they say will never be heard, since the day's action is inevitably spliced and condensed to fit a two-hour highlights show with a coherent narrative. It's hard work, with the chaps usually pairing up for hour-long stints at a time. For Peter, this was a particularly difficult format and not the sort of commentary on which his reputation was built.

More suited to longer, slower broadcasts, Peter always made great use of whatever time and space he was afforded to express himself. He liked to take his listeners with him as he discoursed on this and that, always offering enlightening or funny insights regardless of the subject matter. Highlights shows, on the other hand, are ruthlessly edited, meaning there is little time to meander and less scope for the classic commentary on which the Alliss name was built. Thankfully, a book affords Peter all the space he needs to take us on one of his famous detours, revealing what he was really thinking as he returned to one of those places where it all began…

WHEN the R&A announced the Open Championship would be returning to Royal Portrush, an air of great expectancy ran through the golfing world. Certainly, sixty-eight years is a long time between engagements, and naturally, there were some who were not totally sure whether this was a wise move or not. There were four main points for discussion: access, accommodation, the weather coming in off the Atlantic (which no one can control, of course) and whether we would end up with the 'right' winner. If all these factors worked out, and the stars aligned, I knew 2019 would surely be a contender for the greatest Championship of modern times.

Many preparations had to be made to accommodate the ever-growing infrastructure. This process was made even more challenging than usual by the fact that so much of the equipment and staging had to be brought across the Irish Sea in containers. More significantly, course alterations had to be made.

As it turned out, this latter bit was relatively easy. The original 17th and 18th holes were two of the dullest, especially in comparison to the grandeur of the rest of Portrush, so losing them and creating two others, pretty well in the middle of the course, was no great hardship. The beauty of their design and construction was a huge bonus, and I had been very much looking forward to seeing how this new layout fitted in with the natural landscape. I was pleased and relieved to see that it all meshed together perfectly.

Returning to Royal Portrush for an Open Championship after so many years brought back a flood of memories. It took me some time to remember how Alec and I had travelled from Bournemouth to Belfast and on to Portrush the last time out. I worked a bit of Sherlock Holmes magic and finally came up as near as I could to our travel arrangements all those years ago...

First would have been the bus from our house in Ferndown to Landsdowne in Bournemouth, which is close to the train station. My brother and I would have walked the couple of hundred yards with a set of clubs and a suitcase each. Then the train to Waterloo, a hop across town and on by train to Holyhead, followed by a ferry to Dublin and an Irish Sea crossing which I remember as being rather rough. There was a train to Belfast, and then it was a question of catching the bus to Portrush and settling in at a small hotel within a mile of the course. At last, we were ready to go.

How different from 2019, when I travelled with no golf clubs and no brother, just a long-suffering wife. Jackie and I made it thanks to our super secretary Frances, who, along with help from the BBC, arranged all ticketing, booked the use of wheelchairs through airports, sorted chauffeured cars et cetera – she fixed the lot. And I'm pleased to report these travel arrangements worked very well. I'm amazed, considering how many people these days require assistance at airports, how smoothly it all runs. Occasionally there's a delay, but these hold-ups rarely last longer than a few minutes.

The BBC, with its reduced position in the world of sporting television, now operates from that aforementioned Portakabin. The place is decked out with a set of tables and chairs which would not look out of place in a 1949 NAAFI. We are graced with small refrigerator, what I think is a George Foreman grill and various groceries and snacks, some of which are quite fattening.

Sadly, some of my former colleagues have passed on to the great country club in the sky, but the ones that remain are just as affable, kind and considerate as any that had gone before. Working with Ken Brown has always been a pleasure. Ken may be something of a loner by nature, a man who likes to make his own travel and accommodation arrangements, but he is a wonderful colleague and has entered wholeheartedly into the BBC family, although his ties to other networks are still strong. He has a good sense of humour and is a meticulous broadcaster who cares very much about the end product. He has been a great help and a staunch supporter, for which I will always be grateful.

Andrew Cotter is a man for all seasons: rugby, tennis, golf, athletics... you name it, he can handle it. As such, he has developed into a first-class all-round broadcaster. Again, rather like Ken, he believes in the old saying that he who travels fastest travels alone.

Eilidh Barbour, meanwhile, is the new face of BBC golf. Following Hazel Irvine is no easy task, but her bubbly personality carries the day.

Jonny Bramley, Michael Jackson, Chris White, Matthew Wayne and many others make it a pleasure for me to go to work – as have, in the past, Paul Davies, John Shrewsbury, Bruce Critchley, Clive Clark and Mike Hughesdon.

Working with people you like really is half the battle, and I have been very fortunate in this regard. It was the same when I worked for many years for ABC in the United States. I was made so welcome, despite being a stranger in a strange land, so I'd like to offer a big thank you to the likes of Terry Jastrow, Jim Jennett, Jack Graham, Judy Rankin, Jim McKay, Jeff Shapter and all the others in the crew who played such a large role in my life within the world of televised US sports. Collectively, their helpfulness, encouragement and sense humour towers beyond description, and I remain hugely thankful to them all.

But back to Royal Portrush and the 2019 Open. During that trip I could not help but notice a great increase in the proliferation of facial hair among both young and old. On some it looks reassuringly dashing and almost, dare I say, romantic, while on others it looks grey, thin, and grisly – desperately in need of a dab of Supergrow. On young chins one can find something known as designer stubble, although in many cases it looks like the wearer is in need of the cold steel. Others sport just a wispy bit of hair that makes them look ten years older. They call it fashion, apparently. Lowry, incidentally, was the first bearded winner of an Open since Bob Ferguson triumphed at St Andrews in 1882. So that's 137 years between these two champion golfers – a long time to grow some facial fuzz.

I hope it won't be too long before The Open returns to Royal Portrush, although the scoring was perhaps lower than many thought it would be. Could that count against it? I don't think so. As things turned out, it won't go down as the greatest Championship ever, although it can boast the second biggest attendance in Open history, the 237,000 who crowded into Portrush giving way only to the 239,000 who watched Tiger Woods at St Andrews in 2000. However, if a few things had been different – the weather and a closer pursuit of the winner, for example – it would have been a damn close-run thing. But before all this would come to pass, I had to get there, and for me that is not so easy these days.

I set off with Jackie on the Monday of Championship week to give myself a couple of days to sniff the air and paw the ground like the old warhorse I've become. As the week unravelled, it became ever more fascinating. For some unknown reason, the BBC decided to book me on a late flight to Belfast which meant, sadly, I was unable to get to the club in time for the R&A dinner held on the Monday prior to the Championship. I sent my apologies and hoped everyone understood.

The short flight from Heathrow to Belfast was very easy. Jackie and I found ourselves booked into the Roe Park Resort in the pretty town of Limavady. It's a hotel I am very familiar with, as I had stayed there on multiple occasions when working on the British Seniors, which was played in the late 1990s at Royal Portrush. I like it very much. Safe to say, things were off to a good start.

On Tuesday morning we were picked up at 11:15 for the forty-minute drive to Portrush. This is the one day when there is a little time spare to take a look around and enjoy the delights of the R&A's Trophy Room – a haven of excellent food, fine beverages and old friends. I was also able to marvel at the huge infrastructure which had been put up over the previous months. It really is something these days. In advance of the tournament I had contemplated how things might work out at Portrush after such a long absence. Would the traffic flow? Would the spectators get around the course relatively easily? Would the Park and Ride facilities work? Would there be enough accommodation? So much to see and ponder.

Well, for starters, the Trophy Room was quite magnificent. It is so good, in fact, that Augusta has produced its own version for the Masters. The facility at Portrush has grown over the years to accommodate R&A guests from far and wide. The first person I ran into was Sir Paddy Hine and his delightful wife. Paddy, as a young man, had dreamed of becoming a golf professional but ended up as Air Chief Marshall of the Royal Air Force. Quite a decent career swap, I'd say. He had just celebrated his birthday and looked fit as a fiddle. Everything seemed to be running smoothly, but it was early days.

On Wednesday there was a change in the weather. After three days of sun, things turned overcast, and the rain came pelting down now and again. We carried out our annual charity wheelchair presentation in the tented village, and it was thankfully a great success. The delight on the faces of our three young recipients and their families was, as ever, a sheer joy to behold.

I have been heavily involved with this initiative since George Makey came up with the idea some forty-five years ago. George, a banker at the time, was a member of Parkstone Golf Club in Dorset, where my brother and I were the club professionals. The aim was – and still is – to raise enough money to offer state-of-the-art wheelchairs to youngsters whose families otherwise could not afford them. Since its beginnings, the charity has raised some £10million to spread this happiness. It is extremely moving to see the joy on the faces of youngsters when they realise they have a powered wheelchair and so have some freedom of movement for the first time. For some years now, the R&A has very kindly allowed us to make these presentations on-site, and more often than not, this is the highlight of my Open week.

Jackie and I also attended the R&A captain's lunch, which was quite splendid. The great and the good were there – from Augusta, Australia and all points to Chipping Sodbury. To everyone's relief, the rain stopped at four o'clock, in time for the massed greenkeepers to do their final preparations. All, it seemed, was well on the eve of the great competition.

At precisely 6:35 a.m. Darren Clarke struck the first tee shot of this much-anticipated Open. What an ungodly hour to start! I don't think any other sporting event begins so early, other than perhaps ocean racing. Clarke's participation in the build up to the Championship had been excellent. He's very much a Portrush man; his home overlooks the course, and he campaigned vigorously to have the Championship return. No wonder so many people were hoping he would qualify for the final thirty-six.

While Clarke opened with a momentarily reassuring birdie, the movement of traffic through the little town looked to be very good. Inevitably, there was a massive police presence. All these officers were smiling and helpful in their manner of dealing with such a massive influx of people, so annoyance was at a low ebb. Still, it always comes as a bit of a shock when you notice every officer has a gun at their waist. I knew this would be the case before I arrived in Northern Ireland, of course, but it's still an eye-opener every time.

Then came a sprinkling of rain. I thought those players cursing the early start might have ended up with the best weather of the day. At around two o'clock, just before Rory McIlroy's tee-off time, the rain increased. The R&A starter announced, 'On the tee, Rory McIlroy.' Everyone held their breath as Ireland's most outstanding golfer prepared to enter the lists. He was taking an iron for position and safety, and why not? You can end up out of bounds on both sides of the fairway, but its width, plus the rough either side, meant he was aiming for a target at least fifty yards wide. Then the unthinkable happened: he hit it left and out of bounds. Oh, woe is me. His troubles continued, and following a catalogue of errors, he ended up taking an eight on this relatively benign opening hole. One hole down, four shots dropped. Cue raised eyebrows all around our commentary HQ.

Broadcasting friends - old and new: Judy Rankin (top left), Terry Jastrow (top centre), Jim McKay (top right), Eilidh Barbour (right) playing in a ProAm with Martin Slumbers, Chief Executive of the R&A, Andrew Cotter (below), Hazel Irvine (below right)

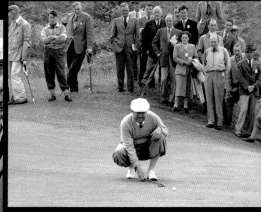

TOP LEFT: Max Faulkner with the claret jug after winning the 1951 Open at Portrush
TOP RIGHT: Bobby Locke at Portrush in 1951
ABOVE: The Claret Jug returns to Portrush
ABOVE RIGHT: Darren Clarke drives off the first tee to get the 2019 Open under way
BELOW: Shane Lowry finishes six shots ahead of his nearest rival
RIGHT: Congratulations for Shane Lowry from playing partner and runner-up Tommy Fleetwood

It was a dreadful start, but McIlroy's problems didn't end there. He signed eventually for a 79. He wasn't alone, however, since many other big names were struggling. I'm thinking of Phil Mickelson, Bubba Watson, Tiger Woods, Adam Scott and David Duval, who is a lovely chap and a former Open champion but one who appeared to be playing off a 16 handicap that week. One 66 and a 67 were the best scores of the opening day. Then came a plethora of 70s; the early scoring was tight.

Showers were forecast for the second round, and it was pleasing to see that Brooks Koepka and Tommy Fleetwood, two of the favourites, were in good shape. Fleetwood continues to improve in a quite remarkable way. His progress over the last four years is as good, if not better, than anyone else in the world of golf. Meanwhile, the organisation was superb on every front, although there were one or two complaints from local shopkeepers who said much of the pedestrian traffic was being directed away from the centre of the town, to the detriment of local business. The Park and Ride facilities, however, worked remarkably well. They must have commandeered every double-decker bus in Ireland, and considering how relatively narrow the roads are in and around Portrush, everything seemed to come together superbly.

It's always interesting looking at the latest golfing fashions. At this Open, I'm afraid to say, they seemed very dull. I saw a great number of players in black waterproofs and baseball caps, making it difficult to identify them from a distance. Hardly anyone wore pastel shades or, indeed, dared to don anything colourful. Oh, for the elegance of Bob Charles and rainbow outfits in the style of Doug Sanders. The gallery also seemed to be dressed mainly in black, particularly while the rain was coming down.

Graeme McDowell was going well, but he lost his ball off the 18th tee and was caught out by the new three-minute rule. Just twelve seconds too late the cry went up – 'Here it is!' – but sadly McDowell was already on his way back. Darren Clarke was on the verge of qualifying for the final thirty-six when all sorts of trouble hit him on the last couple of holes. In the space of twenty minutes he went from Dr Jekyll to Mr Hyde, and woe betide anyone who got in his way as he left the 18th green. He's always been like that, Darren. Sunshine one moment, storms the next.

Tom Lehman bid everyone an emotional farewell. The American has reached the age of sixty, so he will no longer receive an invitation to play in the Championship he won so memorably at Royal Lytham in 1996. Meanwhile, many big names had already put themselves out of contention, but Shane Lowry played beautifully, his short game pulling him ahead of everyone else. The whole of Ireland was excited – there are no borders in Ireland where golf, like rugby, is concerned – but could this local hero keep it up? Justin Rose was still going, too. After a shaky start, he finished well, coming in with a 69.

Justin is an interesting golfer. When he turned professional, immediately after finishing fourth at the 1998 Open, he famously missed those twenty-one consecutive cuts on the European Tour. At the time I felt, as did many others, that he was finished… but no! He rose Phoenix-like from the ashes to establish himself as one of the finest of English golfers, winning the US Open, an Olympic Gold Medal and making number one in the world rankings. He always comes across as a decent, likeable man, but beneath this niceness he is clearly very, very tough. Could he now add an Open Championship to his impressive list of achievements?

To great excitement, McIlroy, determined to at least make the cut after such a disastrous and morale-sapping first round, was burning up the course. He was urged on by the galleries but ended up with a 65, which was unfortunately just one too many. He left the final green with cheers echoing in his ears and tears in his eyes. McDowell got through, but Clarke and Harrington went out. The qualifying score of one over par, 143, was very low for an Open. Meanwhile, Ryan Fox from New Zealand had a spectacular round of two halves – 39 and 29 – to show what was possible if you kept your head and found a touch of good fortune.

Come Saturday's third round, the weather was good. It was reasonably calm, warm and generally benign. No one appreciated this more than Lowry, who simply blistered around the course in 63, putting magnificently but also enjoying some strokes of great fortune when several misdirected drives ended up in hittable places. There has never been an Open champion who did not find himself blessed by a touch of good luck. Everything was building up very well for Sunday, although the field was spreading out. Already it looked like a four-horse race.

There is no sport where luck does not play a part – for better or worse. There are moments when one's mental strength becomes the most important attribute of all, and golf being a pedestrian game, there's a lot of time to think. For some, there's too much time. Here's where doubt can creep in, affecting not only the swing but the player's general demeanour. Although many experts go on about the importance of muscle memory and an automatically repeatable swing, this is an assertion I don't totally believe in.

What I want to know is why can't a player perform in a final round with something closer to the freedom they have during a practice round? Are they too excited, too nervous? Do they want it too much? Are they actually afraid of success, daft though this may sound to the uninitiated? As you ought to know already, I do feel that the modern player spends too much time on the practice ground, beating ball after ball, and not enough time just playing the game. In my day, we practised less and played more, and it seemed to work out okay.

Whatever the truth, I know that what marks out the greatest players is their ability to play these all-important final rounds with something close to a freedom that the others can only admire. It is, indeed, what makes them great. I see perhaps twenty-five talented young players today – all under thirty years of age – who I would love to see relax more on the course. Golf, by its nature, just allows so much time to get into one's own head. If only they could cope better with all this time, then I am convinced these players could indeed take giant strides forward.

The Sunday weather forecast was not good, with the really bad stuff due in the afternoon. In response, the R&A brought forward the tee times – an unusual move for an Open but, in the face of a severe Atlantic storm, a wise one. Eddie Pepperell, one of my favourites, stepped out on the last day in a very dull outfit. Now, Eddie has a ready wit and a certain charm, but blacks and browns together with deep autumnal shades were not a good look. He'll be disappointed with his result, but hopefully he will learn and fight another day. Inevitably, there where were some high scores as the wind grew ever stronger: Dustin Johnson with 76; Xander Schauffele, a favourite, with 78; Matt Kuchar's 79; McDowell with 77; and Sergio Garcia with 78. Francesco Molinari, meanwhile, mounted a creditable defence of his title to finish three under par. He never really threatened, but it was a decent riposte for a returning champion.

The crowds, as predicted, were enthusiastic and generous in their applause. I was told the local police arrested no more than half a dozen people for drink-related offences over the week, so even here there were no serious black marks against the Championship.

It was quite staggering to see the amount of effort put into the television coverage by Sky, opening up at 6:30 a.m. and finishing some ten or twelve hours later. The BBC, meanwhile, did its very best not to let anybody know we were doing the highlights. I was frustrated to meet several R&A officials, festooned with badges, who exclaimed, 'Peter, how nice to see you! What are you doing here?' Wearily I told them I was working for the BBC, helping to produce a two-hour highlights show every night. And not just any highlights show! We're talking about a broadcast that averaged over a million viewers each evening – three times the Sky audience. This must be disappointing for them, considering the amount of effort put into their production, but then I learnt long ago that they're only interested in selling dishes. You can't control what people watch.

Anyway, the leaders got off to a shaky start. Lowry holed a nice putt on the first green for a bogey. Fleetwood missed a similar length, eight or ten feet, for a birdie. You could argue, with the benefit of hindsight, that the fate of the Championship was settled there and then. Regardless, there can be no doubt Lowry played the best golf among the leaders on that final day. Yes, he had moments of good fortune and others were unlucky, but that's the way things are and always have been. The Irishman is a deserved champion and one who will carry the mantle very proudly and with honour.

So what conclusions can be drawn from that 2019 Open Championship, all of us having made the pilgrimage back to Portrush after sixty-eight years? All those years of planning and preparation – did they come to fruition? The answer must be a resounding, 'Yes!'

If you'd had a magic wand, the weather might have been a little more consistent and Lowry might have been chased home by McIlroy, only to prevail on the last with a five-foot putt. If – and I say 'if' – that had happened, it would have been, in my opinion, one of the most entertaining, spectacular and enjoyable Championships I have ever been to, and I've been to sixty-nine of them. So, if Portrush is considered a great success, how about the chances of Royal Porthcawl getting a chance to see if they can produce a winning formula? There is no doubt that the course, with some tweaks, can be good enough, but do they have everything else they need to stage one of these great jamborees of golf? So far, the R&A, in their infinite wisdom, think not. A pity, but this decision is understandable. Perhaps a new access road and more space for all the infrastructure is needed, for The Open is about so much more than just the course.

Soon it was time to make the journey home, starting with a car ride to the airport. We had an interesting driver, who took us cross-country from Portrush to just north of Dublin, offering a delightful view of the countryside on the way. Conversation flowed, as it as it so often will in Ireland. The staff at the airport were smiling and helpful, and they were full of conversation regarding The Open. There were clear skies for our flight home, and we were afforded a great view of the Wirral and the fine city of Birmingham. Then came the run in to Heathrow from the east, right over London. The view, as ever, was magical. A splendid week, but it's always nice to get home.

Could another Open be on the cards for me? Who knows, although I would very much like to make it through to St Andrews in 2021. The Open there is always extra special, and for me, it would complete a very big circle in my life. As long as there are people ready to offer a helping hand, and as long as I'm wanted there, it's a distinct possibility. I certainly hope so, anyway.

Meanwhile, while glad to be home and, I must admit, a trifle weary, I turn my attention to the Solheim Cup. Staged at Gleneagles, these matches are set to be my next assignment for my beloved BBC.

It is indeed a grand life if you don't weaken, and I trust you've enjoyed finding out about bits of mine. Always remember: it's better to be lucky than good, although it's better still to be both.

Happy golfing.

EPILOGUE - MY PETER
BY JACKIE ALLISS

THE course at Dalmahoy in Scotland was closed. It was pouring with rain, and golf was cancelled for the day. It was 1965, and I was working for Gallahers Tobacco Company, representing the firm at the Senior Service Tournament it sponsored. It was my first ever time on a golf course, and as the rain came down I found myself sitting in the clubhouse with the promotional girls, chatting to the frustrated golfers. I spent much of my time translating for Jean Garaialde, who spoke very little English, but David Thomas, Guy Wolstenholme, Bernard Hunt and the famous Peter Alliss were all there too. I remember his wonderful smile, his tanned face and his beautiful hands; I was head-over-heels in love. I was twenty-two years old.

I can't remember what I ate at dinner that night, but I can remember Peter holding my face in his hands when we said goodbye.

'It's a good job I don't live near you,' he said. 'If I did, I would fall in love with you.' It was too late for me, of course.

Play was cancelled the next day. Peter had already gone, and we Gallahers girls were put on a plane back to London. I cried the whole way. Some nine months passed before Peter phoned out of the blue. The rest, as they say, is history.

Peter was married and separated, and those early days were complicated. In 1970, however, we moved to a lovely farmhouse on the 17th fairway at Moor Allerton Golf Club in Leeds. Here we started our life together. We had no money, due to the divorce, but we had each other, and our days were filled with laughter. We were fortunate to be surrounded by great friends, who have remained close over these past fifty years. I remember our first ever Christmas; we threw a Boxing Day party for twenty-odd people, with Bollinger for everyone. Our guests thought we were so generous, but the truth was that Peter had recently done some promotional work for the boss of Bollinger, Anthony Leschallas, and so we had been given a load of bottles as a thank you. It was a good job, because back then we were so poor that we couldn't afford to buy wine.

We had ten great years in Yorkshire, although they were tinged with sadness. Sara, our firstborn, joined us in 1972. Our second daughter, Victoria, was born severely disabled, and her needs were so complicated that we couldn't look after her by ourselves. Then our son Simon came along in 1975. Those years showed me Peter's strength and compassion; I was wrapped up in my own world, with two children in the house and one sick child in a children's home. Peter gave me my headspace and his strength, and he was there beside me all the time, supporting me and keeping my courage up. In 1980 we moved south. We brought Victoria with us to a home in Hindhead, where she stayed until her death in 1983. Five months later, our second son, Henry, was born. So much sadness touched with so much joy.

Life in Surrey was very different. Peter was in high demand, and he was travelling and working in the States for weeks on end. I was fortunate that I could travel occasionally with him as he went about his various broadcasting duties.

Peter was happy and very busy, and I was happy and branching out. With his backing, I became a magistrate. I think I have always been a frustrated lawyer, and I found the work absorbing and hugely interesting. On the night of my swearing-in, Peter remarked: 'I've never slept with a magistrate before.' He really did find humour in everything.

Peter loved his home, and he was always pleased to get back after a trip. He would often drive all the way from Scotland to Surrey rather than spend one more night away. It helped that our house was usually full of interesting people from all walks of life: local friends, celebrities, sportsmen and women and various reporters, who were forever after comments from Peter because they knew they were guaranteed an interesting response, whatever the subject.

We were living in the era of big dinner parties, and Peter loved nothing more than to entertain. Our friends came from all over the country, and I was blessed, on Simon's first day of nursery school, to meet Pauline and Jack Buchanan. They have been firm, supportive friends over the past forty years, understanding our somewhat topsy-turvy world and, as godparents, supporting me and the children through thick and thin. Later, while filming *Pro-Celebrity Golf*, we met Terry and Helen Wogan. (Remember that sensational putt across the green?) Terry and Peter shared the same sense of humour and love of the ridiculous, and our Sunday lunches were soon infamous. There was always far too much good red wine and delicious food, as Helen is a wonderful cook. We watched their children grow up and they watched ours. Terry was godfather to Henry and was very hands on. How we laughed when Peter asked Terry to officially open our hen house, with a ribbon-cutting ceremony and a photographer to record the occasion (I still have the photo). Terry's death, seven years ago, hit Peter so very hard.

Peter was an avid newspaper reader. He read very few books but loved all the old movies: Westerns and all the old musicals, such as *Seven Brides for Seven Brothers*. I swear he knew every word and every tune. He said it all went back to his childhood, when he used to visit the cinema in Parkstone twice a week. To his dying day, he loved the magic of entertainment.

I should add that we have a parrot, with whom Peter had a love-hate relationship. Charlie – the parrot – bit Peter frequently, and consequently Charlie swore very loudly in Peter's voice several times a day. Peter also taught him to whistle the theme song of *Hancock's Half Hour*. This came in handy when Peter inadvertently left the cage open and Charlie went flapping away, up and over the treetops. The only way we found him was by whistling that song.

I started Alliss Promotions after running several charity golf events with Peter's help. No, I never did learn to play, but I do love the game. One day, Peter looked at me and said: 'I think I need to set you up in a company, as you are costing me a fortune.' With me, he became a patron of several medical charities, and my world opened up to celebratory golf days. For many years, working for the British Orthopaedic Society and GUTS, I was running upwards of eighteen or twenty tournaments a year. Peter was always at my back, telling me I could do whatever I wanted to do and promising he would always help along the way. My love of cookery led me to publish my first cookbook, and shortly afterwards I was asked to film six programmes with celebrities for ITV. Peter was the one who said to me: 'You can do it! Be yourself; you're a natural.'

Thanks to Peter's support, I also achieved a personal ambition to fly and earned my Private Pilot's Licence. Maybe, at heart, that was the one thing Peter was not so keen on. I think he was worried about my safety, although he flew with me several times in my little Robin plane. I loved flying. It was the perfect escape to fly my children down to the Isle of Wight for a day on the beach and to come home tired, happy and covered in ice-cream. I also did a parachute jump for charity, and that was probably the only time Peter really put his foot down. He threatened to divorce me if I did it again, and the BBC offered to double my total take if I didn't jump. But I did jump in the end, and I have no regrets.

I travelled to the States occasionally over the years, and when Henry was born we took him with us until he went to playschool. The *Pro-Celebrity Golf* days at Turnberry were wonderful times for us all, and they gave us the opportunity, as a family, to be together. Family holidays just didn't happen, as Peter was always away working during school holidays. Peter used to say: 'Maybe I'm not a great father, as I can't swim and I can't play football and I'm never there for parents' evenings, but I am a great provider and they do meet a wealth of wonderful mix of people from all walks of life.'

Neither of us could ever forget the day at Turnberry when Sara rushed into our bedroom breathless with excitement. 'I've just come up in the lift with Miss Ellie's husband!' she said. Then there was the time when Henry, aged two, was discovered hanging over James Hunt and his wife Susie's bathtub, having momentarily escaped from our beloved Grannie T, who looked after them. Peter loved it all. He was in his element when filming; those were the times when his natural love of people, his powers of observation, his sense of humour and his penchant for the ridiculous were all able to flow freely.

It was the same when the World Golf Hall of Fame got in touch in 2012. They wanted to honour Peter's contribution to the sport by inducting him as a member.

THREE AWARDS THAT MEANT A GREAT DEAL TO PETER

ABOVE: Presented to Peter Alliss... With grateful thanks for your support of The Open Championship and the game of golf around the world

BELOW: To Peter and Jackie with thanks for your contribution to BBC golf

RIGHT: Peter Alliss World Golf Hall of Fame Inducted May 7th 2012

Dave Cannon, leading golf photographer and friend of the family recalls a memorable assignment:

The phone rings at home just a couple of days after Henrik Stenson's fabulous win at The Open. 'Ah hah Cannon its Peter here. I have a little task for you. My lovely Jackie breeds Weimaraner dogs and we have a litter of twelve very frisky Weimaraner puppies that we would love photographing before they leave us. This will test your mettle.'

Having a pair of similar German Short Haired Pointers of our own I knew how challenging this might be. We have a gorgeous studio picture of our first one, she was one of nine puppies and I clearly recall the breeder telling us a hilarious story of how they spent hours chasing errant pups, hurtling all over the photographer's studio trying to get these frisky pups to all sit at the same time. So, I knew I was in for a challenge. I tried to lower Peter's expectations and recruited my wife to act as a willing but bossy assistant, just what I needed.

Little did we know how much fun we would have – nine puppies were clearly a challenge but twelve – I knew it would be almost impossible to get nine to sit in a row let alone a dozen. As it happened it took all our cajoling, and ultimately dog treat bribery to get all the little rascals into one picture. Whilst we came away with a tinge of disappointment that we had failed in the main mission to get all twelve looking at the camera, we still remember fondly that afternoon in Hindhead and the smiles with those lovely young dogs (six was the most we managed to get on the bench and their laps at the same time) wriggling on Peter and Jackie's laps and the obvious delight of the proud owners. How lucky I was to know Peter well enough to be asked to spend time at their home capturing their joy of such a wonderful litter.

He didn't want to go to Florida at first, but I persuaded him. Invitation accepted, the organisers asked for a copy of the speech he intended to make. There was total disbelief on their end when we said Peter didn't intend to write one. They pointed out that they always had prior knowledge of an inductee's speech. 'Not this time,' Peter said. When the time came, his off-the-cuff speech was superb. Many said it was the best ever. That was my Peter, and I suspect that wonderful monologue will forever be a favourite on YouTube. He was an easy-going man with time for everyone. People just liked him.

We had so many wonderful times together. We were even invited once to a state banquet for President George W Bush, a mad-keen golfer who admired Peter. We went to Buckingham Palace in Peter's beloved Bentley with that infamous PUT 3 number plate. It was such a magical moment to pull up at the palace and walk up the carpeted steps, guardsmen flanking us on each side. Then these soldiers started quietly whistling the theme tune to the BBC golf coverage. One or two muttered through the side of their mouths: 'Hi, Pete.' We almost didn't make it for laughing. It was such an amazing experience – one given to so few – but it was not so lovely some hours later, when we got into the car and it wouldn't start. Helped by palace staff and the AA, our driver eventually got us home.

When our children left home to begin their adult lives, I began to accompany Peter to more tournaments. He liked having me there, and in later years, as his legs gave him more bother, he needed me. It was special to be accepted by the BBC team back in the days when the Beeb was still a major broadcaster. During big weeks, like The Open and the Masters, it was like being in a great big family full of lovely people. We stayed in rented houses, and most nights, Chris White cooked great vats of chilli and other appetising dishes for the hard-working team. There were BBQs and plenty of booze, and I used to take dishes of homemade pâté and fruitcakes. Peter held court in his imitable way, keeping the assembled company in stitches. The last time we were out at the Masters in Atlanta, in 2019, the team threw a special supper for Hazel Irvine. She was retiring from golf, and it was a very emotional evening with lots of speeches and lots of laughter. Then Peter made the comment that this possibly could be his last Masters. Everyone protested and said he would be there next year, but his words turned out to be strangely prophetic.

Peter's death on Saturday 5th December 2020 was as unexpected as it was devastatingly sudden. He had not been seriously ill beforehand, although his legs were a little suspect. He had grown a rather fetching beard, and our son Simon had been over that afternoon with the clippers and various lotions. I went out Christmas shopping with my daughter-in-law Kelly, and when we returned, the two of them were having a fine old time in my kitchen. Peter had a towel round his neck and Simon was asking if he would like 'anything for the weekend, sir?'

Their laughter was very special, and in that moment I didn't know it was to be the last time I would hear it.

Peter and Simon had a couple of whiskies, and then Simon left to go home for his supper. Peter and I had dinner and watched some television. At ten o' clock he said he thought he would head up to bed. A few minutes later I heard him call my name. I came running, and I found him on his knees in the hallway. I took him in my arms. He didn't say anything. He just looked into my eyes and then closed his. It was all so sudden. His doctor, Ed Leatham, told me that although he didn't speak, he would have known I was there. I cling to that thought. I am just so grateful that he died with me, that it happened so quickly, and that I was able to tell him I love him.

The house is different now. It looks the same, but it's quieter. We all miss the laughter and the sheer presence of him. I really don't think there was ever a day when he didn't make me laugh. Like all couples, we had our barneys now and then, but they never lasted long. And afterwards, he would always come up to me, put his arms around me and say, 'Shall we be friends again?' And that was that. He was a real romantic, and he liked to leave me notes in strange places, all of which give me great comfort now.

Peter and I had such an amazing life together. I never wanted anything else but him, and I do believe he felt exactly the same way about me. I feel so very blessed to have my memories and to have shared the laughter, which I can still hear echoing in the house. I am grateful for my family, who have been a staunch support, and for my my grandchildren, who keep me smiling through the tears. I am so very blessed to have shared over fifty years with such a unique and special man.

Peter's funeral took place on 7th January 2021, a cold, locked-down day. When his coffin was carried into St John the Evangelist Church – not a mile from his home in Hindhead, Surrey – resting next to the flowers on his coffin was one of his golf clubs, and perhaps a microphone should have been there too.

Absent were the many hundreds of friends and fans who would have wanted to attend, for Peter was a man whom many felt to be something of companion, even if they had never met him. As it happened, there were just nineteen of us, close family and very close friends. It was a beautiful service, replete with flickering candles and a pervading sense of peace and tranquillity. The choir was stunning, and their music filled the church. I do believe Peter would have appreciated this beautiful, simple service, surrounded by those he loved.

ACKNOWLEDGEMENT

I cannot close this book without recognising the huge input by journalist and friend Bill Elliott. When Peter talked about writing 'the ultimate book' he said he wanted to write it with Bill, a golf writer he has known for many years. The dream became a reality, starting in late 2018. It was rudely interrupted by Covid and then, sadly, by Peter's death in 2020.

My abiding memory is of the two of them giggling away in Peter's study as they reminisced about golfers they knew, tournaments they had attended and personalities whose paths they had crossed. In other words, they had fun together – although neither knew how this long journey would end. I thank Bill so very sincerely for all the help, dedication and, indeed, love he gave Peter to get this book completed.

He has been a tower of strength along with our publisher Adrian Stephenson, Lennard Publishing, who enthusiastically picked up the draft and ran with it. Adrian, an old friend of many years, has cajoled, suggested, amended and chivvied me over the past twelve months and when I was flagging he was enthusiastic in suggesting new angles to finish the book.

I also must mention Peter's long-time assistant, Frances Dowty, who patiently typed and retyped the manuscript as Peter and Bill improved things.

I thank them all for allowing the family and I to realise Peter's last dream to have the book published, just as I am so grateful to the men and women from the world of golf and beyond who so eagerly added their own thoughts on my late husband when the book was revamped following his death. Peter would be very pleased with you too for reading it.

Thank you,

Jackie